The Truth behind the Mommy Wars

Who Decides What Makes a Good Mother?

MIRIAM PESKOWITZ

Seal Press

The Truth behind the Mommy Wars
Who Decides What Makes a Good Mother?

Published by
Seal Press
An Imprint of Avalon Publishing Group, Incorporated
1400 65th Street, Suite 250
Emeryville, CA 94608

Library of Congress Cataloging-in-Publication Data
Peskowitz, Miriam, 1964-
   The truth behind the mommy wars : who decides what makes a good mother?
/ by Miriam Peskowitz.
       p. cm.
   Includes bibliographical references.
   ISBN 1-58005-129-4
     1. Mothers—Psychology. 2. Mothers—Attitudes. 3. Mother and child. 4.
   Parenting. I. Title.

   HQ759.P4685 2005
   306.874'3—dc22

   2004030249

   ISBN 1-58005-129-4

   9 8 7 6 5 4 3 2 1

   Cover design by Gia Giasullo, studio eg
   Interior design by Margaret Copeland/Terragrafix
   Printed in Canada by Webcom
   Distributed by Publishers Group West

For Myra and Samira.

CONTENTS

INTRODUCTION

Rachel doesn't have children, but chances are good that a few years will see her and her actor-husband, Yuri, pushing a stroller down the streets of Chicago. Meanwhile, she's just back from a trip to old haunts in L.A. and San Francisco, where all her friends have babies and toddlers. She's trying to sort out what she's just seen.

"Everyone loves their kids," she tells me. "And at the same time, every mother I know is upset. The working moms are miserable and run down, and want more time with their kids; they think the stay-at-home moms have it easy, being home with the kids all day. The stay-at-home moms are at loose ends, and they feel lonely and isolated. They're with the kids, and feel lucky, but they want more autonomy; they envy the working moms that way. Sometimes they're bored, too, though it's hard to admit, and they want their old identities back—something more than life as a mother and a wife.

"Nobody's really happy," she concludes. "And everyone feels very alone in their plight. They feel ashamed that they can't make it all work out right, like there's something wrong with them. Women talk about it, but they don't *really* talk about it."

Rachel's words are the best starting point for this book that I can find. We love our kids, but by and large, we mothers are not entirely happy with the available arrangements for work and parenting. We feel very isolated and alone in all this, sure that the imbalance is a personal failure, not even sure what words to use to describe the problem.

We get so little support and understanding for the different types of parenting and working lives we lead.

Myself, I never planned on being a stay-at-home mother. I'd been running the fast track, and though I paid lip service to the importance of a well-rounded life, a career was what mattered. My husband, Rob, and I lived in a two-bedroom apartment; since my job was in a city an airplane ride away and Rob traveled a great deal for work, the airport was our second home. When my daughter was born, it became clear that our previous lives didn't have much room for a baby—our lives would have to change. Consequently, once I began caring for Samira, I had to be initiated into a world I hadn't really known existed. And I was thoroughly surprised by what I found: 10:00 AM playgrounds filled with women and children. Weren't we all supposed to be at work? Was this the 1950s, redux? I was confused. Diapers and the details of infant care aside, I found myself in a world that prides itself on its progressive values and the public advancements we women have made, but whose daytime playgrounds are filled almost exclusively by mothers and their kids. One May day, when my daughter was seven months old, we strolled over to the City Hall bandstand for a noon concert of Irish music. I never knew who went to these concerts; I assumed the audience would be all the folks who worked at City Hall and in the nearby office buildings. I was wrong. The bandstand lawn was filled, jam-pack-filled, with mothers and small children. Wherever I looked, I saw women and babies. None of it really made sense.

Don't get me wrong: I enjoyed my years at home. Immensely. I had tons of fun, and spent long, lovely afternoons with my daughter, her tiny pals, and my new mom-friends at my neighborhood playground. I did all those new mom things. I found a playgroup. I tried out the now-caricatured baby massage classes. For years I had worked maniacally. Life at home with a baby, even on its hardest days, felt like a midlife retirement. We lived in a relatively warm climate and I loved being outdoors so much of the day and year. I'd go on long walks. I'd visit art galleries and nurse my daughter in the dark of video installations. After years of total ambition and career focus, I was able to relax into other parts of life, to learn my city and my neighborhood, to feel at home, to live the whole life that I believed in. Raising a young child is hard work, but for me, this kind of hard work at least didn't carry the stress and anxiety I was used to bearing, and I appreciated that. Being at home with my child that first year was great; the stress only reappeared when I tried to integrate life as a mother with keeping up professionally.

Despite how much fun I was having, the big picture of how our lives as mothers collide with competing expectations about motherhood and work kept disturbing me. From the beginning, I couldn't believe that desiring some relief from work for a few years while my daughter was young would mean I could never work in my profession again, or that I would lose so much ground. The professions are rigidly unforgiving of those who step off track. From day one, my enjoyment was accompanied by this worry.

This uneasiness gnawed at me, followed me down the street, and nipped at my heels. I spent time with women who always knew they would stop working when their kids came along, and parts of life with them seemed natural. I spent time with women who never imagined their work lives would miss a beat when and if they had kids, and parts of life with them, too, seemed natural and normal. I remember long, solitary stroller walks with my tiny daughter tucked into her three-wheeled stroller, walks that stretched for miles down the utopianly named Freedom Trail, sure that I shouldn't be split in two, knowing that something had to give, and trying to piece the clues together.

I knew enough about the history of women and work to see the troubles of new motherhood as more than an identity issue. The struggles of mothers are a labor issue, and as I explain throughout this book, it helps to see them through this lens. Because the media offerings for making sense of motherhood and work were so meager, I started looking around and asking questions, searching the Internet, and making phone calls. The frustrations of motherhood can be a hard topic to broach. Mostly we're just busy with the kids, or with work, or both. These frustrations are also painful. They're laced with questions of how love translates into time and care. Sometimes we mothers don't want to talk about the trade-offs, about how we aren't getting what we need, about how it's disappointing, and why. Sometimes we just want to get through the day. Mothers are supposed to be competent and reassuring. We fix things; we make the world right for our kids. We protect. Mothers are the classic good girls, so it can be hard to voice anger and disappointment. Even as we spend so much time teaching our children to play fair, and trying the best we can to get life to provide a fair shake for our kids, it can be hard to turn around and say, It's not fair for mothers. We mothers are not getting the support we need—no matter whether we're working, or at home, or doing both part-time—and we're making sacrifices that we don't need to be making.

Like many mothers, I didn't quite know how to make sense of this. It's easy, at first, to think this is just an identity issue, as in, "Can I really be a modern woman and also raise my kids?" I soon learned that this is not at all the right question; motherhood is only partially an issue of identity. The frustration we experience in our parenting and working choices is about identity and desire, but it is also about our workplaces, and particularly about the refusal of most American workplaces to deal creatively and humanely with family life. I also learned that, mythologies of superwomen aside, the majority of mothers in America don't work full-time—upwards of 60 percent of us don't, and many have been shocked when I've told them these numbers. For mothers of infants, this rises to a staggering 76 percent. That's three-quarters of us who leave the workforce—and its benefits—at least temporarily to raise young children. Sixty-seven percent of mothers of preschoolers work part-time or are home full-time with their kids. Not till children start elementary school do the numbers drop and more mothers return to the workplace. Before I had a child, felt the frustration, and went looking, I never knew. That the statistical numbers don't match our collective mythologies of motherhood is one of our society's better-kept secrets.[1]

Once I started asking, I learned, first, that it wasn't just me, and second, that when given half a chance and a few minutes, most mothers and fathers desperately want a chance to talk honestly about their lives, whether they're hip down-market urban parents or well-coifed suburbanites, Wall Street moms or welfare moms, doctors or daycare workers. Mothers and fathers are upset, and they're angry. In the words of one Seattle mother, "I'd *love* to talk with you about this issue. I probably have too much to say. . . ."

Once I started listening to mothers and fathers around the country, I learned that our lives at home are much more complex than the sound-bite versions. Some parents are well educated and living very comfortable lives. Some are following creative and intellectual passions, but living barely middle-class lives. Some have little formal education and are raising families without having the privilege that advanced degrees can bring. Some women work in small offices and factories and on sales floors; some are trained in classic female professions like nursing and teaching. Some have always been single, some are newly so.

Many decades ago, women's frustrations with mothering were called "the problem without a name." Today, the frustration women and men express at the relatively limited options for combining parenting with working is, perhaps, the problem with too many names. Mommy Wars is one particularly troubling name given to it. "Work-family balance" is another. "The stay-at-home mom explosion" or "the new stay-at-home moms" are other terms I've heard. The problem, at its heart, is that mothers and fathers want to spend time with their kids, perhaps stay home during their youngest years and work reduced hours later on, and the workplace in general doesn't allow this. The typical workplace bets on having workers whose lives and children don't get in the way of work.

The parent problem is exacerbated by the media's Mommy Wars, those periodic articles and daytime TV episodes that report on the lives of mothers as if our largest problem were each other. Mommy Wars reports divide women into two groups, working moms and stay-at-home moms, and set them against each other. Remember Barbara Bush and Hillary Clinton squaring off to see whether stay-at-home moms or working moms made better chocolate-chip cookies? Clinton had remarked that as a lawyer and working mother, she hadn't "stayed home and baked cookies." Based on the comment and uproar that followed it, *Family Circle* magazine stepped in to transform the statement into an actual bake-off. Clinton and Bush were both asked to submit cookie recipes. *Family Circle* readers then baked them at home and cast ballots on their favorites. (Clinton's oatmeal chocolate chips won.) This was a key moment in the media-fueled Mommy Wars.

Far from helping us understand the social and political stakes of motherhood, the media's Mommy Wars obscure the issues facing us. They transform parenting into a style war. Report after report, from the nation's newspapers and TV stations, asks whether stay-at-home moms think they frost their cupcakes more expertly than working moms—or whether working mothers think stay-at-home moms are stupid, plot ways to keep working moms from being involved in the PTA, and don't really watch their kids since they spend too much time doing Pilates. Usually reported in women's magazines, or Sunday magazines, or style sections, these flaps keep our energy diverted and our frustrations quiet. They prevent mothers from feeling empathy for each other. They diminish the parent problem by expressing it in the trivial terms of catfights, while a real proposed solution, the introduction of the Family and Workplace Balancing Act of 2004 by Congresswoman (and former welfare mother) Lynn Woolsey, gets no press outside Woolsey's native San Francisco Bay Area.

The truth behind the Mommy Wars punditry is that in real life mothers don't split easily into two categories. Mothers tend to carousel into and out of the workplace, or expect to. Many of us move back and forth between working and staying at home. We don't fall neatly into a single group. Many of us work part-time, and this receives little media attention. Another truth is that mothers are actually much more helpful to each other than media reports would have us believe. Most mothers want more support for the different ways in which we combine work and family life. The truth behind the Mommy Wars is that in real life mothers are casting about for lives that feel sane and safe, and we need more help than we're getting.

Stories from real life undermine the Mommy Wars, and this book is filled with tales of mothers and fathers and how we plot courses through the maze of work and parenting. Plenty of ordinary women and men heroically navigate the labyrinth that makes raising good kids and living a good life both supremely simple and really, really hard. Because in all the Mommy Wars hubbub over who's the better mother, we miss what's at stake: millions of women and men and families and kids trying to sort their way through the ancient philosophical questions of what constitutes a good life.

The women and men whose stories fill this book are nearly as diverse as our country. Though they are not identified racially or ethnically, readers should know this, because too often our debates assume that all mothers are white and affluent and well educated. Some of the women have been, or currently are, on welfare and other forms of state assistance. They live in places as different as rural New Hampshire and Atlanta; Montana and Wisconsin; New York and Philadelphia; San Francisco, Portland, Seattle, and more. I picked their stories for this book because the usual media coverage focuses on lawyers and corporate women who have quit jobs to be full-time mothers. I want to present a richer story, to express the wonderful messiness of everyday life as a parent, vacillating as it does so quickly between love, joy, and aggravation.

In these pages you'll meet a range of women and men who make choices about parenting without necessarily having a financial cushion, who work a range of jobs and professions, and who see value in reflecting on what work and parenting mean in their lives. Many of them are looking for a middle ground between the public life of work and the private and domestic world of being home with kids. Many are trying to work part-time, or build businesses from home, or find other ways to craft lives that combine work and parenting in ways that feel right for them. What they all have in common is that today's mothers and fathers are caught between a cultural assumption of an egalitarian society and a cultural reality that is not exactly egalitarian. This is the parent problem, the contradiction that is hard to name. The parent problem is not a working-mom problem or a stay-at-home-mom problem; it affects us all.

Cecelia was thirty-six when she was pregnant with her first child. By then she had built a great career in New York publishing. After her first child was born, though, she left her job. She hadn't planned on this ahead of time, and when I asked her about it, she was very forthcoming. She was fully established in her career, she said, and she felt a certain amount of freedom—freedom to take a break from professional ambitions so she could focus on her pregnancy and then on her daughter. She didn't decide whether to return to work until after the baby was born. As a new mom, for a host of reasons, she decided that returning to full-time work wasn't the right option for her. She had no intention of giving up work entirely. She felt confident that she could return to full-time editorial work whenever she wanted. She knew that her skills as an editor would lend easily to freelance work, and while she was pregnant, she had already secured a book contract. She also had some ideas for starting a home-based editing business, Idea Architects, with an old friend who was a work-at-home dad of three.

While Cecelia seems like a woman who has it all, with choices and good options, upon closer inspection, her decisions regarding work and motherhood were also not entirely choices of her own making. She quit her job because she didn't want the kind of life where, in her words, she and her husband both left the house at 8:00 AM and returned nine or ten hours later to put their child to bed. That wasn't her vision of life, and it would require more discipline than she had as a "frazzled, sleep-deprived new mother." Cecelia left her job because she wanted some relief from work and to be with her kids. Her employer wasn't open to job flexibility; her only option was to quit.

Many women move into and out of the workplace. Some call this "sequencing" but for many mothers it's more like a carousel. Cynthia has two elementary-school-age children. When her kids were small, and so she could work near them, she had gotten herself certified to start a family daycare. But as she was getting ready to start, Cynthia took a job at one of the toniest daycares in the city. The perk they offered was the opportunity to place her children in the classes, in a stimulating environment she could never have afforded had she not worked there. But a terrible accident meant the end of that job and the end of her working life for several years. Cynthia was eligible for disability payments and she accepted. Another city program helped pay the tuition at her children's school. When she partly recovered, after having learned how to walk again, she did not work.

Cynthia wanted to be around to pick the kids up from school, hang out with them in the afternoon, and cook dinner each night; to complicate matters, she and the children's father separated shortly after she was back on her feet. When her health improved and life felt more normal, Cynthia looked for part-time, part-of-the-year work that could fit her kids' schedules. That summer, Cynthia worked at a camp where she could also enroll her two kids. The following year she was hired to direct a before- and after-school program, and she jumped at the chance to use her skills to make the program work. The downside was that her hours off matched the exact hours her two children were in school. After several months she asked her boss if she could work part-time. The answer was no: all or nothing. Again, she got on that motherhood carousel and left the workplace.

Scottie is the devoted stay-at-home mom of two daughters. She's the super-energy mom, the kind who organizes playgroups and collects money for organizations that purchase cribs for low-income mothers and their kids. Scottie holds an advanced degree in French literature and taught high school French for many years. She proudly considers herself a feminist; she's also a devout member of her Methodist church. When I asked her how she had come to be a stay-at-home mom, I had already heard many stories of women who'd found a back door into stay-at-home motherhood: a 24/7 job that left little choice; an office day that began at 7:45 AM, or 5:30 AM if you count the commute, and stretched to 8:00 PM; a boss who allowed no flexibility, no telecommuting, or no release from the demands of overnight travel; a daycare or babysitting situation that fell apart; a personal breakdown about to happen.

Scottie always knew that when her children were born she would quit her job. As she said to me in her broad and reassuring Tennessee accent, "I'm big into the idea of seasons in our lives." For Scottie, teaching was a vocation: "It's a calling, and it requires all of one's energy to be teacher, counselor, listener, minister, friend, resource for everything from getting into college to coping with rejection by the cheerleaders." The season in which children are young is wonderful and short, and she didn't want to miss it because her attention was divided between her own kids and the older kids at her school. In quite spiritual terms, she wanted to attend to life—a single life purpose that didn't have to be mixed with fifteen competing priorities: "I knew staying home was a specific chapter in my life. It's a luxury to be at home—not so much for the kids, even, but for me, because I knew it would be such a brief time."

When Scottie's daughters were two and three and a half, she found a job teaching French one evening a week at the community college nearby. "It is so all-consuming to be at home with young children. It's so easy to lose one's soul," she told me. Scottie really wanted to be a full-time mom, and as her kids grew she also wanted some interesting and decently paid part-time work. This, it turned out, was a hard combination to find. Our country lacks quality part-time work. One of the trade-offs the majority of mothers make in leaving the paid workforce is that we take a wage hit, lose the seniority we've accrued, and face the lack of decent part-time jobs. Scottie wanted to be a stay-at-home mom. She chose this freely. However, she didn't choose how hard it would be to find rewarding part-time work for fair pay when the girls were older.

Michelle and her husband had tried for a long time to have a child. They submitted to round after round of fertility treatment, unsuccessfully, and then registered to adopt. Finally, their baby, Jakob, arrived and was adopted into their family at birth. It wasn't, professionally speaking, the most convenient time. Michelle had just finished her doctorate. She had accepted a prestigious job in North Carolina and was about to move. But when faced with moving, when Jakob was four months old, she decided to stay in Philadelphia near family and friends.

"Community is really important," she tells me. She sits calmly, cross-legged in a comfy chair. It all seems quite commonplace until I realize that she is breastfeeding her adopted son, almost miraculously crossing the boundaries of nature and nurture. She gave up the job, and now she's with Jakob full-time. She has given up a great deal, she knows it, and I ask her about this. "I could only imagine it being too stressful," she begins, "to juggle work and childcare. It just seemed too much. There's no way we could have afforded a babysitter. And I really didn't want him in daycare." Michelle and her husband live in a small rental apartment. They share one car. "We keep life simple," she says. She tried working part-time at a university writing center in the evenings while Michael was with the baby. It was too hard to be with the baby all day and work in the evening at a job that demanded intellectual effort. The job lasted only a few months.

In our conversation, Michelle doesn't try to make it all even out. "I can't predict where my life will go, and I worry about being able to balance parenting with decent, interesting work," she says. "But I am doing this with a feminist consciousness. It's a choice to make a family work, to make it fun. I wanted this baby for so long. . . . I want to spend time with him. I want to be with him." She ends our conversation by telling me about something the baby's birth grandmother said when Michelle told her they wouldn't be moving to North Carolina after all, and that she would be home with him. "I thought we would have figured this out for you by now," said the grandmother, a research scientist now in her fifties. She knows the history of women in our country and how hard we've fought to get ahead, and what Michelle is losing even while she's gaining something else.

Women like Michelle simply want to be with their kids—not because they have to and not because being a caregiver is somehow biologically linked to female essence. She is not responding to anyone else's sense of what women and mothers should do; in fact, her choice doesn't fit with her broader family's sense of what educated women should do. Of course what is really painful is that a decision like this, based on love and care, is not valued and supported in our society. Michelle knows what she has given up. Michelle knows that for all this she has gained something less tangible: a sense of shifting life for the love for one's child. In the biggest possible sense, this is good, right, and wonderful. Love should be the core and center of how we act. It shouldn't have to be canceled out by such total loss in the public sphere. This only continues centuries-old traditions in which family duties conflict with women's desires to have more, to have both. Men have always had work and family. Part of the parent problem is that women don't have this option in the same way, and we need to be able to sort out the reasons why.

As if struggling with work and family care issues weren't enough, mothers are bombarded with judgment, no matter what we do! Our society has no consensus on how children should be raised, the effects of childcare, and the effects of homecare. That's a good thing; there are, in the end, lots of good options for caring for kids. The negative is that all mothers eventually come under criticism. It seems there's no safety zone for escaping the judgment.

Helena starts talking about her life as a mother and the words pour out. Her six-year-old daughter is in first grade, and her three-year-old daughter is playing nearby. In her years as a mother, Helena's been a student and worked in schools. She's been a stay-at-home mom and she's worked part-time and full-time in different measures. "People are so critical of mothers," she says. "My mother-in-law never worked outside the home. She's critical of me for not being able to do all the things she did, even though I've always worked and I have two children. She feels bitterly that I won't take the kids on eight-hour road trips whenever she wants to see them. She'll say, 'I drove the boys on long car trips every year.' She thinks I'm a failure as a mother because I can't do everything she did. The bar is set so high. But she never worked, so she doesn't understand. My house isn't as clean as hers, but she doesn't work and she had a housekeeper all her life."

Another family member also doesn't understand. "We were talking the other night and I was telling her how we live in the city and the schools are bad, and even though we get tuition aid, paying for schools puts a big financial strain on our family," says Helena. "She told me not to complain—'You're choosing not to earn as much as you can possibly earn, so how dare you complain.' She doesn't get it. I didn't want to work full-time because I have two young children. I don't see how I could be the parent that I and my husband believe our family needs. We don't want our children in daycare for forty hours a week."

Both Helena and her husband feel that a kid's early life is important, and that you only have one chance at it, to run around, to be with your kids before school begins for real, to play and relax. If they have to wait on some of their financial aspirations, they feel it's worth it.

"Both of us are as available as we can be," Helena explained, "but for many years, I had the milk so I stayed home. Last year when I worked full-time, Charles left work at three and picked up the girls. I got home at four, and he'd go upstairs and work at home for two more hours. It totally disrupted his workday, but that's the way we could make it work so the kids wouldn't be in care till five o'clock. He works for a small company that's flexible. 'Family first' is one of their values, so he can do this. It's a trade-off for him. He's looking for a new job now, and he'll end up at a larger company. We know that though he'll make more money, there will a trade-off in terms of less flexibility for our family and his life as a father."

The parent problem is multifaceted—affected by workplace convention, by the expectation that the perfect worker is unencumbered by family responsibilities, by the constant media staging of wars between working moms and at-home moms, by government regulations on health benefits and part-time work. It's affected by our centuries-old belief that women are caretakers and men gather resources for the family, and by the more recent attempts to change these gender roles. Still, families struggle to sort out the intimacies of how to divide the often invisible labors of domestic life.

When Mariella's daughter was born, she had just been offered a job curating a public art gallery. It was close to a dream job. After childbirth, though, she was blown away by how much she wanted to be with her daughter. Her husband had been offered a fellowship that would deposit them in Berlin for a year. With a sense of abandon, they went, toddler daughter in tow. Now, four years later, their daughter is in school, and Mariella's on to the next stage of her life, repairing her life as an artist, making new art, and sending slides to galleries. Her family doesn't have much money. They rent part of a house on a busy street and they drive a single, older car. Once her daughter started kindergarten, Mariella began teaching art and design classes around town. She worked first at a nearby college, and after several years landed a good job teaching art at a high school, choosing this so that her work hours would overlap with her daughter's time at school.

Mariella explains why she put work aside when her daughter was born: "It wasn't exactly a choice, it was something less chosen, and more private. My mother was a social worker. She worked all the time. I wanted to wake my daughter up and put her to bed and see her all the day through. That's the kind of relationship I want to have." When I pose to her the problem we all face—that in leaving our work we are unwittingly turning back the hands of feminist progress—she offers this answer: "No, I can't really take responsibility for all of that. Mine was a feminist choice, well, not in the usual sense. It was a feminist reaction, if anything, an uneasiness."

Mariella chose to be home during her daughter's preschool years; she didn't choose a world in which most fathers still do less than their share of housework and childcare, something we knew was true anecdotally and which was recently proven by the government-funded American Time Use Survey, which confirmed that mothers spend twice as much time as men on chores and childcare. She didn't choose how hard it would be five years later to find studio time and rebuild her reputation as an artist, or to find work as a teaching artist with a four-year résumé gap.

Mothers don't want to lose their souls, as Scottie said so eloquently, when they choose to parent full-time, and neither do we want to lose our place in the working world to do such an ordinary and necessary part of life. We need to create a culture that doesn't see parenting and mothering as such an all-or-nothing choice, that gives us more space for interlacing these parts of our lives. As one woman remarked to me, "When I take my granddaughter to the playground, the mothers are lovely, but they seem to feel like they can only be mothers, that they can't talk about the other parts of themselves. They're all well educated and they've done interesting things in their lives. It's as if they've bought into the old idea that motherhood is exclusive, that it has to chop off the rest of your life, that it can't be integrated."

The parent problem is always portrayed as a women's issue, which it both is and shouldn't be. Mothers are more likely than fathers to experience it despite the growing numbers of stay-at-home dads. Still, it's us mothers who by and large do more of the childcare and more of the daily chores associated with childraising and housekeeping.[2] As Mariella noted with verve, "There were things that the feminist movement never got to. For example, they never got through to my husband. I'm just tired of fighting over the division of household labor." It's still more likely for mothers to make job sacrifices, move into and out of the workplace, downshift their careers after the kids arrive. More women than men bear the economic brunt of job sacrifice that comes with parenting, and we're left more vulnerable as a result. The parent problem happens at home and it happens in the workplace. The parent problem is a serious, structural problem. It's a remnant of an economy that saw men as central and ideal workers and relegated women to supporting roles at home.

The parent problem affects women of all classes. The public media face of it, certainly, is affluent and white—professional women with fancy degrees and jobs that demand sixty-hour workweeks, travel, and evening commitments. Caitlin Flanagan, writing a series of articles about motherhood in the *Atlantic Monthly*, famously told professional mothers to be quiet and think about how hard life is for women who work in factories. Elizabeth Kolbert, in the *New Yorker*, opined that these are problems for those of us who really have no problems, and really, that we should stop whining. Yet, the parent problem affects all of us despite the lack of media interest in the rest of the mothers out here. It's not a zero-sum game. Money can make the problem go away for a while, but as the media's focus on professional and affluent women shows time and again, all the money in the world can't get your old employer to hire you back to your job part-time or when your kids are in school or whenever you're ready to return. Money, apparently, can't solve this issue of work, family life, and gender.

All of us are pieces of the same story—all of us living in the same gender culture, the same society that still gives the responsibility of childraising and domestic life to women. Julie Press is a sociologist at Temple University who has just completed a study of poor and middle-class working women and childcare. "We treat children and their care as an individual problem," she says. "Our national policy sees the care of children as something essentially private, without national benefit. We have fewer regulations on childcare than on the people who do your hair or your nails. What we need is a national conversation about all this."

This book about parenting is not about our kids, it's about us. You won't find creative lunchbox ideas, menu planners, tips to make bedtime easier, or clues to get kids to stop tantrums, use the toilet, brush their teeth, or say thank you to adults. You also won't find judgment or castigation for your choices as a parent because we're all in this together, and we need all the friendly support we can get. I promise never to offer advice on how best to raise kids; on that count, I'm navigating along with everyone else. You won't even find many stories about my own daughter, much as I love to tell them to anyone who will listen. No, this book about parenting is about us parents, about mothers and fathers, about a new generation of parents caught between a rock and a hard place, as they used to say, of work and family, paychecks and parenting, living in a society that takes more and more hours from its workers ("productivity" it's called), demands very strict career paths based on a century-old model of American family life—without offering much security—and offers bewildering and contradictory messages about what mothering and parenting should be ("Bake cupcakes!" "Bring home a six-figure salary!" "Buy the right baby products!"). Think of this book as an extended moms' night out—where we get to hang out, drink beer if we want to, and tell secrets. Where we can boast about the good and bitch about the bad and spin homespun visions from the playground and the kitchen table for how life can be better. I offer this book as a guide through the confusion and the conundrum of work and parenting in twenty-first-century America.

The chapters that follow chronicle what happens when we start to talk about the work we do as mothers and how we feel about it; about the public world of motherhood and the cultural images that surround us; and about the social change coming our way when we see parenting and family as truly part of the larger world. Changes are also imminent when we see our personal decisions as part of larger trends and when we ask our shared institutions—our workplaces, our state and federal governments, our newspapers and magazines and websites—to start counting the labor of parenting, to move beyond the old terms that divide life into public and private spheres that value only the wage-earning public life and devalue the domestic work of parenting and housekeeping. This work is what keeps us together day after day, the work that keeps us clean, fed, clothed, that packs the kids' lunches, feeds them dinner, keeps up with their teachers and homework, and trots them off to swimming, or art class, or music lessons, or playdates with friends, or to whatever else adds spark and magic to their lives; the work that raises them up to be good adults.

These are profoundly real issues; how dare they get diverted into fake wars over who frosts her cupcakes better. At the moment, this problem falls more heavily on women's shoulders (it doesn't have to stay that way; we hope that men will continue to take more of a role in raising kids), and that makes it one of the most pressing feminist issues around—that makes it *the* issue that could lead us into a new feminist moment.

We inherit from Western civilization a series of terms and oppositions, words like "public" and "private" and "domestic" that powerfully obscure very real connections. We're told that family life is private, even as our daytime talk shows mercilessly air family life's dirty laundry; even as politicians make laws about who can marry, how families are taxed, how healthcare will be disbursed, when children must start school, and how old they have to be to give up their car seats. Families are very much the focus of public attention, just not always in the most helpful ways.

We also inherit a sense of American individualism—something very helpful and inspiring in some situations, but poorly suited, it turns out, to caring for our families. What we need to do is to begin to see our families and our decisions about care and work in broader terms than are usually available in our headlines and magazines—and in our society at large. This book is a start.

CHAPTER 1.

Do Real Women Have Mommy Wars?

"Working moms should hide in shame for
putting their kids in a filthy daycare center."

"Stay-at-home moms get their nails done all
day long."

"Working mothers are selfish."

"Stay-at-home mothers waste their education
and throw us back to the 1950s."

These comments aired recently on daytime TV on a show that separated working moms and stay-at-home moms—literally seated
them on opposite sides of the aisle—because, as we all know, "there's a
big division between them." Nowadays, all over the media it's the
Mommy Wars: Mothers are either working full-time and are uninvolved,
absentee parents, or full-time homemakers, nonintellectual, hovering,
and provincial. In the Mommy Wars version of motherhood, the women
in each group have nothing in common with the women in the other;
they share no values. Instead, battles rage. Both sides are embittered and
entrenched—so much so that on the *Dr. Phil* show from which the above

quotes were pulled, workforce moms and stay-at-home mothers were physically separated, like hitting toddlers who couldn't share.

Mommy Wars reports insist on two essential kinds of mothers. Parenting choices last forever, the reports presume. Stay-at-home mothers never return to the workplace. Ardent working women committed to their jobs never up and quit because they get no support.

In real life, mothers move into and out of the paid workplace. Most mothers—upwards of 60 percent—work less than full-time. Not so in the world of the Mommy Wars, where the problem is never with the workplace—it's just that these two types of mothers don't get along. They never switch places; they never show empathy, only judgment. Neither group, we should suppose, gets along with the 18 percent of women in America who don't have children. If only these different moms could love each other, well, the frustrations of motherhood would be solved. Lots of newspaper dailies and magazine issues are sold on this premise, and daytime TV pitches us the Mommy Wars like makeovers and insta-therapy.

Yet, I don't find my life reflected in the hype. When I hang out with my neighbor Mary, a lawyer who has a seven-year-old and twin toddlers and works long hours in an office downtown (as does her husband), there's no animosity. We like each other very much. Same with Ellen, a single mother, across the street; or Chris next door with her two teenage daughters. When my daughter was very young and I was at home more, my two closest friends in the neighborhood both worked full-time. Susan had left one job when her first child was born. Like me, she worked several states away from the house she shared with her husband. After a year off, she got lucky and found a good job that was nearby, but lacked the security of the job she had left behind. Lisa was a former international entrepreneur who had spent many years running an import/export business in Southeast Asia. Her business had fallen victim to the Asian recession around the time she married and had her baby. Now divorced and the mother of a toddler, she works from her basement as a sales rep for a British ceramic tile company. We all met at the neighborhood playground. Of my two longtime best girlfriends, neither has children. So much for the Mommy Wars.

Despite experiences like mine, which many women share, however, the term Mommy Wars still supplies the most widely available description of our lives as mothers—lives in which we are isolated, defensive, guilt stricken, and tired. Instead of encouraging us to band together, voice concern, and work for change, the Mommy Wars prompt us to judge and undermine mothers who live their lives differently.

Let's be clear: Women do envy and dislike each other (as do men) for various reasons. Envy is endemic in our society, and our society seems particularly mean spirited these days. We are encouraged to express nastiness instead of yielding to our better and more empathetic instincts. When I ask whether real women have Mommy Wars, it's not because I think we're all saintly. I'm attempting to separate our true instincts from the images public culture and media create *for* us, images that we mothers sometimes adopt as our own, images that take our more diverse and complex experiences and sculpt them into something more singular but which ignore the more humane and community-building parts of our lives. The most widely available images of motherhood are not positive reflections of mothers' existence—in fact, they are often poisonous.

To illustrate the strength with which media shapes our lives, let's take a look at an example that we're no longer as closely enmeshed in: the Soccer Mom. Remember her? Before the current at-home mom vs. working mom media-fueled Mommy Wars, there was the Soccer Mom, a sporty '90s incarnation of motherhood who drove an oversize, gas-guzzling minivan. She was the appointed representative of middle-class motherhood. The mother we were supposed to be and the mother we were supposed to define ourselves against. She's the caring mom—she drives her kids around—crossed with the consumer mom. When she's not at the soccer field, she's filling up at Sam's Club. With her gas-guzzling SUV or minivan and her perfectly applied makeup, she was also a straw woman, the symbol of all that's supposed to be wrong with suburban culture. Soccer Mom carted troops of kids round to leisure-time sporting activities and hauled the groceries to feed them after the game. Her first priority was family—and fulfilling their consumer needs.

We barely mention Soccer Moms anymore. They've become anachronistic, at the very least—I noticed that when my sixteen-year-old niece recently used the term. She wasn't complaining about her own mom, an immigration lawyer who can't find it in herself to bill her clients enough to afford a minivan. Molly's mom doesn't fit the Soccer Mom stereotype, despite having cheered Molly's soccer teams from many a sideline on a finger-numbing Saturday morn. To Molly and her friends, Soccer Moms are simply mothers who drive minivans—problematic to sixteen-year-old new drivers who wouldn't be caught dead driving their moms' uncool cars.

Soccer Mom had devolved into Minivan Mom, a mother defined by her choice of car, frumpy clothes, or (from a teen perspective) bad hairstyle. Social stereotypes of mothers are created and they become quite powerful, even though we know better. Often we mimic media images of who we are supposed to be—again, even when we know better. But who creates these mother images in the first place? Who, for example, created Soccer Mom and with what intent?

Soccer Mom didn't always exist. In fact, she was willed into being in the 1980s as a tool for winning political elections. The earliest attestations of the phrase take us back to 1982, when "Soccer Moms" merely meant organizations of mothers who raised money to support their kids' soccer teams. These mothers' auxiliaries sold chocolate bars and organized cupcake sales so the kids could have new uniforms, while the dads mostly coached and refereed. Picture them as the classic Women's Auxiliary doing traditional, female, behind-the-scenes work to make sure the players got trophies and end-of-season pizza banquets. These clubs reached the national news when a certain Joseph Decosta, the thirty-four-year-old husband of the treasurer of the Soccer Moms club in Ludlow, Massachusetts, looted $3,150 from the cashbox. The consequence was a month in jail, full restitution of the funds, and a mention on the Associated Press wire of October 14, 1982, picked up by newspapers throughout the country. "Soccer mom" was a literal, specific description of someone who "stood on wet grass at 7:00 AM on Saturday mornings drinking cold coffee on the sidelines," as penned by Renee Peck in the *New Orleans Times-Picayune*. For Peck, herself a Soccer Mom, it meant "weekend treks to places like Birmingham and Jackson . . . a minivan that smells like a locker room . . . filling up my car with gas (regular, self-serve) three times a week." Soccer Mom had not yet become political and mythic, larger than any one mother could be.

Indices of American magazines and newspapers show that the Soccer Mom barely beeped the radar until 1995, when she appeared in a handful of articles, most about a certain Susan Casey, a Democrat running for the Denver City Council. Casey used the term to reassure voters that even though she was an accomplished and well-educated woman, voters could trust her to be just like them. The phrase cut to the heart of anxiety about women's achievements, and it cut against stereotypes about smart and accomplished women—that they can't manage professional success and family love simultaneously. What Casey meant was: "I have a PhD and I've managed national presidential campaigns, but when I wake up in the morning and go to bed at night, my heart and soul are with my family." It was as if she were saying, "Don't worry if I'm really smart, I still love my family like ordinary women do." Casey won that election and represented southeast Denver on the city council; she was reelected in 1999.

Casey wasn't looking to coin a phrase that would hurt and demean women. When asked about it after the phrase had lit up the national stage, she insisted she had meant no gender stereotype. Soccer Mom was a way of showing Denver voters just how ordinary she was, she said. And Soccer Mom accurately describes a good deal of what Susan Casey was doing as a mother. Her son Conor, now in his twenties, was no ordinary thirteen-year-old travel-league player. Soccer was his thing. An excellent athlete, he competed on the United States soccer team in the 2000 Olympics in Sydney and now plays professionally in Germany. Susan Casey really *was* a Soccer Mom, in the most descriptive and literal sense.

All that was to change in the 1996 presidential election, which pitted Bob Dole against Bill Clinton. In Susan Casey's case, the candidate had been the Soccer Mom. In 1996, Soccer Moms were *the* targeted swing voters, just as "angry white men" had been targeted in the previous election and had installed a Republican Congress. Soccer Moms were the new election season's elusive stars, in part because the political pundits grasped them as a group but couldn't predict whether they would vote Republican or Democrat, and so they fascinated consultants and pollsters. But it was Republican pundit and consultant Alex Castellanos who readied Soccer Mom for election prime time. Castellanos is famously described as one of the fathers of the modern attack ad and as the Republicans' "ultimate hit man." In addition to creating the Soccer Mom phenomenon, he was the architect behind the infamous "RATS" ad during the 2000 presidential campaign between Al Gore and George W. Bush. During a TV spot that attacked Gore's position on healthcare, the word "RATS" flashed across the screen for a subliminal second as the word "bureaucrats" faded into the following scene. After public outcry that this sunk below even the level of decency we now expect from political spots, the "RATS" ad was pulled. When Castellanos worked for the campaign of archconservative Jesse Helms, the former senator from North Carolina, he produced the similarly infamous "white hands" commercial to save Helms from a challenge by Harvey Gantt, a black businessman and politician who had been mayor of Charlotte. This political spot featured a newly unemployed white man crumpling a pink slip in his hands while the voice-over complained, "[T]hey had to give it to a minority." That image lightens and Gantt's head fades in until we see the white man's hands crushing Gantt's head. This is the guy who really created Soccer Mom.[1]

Soccer Mom's origin is based in the recognition of the so-called political gender gap, in which women tend to vote for Democrats. Castellanos told the *Washington Post*, "The biggest change [in political life] is the increasing political and economic independence of women, soccer moms, diner moms, and laptop moms." These women are, in his words, "care and fair voters." To get their attention and their votes, he advised conservative politicians to downplay traditional masculine pre-occupations with guns, violence, and order. They should instead emphasize supposedly feminine concepts like "fairness, compassion, and equality of opportunity."[2] That is, downplay, but not change their positions; it's the same rhetorical tactic that produced "compassionate conservatism" as an appeal to women voters' sense of care.

"The working soccer mom is the swing voter of this election, and she is not going to trust a guy who argues for the need to own an assault weapon," Castellanos explained to the *Wall Street Journal*.[3] Or, in the words of this famous quote in the *Washington Post*: "It's hard to explain to a soccer mom why soccer dad needs a sawed-off shotgun."[4] This "feminization" of politics was not about content, about policies that would make life easier for women, mothers, and families; it was about persuading them to change their vote.

Soccer Mom offered a way for Republican strategists to present a common denominator of women's experience in which driving kids to sports games and cheering from the sidelines was the late twentieth century's addition to the list of women's work. That's why we heard about Soccer Moms and not Soccer Dads; politicians had already predicted how they would vote. Soccer Mom became a uniting symbol for white, suburban moms in hopes of convincing them of their shared issues, and then appealing to them as such. This is what pollsters and pundits do—the idea being that it's easier to convince us that we're part of a group, and then campaign to a group, rather than reach out to each of us on our own terms. As the term became commonplace, its origin in partisan politics was obscured. Soccer Mom was political, though not of her own devising.

In 1996, when the term spread through America's playgrounds, ball fields, and newspapers, being a mother was far from my mind. I was teaching my classes, training graduate students, writing grant proposals, and putting the finishing touches on my academic books so I could get tenure and climb the professional ladder. I lived in North Central Florida and I taught at a large state university. I remember little of the 1996 political race. I do recall that all of a sudden everybody started talking about Soccer Moms, but it wasn't quite clear who exactly these moms were. It was assumed that they were suburban and married. It was assumed that they had some education, and, of course, that they had kids and were white. And by stereotype they drove large vehicles: minivans or the SUVs that were just beginning to be mass marketed.

Later on, Soccer Mom was conflated with stay-at-home mom. Long after the election, the term "Soccer Mom" gained traction as a way to slander any middle-class mother who was super-devoted to her kids, and, as a result, not very hip. At their inception, though, Soccer Moms were not divided into stay-at-home moms or working moms. The division that today has so much currency was off the map of the Soccer Mom. Whether a mom earned her own wages was immaterial.

Of course, it wasn't ever clear who Soccer Mom really was. How could it be? Soccer Mom is a figment: a political mythology, a cliché, a mad attempt to turn women into a cohesive entity. She was followed in short order by other results of political pollsters' ongoing attempts to find and name swing-voter groups. Democratic strategists like Celinda Lake, of Lake Snell Perry & Associates, have been just as active as Republican counterparts like Alex Castellanos in coining terms that divide us by class, race, and gender into clichéd groups they hope will vote for their team. Lake gave us Waitress Moms, who, in contrast to Soccer Moms' middle-class, suburban ease and time for leisure, worked hard. Waitress Moms were working-class, non-college-educated mothers who struggled to make ends meet; Democrats were seeking their vote. Office Park Dads and NASCAR Dads were socially conservative, racetrack-loving men who might sway Democratic on economic issues. These creations had little do with real roles or with how people cared for their kids.

We think that Soccer Mom is just about style and automobile choice, but she turns out to have a complex political history. Who knew? In tandem, media accounts of successive elections turn these new, false "identities" into truth and report them as social trends. What's interesting is that "Soccer Mom" stuck as a popular way to define mothers and "Waitress Mom" didn't. On the one hand, Waitress Moms, and working-class mothers in general, are portrayed very humanely in newspaper articles about family life and particularly in those about how hard it is to find affordable and reliable daycare.[5] On the other, Soccer Mom and her divided successors, stay-at-home mom and working mom, make better magazine cover copy. These mothers are always portrayed as professional, well educated, and affluent. They have dollars to spend and they add sparkle to the style section. Waitress Mom has no extra money, and after the campaign season ends, advertisers aren't interested. But as Soccer Mom was shunted to the more affluent end of the stereotype, she was recognized as an ideal consumer with appeal to advertisers; hence she became even more interesting to newspapers, magazines, television, and websites, all of whom want to court those advertisers.

That the history of Soccer Mom is so wrapped up in electoral politics and strategy helps us realize the falseness, the thinness, of the major motherhood images around us. It makes it easier, I hope, to see how similarly constructed and unreal are the standards of motherhood today—the stay-at-home mom and the working mom.

So now that Soccer Mom has become affluent and dowdy, and stays at home, what about those Mommy Wars? In 1986, an article by

Barbara J. Berg titled "Mothers Against Mothers" appeared on the style page of the *Washington Post*.[6] Berg is also the author of *The Crisis of the Working Mother*. To put the article in context, we need to remember that the mid-'80s were the beginning years of the so-called echo boom; for the first time since the end of the postwar baby boom, the birthrate was starting to rise. This in itself would raise the challenges facing mothers to new levels; this was a postfeminist decade in which many women inherited the sense that public opportunity and economic independence was theirs for the taking, along with a family life in which mothers still did more of the childraising and housework. With more new babies, more women would be worrying about what to do. They had few models of how to work full-time jobs and parent at the same time. Ellen Galinsky, now president of the Families and Work Institute, is quoted in "Mothers Against Mothers": "[W]ith no antecedents, women do not have the comfort of knowing the long-term implications. . . . If they choose one way, there's always the discomforting possibility of having chosen the other. That can cause anger and resentment toward those women who have taken a different path because it leads to heightened ambivalences about one's own choices."

In 1986, women could still express ambivalence, the tensive desire to have it both ways. Motherhood had not yet been hardened into stone-chiseled opposition. And even an article that used a headline of opposition (as well as a graphic depicting one white woman with an infant across her chest and her arm around an older child's shoulder, and another white woman dressed to the nines with a stylish briefcase in hand) could end by pointing to the social and political problems all women face: "Most ironic, however, is that women must cope with living in a society that accepts, but does not completely support, either choice. The homemaker knows how easily she can be 'displaced' and how difficult it might be for her to find a job if she is. The professional must deal with inadequate maternity leaves and the problems of finding childcare. It is in that respect that, perhaps, they will eventually accept one another as allies instead of as adversaries." How little we hear about these social challenges in the twenty-first-century updates of "Mothers Against Mothers."

In 1986, a reporter could still admit that there was a social land-scape for motherhood that made it hard for any woman to parent with ease. In the '80s, as now, the press was filled with articles about moth-ers leaving the fast track. They were largely focused on professional women even though many of the women interviewed in "Mothers Against Mothers" held more ordinary jobs (one was an administrative assistant, another was a resource planner at an accounting firm).

The intervening years have changed the types of articles that are published. We find much less of a political sensibility in today's reports. At the same time, the complexity of society has only increased—and we still have inadequate daycare, rising job demands, questions of how much job prestige and money affect our lifestyles and self-esteem, plum-meting quality in our nation's schools, a gender wage gap that isn't budging, the failure of the mommy track, and the continued resistance to high-quality, fair-salary part-time jobs.[7]

In 1986, feminist dreams seemed closer, more resonant. It's the moment just before "postfeminism" became the new word of the day. By the 1990s, Susan Douglas and Meredith Michaels argue in *The Mommy Myth*, American society saw a conjunction of several trends: the aging out of second-wave feminism; the promotion of the new domesticity, focused on home beauty à la Martha Stewart (*Martha Stewart Living* hit the newsstands in 1991); the continued corporate resistance to women's rightful status in the workplace; and the success of the belief that family issues like childcare and paid parental leave were "private," that each woman could and should handle them indi-vidually. Once a certain feminist political outlook was lost, women and mothers were on their own. There was nothing cultural left to unite, then, except a sense of lifestyle. Sidestepping the task of reporting on real, intransigent issues that could help women continue their jobs,

Douglas argues, the media instead promoted home as the answer and continued the "catfight."[8]

Many years later, in 2002, *New York* magazine published the cover story "Mom Vs. Mom." The story featured Ann, a working mom who felt shunned by a stay-at-home mom at a school fundraiser. Their kids were both in kindergarten, so Ann had introduced herself to the mother and said hello. The other woman responded, "Oh," and walked away. The reporter, Ralph Gardner Jr., remarks, "Ann is certain she knows why her fellow mom dissed her, if in fact she did. It has nothing to do with Ann's confusing on-again-off-again marriage or the disparity in their net worth (Ann is middle-class; the other woman is profoundly wealthy). No, as far as Ann is concerned, the reason the other woman turned tail is that Ann works full-time."[9]

Now, this may all be true (although the article is filled with backtracks—she disses, if in fact she did). The reporter, however, doesn't track down the dissing mother to ask. Perhaps she's just rude. Perhaps she was busy; perhaps she only talks to her circle of friends. None of these are nice reasons—but not everyone's nice, and rudeness alone isn't reason enough for a cover story. Not even following the usual reportorial convention of seeking two sides to a story, the reporter lets Ann's analysis stand. One reason: The article was framed by books that had been published that fall, especially by Allison Pearson's novel *I Don't Know How She Does It* in which the tragicomic investment-banker heroine constantly tosses barbs at the pietistic stay-at-home moms at her children's school and is in turn criticized mercilessly by them. What's interesting about this antagonism is that despite the book's other contributions, and despite Pearson's many radio interviews in which she speaks poignantly about the paucity of options for mothers, this image of women dissing each other is what people remember, even though the heroine's trajectory is more realistic and helpful: She leaves her ninety-hour-a-week job, filled with hateful men who Photoshop female colleagues' heads onto Internet-porn bodies, to find

end-of-book happiness in an entrepreneurial venture that supports
local women's craftwork, working on her own terms.

A similar scene in which moms disdain each other at the school
function is reported by Caitlin Flanagan in "To Hell with All That,"
published in the New Yorker in 2004. Literature becomes life: Flanagan
writes vividly about an auction at a private school in L.A. (and we
might question why the stock setting for these articles is the school
fundraiser). Flanagan's been a stay-at-home mom for a few years, enjoying life at home with her twin boys and their nanny. Now that her writing's being published she wants to hang with the working moms, the
lawyers and TV producers who are to her the mom version of high
school's cool girls. Together, drinks in hand, Caitlin's gang of working
moms starts to make fun of the auction organizer, a stay-at-home mom
who is flustering her way through the presentation onstage. When I
read this passage I cringed. This woman, after all, had spent hundreds
of hours on behalf of the school doing something that would help
everyone's children. I know, on one hand, there is liberation in admitting to being mean and bad, especially when you're a mother and have
that sense of never being able to let loose. On the other hand, the scene
was just plain cruel, and was then penned into an article that uses
seductively beautiful prose to once again pit working mothers against
stay-at-home mothers—an article that discusses women's desires about
work and home as if they were mere style issues, unconnected to a history of feminism, of domesticity, or of the ongoing difficulty of our
workplaces to be flexible and forgiving of parenthood. Very few women
have public voices, and even fewer get to publish regularly in the New
Yorker, so it's a damn shame to waste an opportunity like that by
repeating hurtful things that we already know aren't exactly true.

With all of these stories that somehow sound the same, I'm left
wondering: Is the animosity real? Do we really hate working mothers?
At-home mothers? Perhaps we have read enough of these stories that
we call their responses our own. We hear and see them so often that

they now predict how we will respond to other women, what we'll think of mothers who aren't caring for their children the same way we are. Furthermore, are we all just so angry about our limited options that we toss hate wherever we can? People are mad. Mothers are mad. They're frustrated because the culture is so constricted and because it tells us we have many choices when we really don't have enough good ones. But instead of expressing that dilemma, how often do we vent and take frustration out on other women?

Well, according to the *Dr. Phil* "Mom vs. Mom" show that aired on November 10, 2003, that is all we do. Its largely female audience was divided into stay-at-home mothers and workforce mothers seated on opposite sides of the aisle. Up onstage were Sonja and Leah, the representative working mom and at-home mom, and seated in the front row were the show's two experts, chosen to represent opposite positions on the continuum of how women care for their children, earn a living, and follow their creative, professional, and wage-earning desires. According to the two experts, Heidi Brennan and Joan K. Peters, the conversation during the taping was so compelling, so attentive to all the complex issues of parenting, that the audience was asked to stay for an additional hour, in effect taping two shows instead of one.

Brennan and Peters had conferred briefly just before the show began. Each enjoyed the chance to meet the other. Both women wanted to bridge the gap between different kinds of mothers, not exacerbate it. When the taping concluded, both felt that an important conversation had taken place and looked forward to seeing the final result.

When the show was aired, however, both women were appalled. In place of the relatively careful conversation they'd experienced, the heavily edited show featured an audience of mothers hurling insults at one other. Working moms were told they never see their kids. Stay-at-home moms were accused of turning back the entire feminist movement. If ordinary TV viewers were shocked at the confrontational results of the edited show, so too were Brennan and Peters, and they worked together to take action.

Peters is the author of *When Mothers Work: Loving Our Children Without Sacrificing Ourselves* and *Not Your Mother's Life: Changing the Rules of Work, Love, and Family*. She argues for more egalitarian family setups and less sacrifice for women. Brennan is a public policy advisor for the Family and Home Network, which publishes a small monthly newsletter called *Welcome Home*. Its primary audience is stay-at-home mothers, but as the organization has grown, and listened with quiet intelligence to its members, it has expanded its vision to include all parents who want a bit more time with their kids: mothers who work part-time; stay-at-home fathers; parents who work from home, telecommuting or building small businesses; families where both parents work part-time or do tag-team parenting, with one parent working alternate day and evening shifts. The Family and Home Network advocates on behalf of all these parents. It provides information to members of Congress and keeps a spotlight on media coverage of motherhood in its monthly newsletter, which offers advice and inspiration to parents who are trying to spend more time with their kids. On principle, the network turns down requests to participate in Mommy War events.

Neither of Dr. Phil's experts that day believes that the culprit in the Mommy Wars is ever other women. In fact, it is safe to say that neither Brennan nor Peters believes that the Mommy Wars actually exist as such. Both live in the much more ordinary and quotidian world where average women and men spend their days trying to earn a decent living with fair wages and working conditions, and to raise their children with some balance, grace, love, and calm. According to Cathy Myers, executive director of the Family and Home Network, "[T]here is not a rigid dividing line between mothers determined by whether they are employed or not. Couples share income-earning and caregiving responsibilities. They divide these responsibilities in whichever way is best for them. Parents often adjust their responsibilities as their children grow. Single parents can also share income-earning and caregiving responsibilities with extended family members or close friends. Many have written to tell us of the creative solutions they find to meet their children's needs for consistent, nurturing care."

After the *Dr. Phil* show aired, Brennan and Peters, angered at the editing fiasco, issued a joint statement of disapproval and posted it on the Family and Home Network's website. They acknowledged their different opinions about parenting and childcare policy. However, they emphasized there is no war but a "common struggle to support our families financially and emotionally." They sent out a call for a "mothering movement" that would gather all parents together to call for structural social changes. Their call might serve as a general starting point for us all: What do we—women, mothers, fathers, parents—want? The question is a real one, but it is too often posed in the singular, as if everyone were the same and wanted the same thing, and as though the answer to what ails and annoys us might be reduced to a single, unified response.

It turns out that fathers and mothers want many improvements, and few of them are easily delivered: greater workplace flexibility for parents and support for family leave, part-time work, flextime, telecommuting, and home-based businesses; universal healthcare for children that doesn't depend on a parent's job; successful schools for all kids, since parents report working more hours than they want and take on more debt than they think wise in order to live near decent schools; and new cultural messages that are less concerned with consumption and more concerned with valuing family life in all its forms.

In other words, to make their work less difficult, parents want real, social, structural changes—a shifting landscape that will come from government, business, our shared culture, and personal commitment. Their joint statement is a far cry from the bits and pieces of their conversations that were spliced and edited for the sake of TV combat.

The *Dr. Phil* show caught the eyes and ire of other mothers' organizations as well. Mothers & More was founded in 1985 to support women in all stages of their mothering lives, whether they are at home, working full-time, or combining hands-on parenting with some kind of paid work. Its mission is to raise awareness of the fact that mothers live and work in a society that presents significant barriers to their success as women, citizens, parents, or participants in the workforce. It has a national office, 180 chapters throughout the United States, and more than seventy-five hundred members nationwide. Mothers & More responded to the *Dr. Phil* spectacle by creating its first ever "Apple Pie in the Face" award in his honor. The Apple Pie in the Face award focuses attention on media acts that try to divide mothers, create false arguments between them, or demean their struggles.

On its website, Mothers & More asked its members to take action by writing letters of dissent to the *Dr. Phil* show and by sending letters to the editors of their local newspapers. Because this was an Apple Pie award, it was suggested that members might actually send pies—yes, actual apple pies, the fictional companion of true American motherhood—to the *Dr. Phil* show at 5482 Wilshire Boulevard, Los Angeles, CA, 90036. From its national office in humble Elmhurst, Illinois, Mothers & More launched a conventional agitprop response to yet another chapter in the ongoing attempts to keep mothers fighting each other instead of fighting to make things better for everyone.[10]

Over on the West Coast, a blogger at Hipmama.com also took aim at Dr. Phil:

Hey Mamas,
    Did anyone catch *Dr. Phil* yesterday? I was flipping through the channels and I caught the subject: WORKING MOMS VS. STAY-AT-HOME MOMS and I tuned in.
    It was so frustrating. He had these entrenched, embattled women going at it: smug working mamas on one side and self-righteous

home mamas on the other side. Each demonizing and belittling the other.

This is not the debate mamas need to have. We need to have a debate about how to be inclusive and create support for all mamas and their choices.

We need to create a dialogue about our similarities—working mamas come home to childcare, housework, and cooking. Most of the home mamas I know also work. . . .

The other thing that raised my ire is that these were middle-class to upper-middle-class women who had the privilege of making that choice.

The dialogue we need to have is how to include and help poor, overworked, sometimes uneducated, and often unsupported mamas like the mamas of my husband's students. (He is an inner-city emotional support teacher in an elementary school.) . . .

Shame on Dr. Phil. And thank God for *Hipmama* and like-minded communities that support rather than polarize mamas with stupid labels and accusatory, expert studies.

Once you scratch the surface, our private angst and public debates about mothers and parenting are also intimately and excruciatingly about class, cultural capital, and economic possibility as much as they're about classic gender roles and their complexity. Were it not for the relentless reminders of the few that not all mothers are middle class and up—*Hip Mama* magazine and its website perhaps leading this movement—the national debate would rarely get this side of the story; as it is, *Hip Mama*'s voice is ignored more often than not. All sorts of mothers and fathers need help, and the help we need looks different depending on how much economic ease we have.

If most parents reject the stereotypes being handed down, how do those portrayals come to serve as such pervasive and persuasive models? Politics is part of it, but it gets even worse when we look for Mommy Wars instigators inside the world of marketing and advertising. For the moment, let's not even concentrate on the advertisements themselves, but on the inside reports that ad executives and marketing firms produce and circulate to their clients and to the press—the reports that create the conditions and concepts for the ads that eventually emerge. Mostly, we see the end product, the TV spot or the newspaper layout. But examining the process of producing and marketing motherhood is even scarier and more enraging. And while they sell products, we feel put upon, and they make money.

To begin, let's look at a well-publicized marketing report released in 2004 by Euro RSCG Worldwide, the world's fifth-largest global advertising agency with more than two hundred offices in seventy-five countries. A specialist in advertising, marketing, and corporate communications, Euro RSCG thinks up "Creative Business Ideas," its registered trademark, for its clients. Creative Business Ideas "transform the product, the brand, the company—and sometimes even the business itself," according to its website. As Euro RSCG explains in its own promotional materials, a "Creative Business Idea results in profitable innovation, breakthrough solutions, and industry firsts—maximizing the relationship between consumers and brands."

Euro RSCG markets itself to clients as a company ahead of the game, with a bead on the culture and eyes on the future. To give a little background, back in 2003, Euro RSCG successfully popularized the term "metrosexual" to Americans in order to promote straight men who buffed their bodies, waxed their backs, and would and could buy more hair and beauty products. British journalist Mark Simpson, to describe the man imagined by the beauty industry, had coined the term back in 1994 feeling that it "described this new type of man who was actually part wish fulfillment on the part of advertising and the magazine industry, and had been willed into life." Euro RSCG preferred to disagree: Metrosexuals were not urban fantasy boys whose image was foisted on men with expendable income; they were "an existing demographic that was waiting to be defined." When metrosexuality hit the American press in summer 2003 it spread quickly. Americans loved this European import.[11]

And so it was that in spring of 2004, the trend analysts at Euro RSCG presented five new categories of mothers for their clients to consider. They also press-released their findings and the result was a showing of articles throughout the country. "This year," explained Marian Salzman, Euro RSCG Worldwide's executive vice president and chief strategy officer, "we're seeing the categories of 'working moms' and 'stay-at-home moms' splinter into numerous segments as women depart from tradition to forge life paths that work for them." According to Euro RSCG, the new categories that better describe real mothers' lives are these five: Domestic Divas, Boomerang Moms, Yummy Mummies, Mini-Me Moms, and the Rage Brigade.[12]

Euro RSCG's five categories for mothers emerged, apparently, from an online survey of 1,982 adults in the United States conducted in February 2004. They also come from phrases already bandied about through the British Commonwealth, from Sydney to London to Vancouver. "Yummy Mummy" in particular has been promoted—and critiqued—throughout Australia and Canada as *Sex and the City*-ish: a high-fashion, high-priced version of pregnancy and motherhood. (For its less uptown version, check out this call for a British TV show: "looking for single yummy mummies and their luscious daughters for a series that pits mothers and daughters against each other in a fun new dating series.") Here's the new marketing plan for motherhood:

Domestic Divas want their nannies to raise flawless kids and the housekeeper to make their homes gorgeous. The Diva Mom wants to look like the "perfect mom," but not actually do the work it takes. The Diva Mom role model is Carol Brady.

Boomerang Moms have worked during their kids' early years—in corporate jobs, mind you—and left the workplace only later, when their kids neared adolescence. Perhaps these moms (or their partners?) finally attained the financial security to allow them to leave. Their role models are Karen Hughes and Maria Shriver.

Yummy Mummies (I can barely write this without cringing) are ladies who lunch. Kids are their hobby, and Euro RSCG assures us that they spend most of their time at the gym and the mall, keeping their figures trim and their bodies clothed in the latest fashions, and in fear of being discarded by their successful husbands for younger, prettier versions of themselves. Role models: Catherine Zeta-Jones and *Will & Grace* character Karen Walker.

Mini-Me Moms see their children as fashion accessories to be dolled up and shown off. Think Madonna, Anna Wintour, or Kathie Lee Gifford. (I know—the role models don't exactly make sense to me, either, but that's because they are made up, patched together, and, in some cases, not actual women. They *can't* make sense.)

Maternal category number five is ominously named "the Rage Brigade." How different these mothers are from the Yummies and the Divas: The Rage Brigade includes all women who are dissatisfied with the terms of motherhood, marriage, and work. Perhaps they earn more than their partners, and thus can't easily leave their jobs or work fewer hours. They feel burdened by the time demands on their lives and angered when their spouse doesn't do half the housework. In any case, they can't perform the high-cost vision of femininity that Euro RSCG promotes for its clients. Rage women don't have expendable income or lots of time and desire to shop.

The trend report comes with some predictable platitudes about how of course these groups don't include *all* women, and about how nice it would be for mothers to all get along. Euro RSCG reminds us that mothers just don't get the social appreciation and admiration we deserve. But Diva Mom buys products. That's right: The categories that command 80 percent of the report's attention are affluent mothers with money to spend. Mini-Me Moms will need many expensive outfits for the kids. Yummies need gym memberships and massage and salon appointments and frequent meetings with the plastic surgeon and the dermatologist.

In this sinister vision of family life, mothers are blatantly divided for the sake of sales. The definition of which mothers matter is sharply limited to those who are affluent, to those who can spend, to those who want to be maternal in a high-end, hip, and material way. Seeing how reports like this cravenly create mother groups puts a disquieting, disturbing spin on motherhood's cultural definitions. We think of these definitions as coming out of the air—as vague reflections that generalize and stereotype but still somehow represent reality. But these names and definitions come out of political metaphors and marketing plans.

Time-wise, the Euro RSCG study competed with another marketing survey; this one, from Boston-based Reach Advisors, used sociological generalizations to help companies sell their goods to today's young families. Titled "Generation X Parents: From Grunge to Grown Up," the Reach report offers a snapshot of younger families, and of what parents who themselves were born in 1965 and after—the forty and younger set—like to do with their time and money. The report works by making us forget that parents in their twenties and thirties hold lots of different values and want different things. It works when we forget that "Generation X" was always a controversial title for the group it claimed to represent. Who needs to stereotype a cohort, a half-generation? Who gains? According to Reach Advisors: its clients.

Some Reach report findings: Generation Xers are better educated than their parents, but downwardly mobile and haunted by financial insecurity. Gen-X parents want more family time. They are thrifty; unlike the stereotypical boomer dads who buy Jaguars and brag about how much they cost, Gen-X moms and dads prefer good values (and note to advertisers seeking buzz: They spread the word to their friends when they find a good deal). Further, Gen-X moms marry later, have kids later, and earn more money on their own before doing so.

And what about Soccer Mom—does she carry on? It turns out she's generational history. Only 9 percent of Gen-X moms would use that label to describe themselves, and ad campaigns that target these younger mothers are advised to never use "one-dimensional portrayals" of motherhood. These are likely to be met with "a resoundingly cold shoulder." Gen-X dads, by the way, are no Ward Cleavers. They're much more integrated into the kids' lives. They do more work at home, and there's less of a hard line between a dad's workweek and the weekend with the kids. Note to advertisers and entrepreneurs: Younger dads "are more likely to play a significant role in purchases and activities for their kids."

The Reach Advisors report offers young families' lives on a platter for those who want to sell to them. Which would all be okay, were it not that these types of reports privilege some experiences and ignore others, and then portray the generalization as valid for all. Which would be okay, except that when reporters write stories about families and motherhood, they rely on marketing tools like the surveys of Euro RSCG and Reach—often instead of chatting with real sociologists or, better yet, parents from different walks of life.

CBS News, for example, produced a 2004 Mother's Day segment, "Staying Home with the Kids," that was based on interviews with mothers in several northern New Jersey towns. Also featured were Mothers & More founder Joanne Brundage and Maternal Desire author Daphne DeMarneffe. But when the reporter needed someone to provide an overall picture, the Reach Advisors report served as a good enough authority.[13]

We have large systems of knowledge production in this country set up to provide new information outside of commercial interests—systems like universities and demographic institutes. We should all be incensed by the connection between advertisers and news media when it comes to producing news and commentary on "trends" in mother-hood. These public marketing reports pinpoint high-income con-sumers. By its own description, Reach enjoys "helping clients tackle the complex challenges of serving consumers slightly off the beaten path." But this seems to hold true only when those consumers are well educated and relatively well off. "It's not easy out there," Reach's web-site commiserates. "Especially for companies that aren't targeting the more typical couch-potato consumer at the core of the American mar-keting experience. Instead, it's far more difficult when the target audi-ence spends more time outdoors than in front of the TV. Or when the target audience is a more educated consumer than the norm and has lower tolerance for bad product and bad marketing. Or when the tar-get audience has an income at the top end of the population, but also the accompanying time constraints. That's where Reach Advisors comes in."[14]

Marketing reports are complicated to interpret. On one hand, they need to be aware of the many trends out there in order to advise clients on how to sell and to whom. On the other, they need to create a story and manipulate us into being the proper characters. "The Mommy Wars: Phase 2," from the *2004: Ideas from Trends* report by Saatchi & Saatchi, argues that the Mommy Wars are no longer just about a battle between working moms and stay-at-home moms—especially for Gen-X and Gen-Y mothers. "The Mommy Wars: Phase 2" moves from the style page to a place more interior—a woman's psyche: "Just listen to the terms in which the work versus family debate is now being framed: *choice, challenge, decision, struggle.* The words expressing the emotions associated with this debate are equally loaded: *pressure, ambivalence, stress, anxiety, guilt, insecurity, self-doubt.* . . . The conflict has been internalized; the new battleground is within."

The thing is, this report is smart. It can talk about families who want more family time, and it can talk about the economic pressures that make this difficult to achieve. It concludes, "Two incomes are needed today if a family is to stay in the middle class." Then it asserts, "The issue of whether to be a working mother or a stay-at-home mother is a highly charged one for young women. Anyone who markets or advertises a product that touches on motherhood, children, work, or the role of women within the family must realize that women are in a state of heightened sensitivity around this issue. Whether the product is cereal, toothpaste, detergent, or cars, women will scrutinize each communication because it touches the conflict within." Not that we might scrutinize each communication to see if it expresses a family-hostile or antiwoman perspective, but that we don't want it touching our inner conflict. We can't be mad in this view; we mothers can only be interior, vulnerable, and emotional.

If you can bear to keep reading, here's how the trend report ends. It turns particularly chilling as it suggests that continued media attention to mothers' work and family issues is helpful in keeping these interior conflicts alive. Mothers' ambivalences—or, we can say, our frustrations at limited options, time crunches, and social judgment—can be used by advertisers, but not, as many of us would hope, in an effort to raise awareness and promote social change. In its next bullet, "Conflict also presents opportunity," the report goes on to say, "Precisely because this issue is so compelling to women, they will be more receptive to any communication that evokes it. . . . [M]others will be particularly receptive to communications that make them feel more competent and in control as well as those that convey a sense of belonging, that, whatever their choice, others have struggled with it." Ads that reference mothers' struggles will catch our attention.

The report concludes by citing a recent study revealing that 59 percent of U.S. consumers think that marketing has no relevance for them. Trading on mothers' emotions, however, is an effective strategy to get women to pay more attention to advertising: "We pay attention even in this cluttered world to that which touches us emotionally. Because the work/family conflict has been internalized, women continue to debate the issue long after they have reached a decision. It is a guarantee of attention."[15] Consumer attention. The Mommy Wars help advertisers convince us to buy stuff. That puts a different spin on the continuing appearance of magazine articles and TV episodes about motherhood. Are they focusing on our issues in order to enlighte their readers or merely because it helps them sell more advertisements and airtime?

Here's what we've inherited from the Mommy Wars that politics, advertising, and media have helped create and continue: a landscape of maternal judgment and distrust—and a lot of legitimate female anger. On the other hand, most of us know that other mothers aren't at fault. I wish I could say there are no Mommy Wars out there, that it's all a construct, a media and marketing fantasy, and that out here in real life, on America's playgrounds and schoolyards, things are fine. I would like to say these things don't exist, and in a sense, they don't—not in the overblown, simplistic way they are presented. Real women don't have Mommy Wars per se. There may be judgment, jealousy, and envy; harsh, petty words may be launched (the maternal version of "shock and awe"); and gossip, the most uncontrollable force in the universe, sure can spread like wildfire. But this is not warfare. Unfortunately, though, in many neighborhoods it qualifies as normal, everyday language. There's a ton of anger at our limited options. People vent their anger and express it in ways that may feel cathartic but don't change a thing. There are enough hostilities and judgments to turn a green lawn brown.

Everybody's angry, women and men both, because the system doesn't work for anyone. Instead of focusing that anger, it gets spewed at the people who least need it: other parents, and, mostly, other women. Women are always vulnerable, and they're easier targets than, say, widespread business practices, arcane public policies (regarding issues like who gets Social Security and whether family and medical leave will ever be truly available to all who need it), and other hard-to-pin-down cultural assumptions about women, men, love, care, and babies.

The Mommy Wars are the public version of this and they help create it as we take our cues from what we read and hear and see. A woman I met at a Manhattan playground had just quit her job on Wall Street. Her employer allowed no part-time options. As she watched her child move through the playscape, she kept telling me about the Mommy Wars out there. It was difficult to figure out what she meant. She was frustrated, emotionally raw, just getting used to that sea change from working seventy-hour weeks to being a full-time mother at home. And she still defended the brokerage firm she had just left, telling me it was right, there just couldn't be part-time jobs on Wall Street. It was as if she didn't know who to defend and protect herself or her old company.

The Mommy Wars are the terms of a national conversation about motherhood that pits women against each other. They take our focus off real social issues and the possibility of making parenting a bit easier, a bit less sacrificial, for all of us. They erase the fact that the Mommy Wars are often a war against mothers. This phrase keeps going though my mind as I think about my discussions with the Wall Street woman. The lack of either reasonable hours or viable part-time work—either for her or for her child's father, who also held a Wall Street job—forced her onto punishing all-or-nothing pathways.

As parents, we also inherit the way that our democratic culture has become truly mean and, well, *bitchy*. There are few models of politicians, pundits, or other denizens of public culture who talk with each other in tones that are respectful and earnest. Instead, our culture of debate is about arguing viciously, shouting down opponents, and sticking to one's position no matter what. These are not the models we need as parents. We need a more consensual democratic culture that doesn't pit each of us against people who live their lives differently. We need a truly more tolerant and civil culture. Yes, some issues, some protections, are worth fighting for. But others: Oh, in the thick of it, a bit more mercy, graciousness, and kindness to others, a little less emotional violence added to the crazed, hostile world we live in, would go a long way.

There's something else going on, too, especially for those of us who've spent our lives learning and achieving. Something about doing it all perfectly, getting the elements right. And we have to let go of that because parenting isn't an Olympic sport, all jokes aside. It's not a competition. And that's where some countercultural parents get it right (although in my experience the parental counterculture can be just as competitive, only with different standards on organic raisins and the banning of SpongeBob SquarePants). As do many plain-old ordinary parents who out of their own good sense just don't buy into all the fuss over who has the best stroller and whose kid is in the prestigious preschool and whose preschooler can say the numbers up to fifty and whose kindergartner is the first to read.

Motherhood isn't a war and parenting is not a competition. These metaphors of the marketplace and global relations can't help us. Still, competition reassures us. Competition promises that we will succeed, that we will be secure, and that life will be okay. Competition cannot always come through on its promises, however. The raising of children has some securities but many, many more unknowns; we may want to grasp onto the straws that tell us we are doing a good job. When at the last minute I got my daughter into the much-loved neighborhood preschool, I was self-congratulatory. I felt like a successful parent, even though the only difference between this new school and her old preschool—which was much more racially diverse, as it turned out—was that this one was fifteen minutes closer to our house. In the end, it was all about me, not about my daughter, but still I felt that parent-charge that comes with navigating the obstacles and bringing the prize home. Instead of feeling satisfied for our little family, I should have gotten mad that there are so few preschool slots, so few quality preschools and childcare centers, and thus intense competition over limited spaces. We should all be mad about that and out writing letters and opinion pieces and organizing and lobbying for our governments and local institutions to change this. But the day-to-day competition that infuses parenting gets in the way of seeing how we're all in this together.

As Americans, too, we are caught between our belief in our own independence (I do it my way) and our incredible conformity (I do what I read in the parenting magazines, and I do pretty much what everyone else does). This tension—sometimes frustrating, sometimes creative—is precisely the contradiction of our culture. We can't expect the practice of parenting, as we inherit it, as we find it on the playground and on the schoolyard, to be much different. We don't change national culture when we raise kids, after all. Understanding these tensions and cultural traps can be helpful in sorting out some of what makes parenting so frustrating at those times when our better instincts and ideals seem battered by the evaluation and competition that surrounds us. If we can't expect any different at the playground, perhaps the playground can be a place to start modeling something different, something better, such as ways of being that can spread to the rest of our society, bringing it back to some of our profoundly shared goals.

When we really want support and solidarity and empathy, the constant judging of motherhood hits particularly hard. Faulkner Fox is the author of *Dispatches from a Not-So-Perfect-Life: Or How I Learned to Love the House, the Man, the Child*, in which she writes about motherhood in a vulnerable voice. A chapter near the end lands on a topic that may hurt even more than the disparity in domestic work between her and her husband: judgment between women and what it has to do with friendships among women who are mothers. We all want compassion, empathy, and joie de vivre, she asserts, but what we get instead are the myriad ways that women judge each other against the standard of who is more selfish or selfless. If the selfish side were "a totem pole of power," she writes, "professional women [would be] at the top, part-time working mothers and artistic types [would be] somewhere in the middle, and stay-at-home mothers [would be] at the bottom. I felt certain that everyone believed this was the way the pole stacked. Of course the selflessness pole stacked the other way with stay-at-home mothers at the top and professional women at the bottom. As a part-time instructor and writer, I appreciated being at neither pole's end, but I also felt like I was getting slammed from both sides."[16]

As Fox sees it, the judging circle lines up against whether mothers work for pay or stay home with their kids. It also invades the decisions we make about how to raise our children and which of various parenting formulas to follow. She tells me that when she's out on book tours and parents in the audience are talking, they always want to talk about the judgment chapter. Mothers see it as a big issue and not just one created by the media. The tension is regrettable, but it's real. "It's the worst of womanhood, really," comments Fox. "A return to high school, with all its comparisons between girls, its competition over looks. On the playground you see competition over strollers, driven by everyone's insecurity." Some would see playground competition as petty, small, and psychological; Fox disagrees and sees competition and judgment as an important political issue, as a huge impediment that keeps our eye off the ball and stops us from making things better for women and children.

There's something uncanny about the way that the media's Mommy Wars pick up (and pander to and perpetuate) real feelings that women have. It makes many of us uneasy, and we imagine others judging us. Cecelia, the New York editor, remarked to me that even though she loves working from home and being a full-time parent, "when I walk my daughter to school in the morning, I sometimes find myself looking at the mothers who are dressed for the office and running to catch a train, and wondering what they're thinking about me." Many mothers and fathers, whether they're home or going to work, recognize that sense of imagining what others are thinking, especially when we live in communities that express ambivalence about mothers. I'm sure that some of those moms running for the train look at Cecelia and her daughters and wonder the same thing, only in reverse: "What does she think of me for running to catch that train for work?" When this more vulnerable voice that we can share with friends hits media refraction, it can quickly change from "What does she think of me?" to something more preemptive: "I will think horrible thoughts about her (before she thinks bad things about me)."

It makes sense. We envy people who have more, who get more. We envy when we feel vulnerable, when we think that someone else's life is easier, or when we think that the playing field is uneven. We envy when we feel like we aren't getting what we want and need. Shouldn't we all get live-in babysitters if that's what we want? Shouldn't we all have excellent and affordable childcare if we want and need it? Shouldn't we all be able to afford more family leave after the baby's born? Why should only the family with a banker or lawyer spouse or an inherited trust fund or a high-end college education or that managed to make some money in the '90s dot-com or real estate boom, have high-quality home childcare on demand or the financial freedom to quit work entirely? What about me, what about my family, and why are we not getting what we need, what I need, what I want? This is unfair, we think—but then, for women, it immediately turns to the question: Is it unfair or is it just my fault?

The goodies for childraising are rarely about equal access. Thus, the stage is set for envy and guilt. We're mad, we're hurt, and in the awful logic that goes for the worst of human nature, we take it out on the adults around us who are the most vulnerable: other women. Hence, the receptive audience for the public media's Mommy Wars.

But let's go back to that misallocation of family resources—because aren't these also class wars? Finance wars feature high-spending professionals with two parents working and ignore families held fiscally afloat by thrifty plumbers and electricians, who live in working-class neighborhoods with mothers who were schoolteachers only till the first child was born. When so many of the Mommy Wars stories highlight affluent women in two-lawyer households, many people respond by saying, "Too bad, their families will have to live on one six-figure salary and not two." This isn't a good response, and I know from my own experience that financial privilege doesn't make the sexism of a rigid labor market go away.

But what remains in our mind is the privileged darling of Mommy Wars reporting, the character of the once highly paid female lawyer or corporate manager who boxes up her pumps and briefcase, dry-cleans her business suits and sends the whole batch over to Dress for Success, and pulls strings to enroll her kids at a prestige preschool. The Mommy Wars' focus on privileged women occludes the landscape of women at home in a critically important way: *Most at-home mothers are not affluent.* A vast number are more tenuously middle-class, and many are poor. This makes sense when you consider that they're living on a single salary, and not the double salary deemed necessary for middle-class American life.

As an alternate to the typical Mommy Wars story, consider this family: Sarah is an at-home mother and a nurse. Her husband, John, teaches high school social studies. They have three children, two older cars, and a house that needs some renovations. During the school year John works and Sarah's at home; during the summer John's home and Sarah works more. They are gracious people who have made tremendous sacrifice to have a parent home with the kids because that's what they believe in.

How come these ordinary, nonaffluent people aren't the poster children for our discussions of parenting? And if they were, how different would be the ways that we could talk publicly about motherhood, fatherhood, work, parenting, and what it means to live a satisfying life?

I ask Faulkner Fox for her vision of a glorious future; after all, vision is what's behind all the parenting talk, the complaining, the anger, and the playground analysis. This is what the struggle to stay at work, negotiate twenty hours per week, quit entirely, marry, divorce, or bear one child or two or three is all about—our visions of who we are, what comes next, and what is good and worth living for.

"Well, mothers will realize they are not alone. This is an important element of consciousness raising," Fox responds, and her voice slows.

> When people realize they are not alone, that their ideals, their vision is shared, they can start to think structurally—that is to say, "It's not just me as an individual; there are social structures at play, cultural expectations that impact how I feel." Second, I will wish for women to feel less guilty and more able to continue to be who-ever they had been working to become before they had children. Third, I will wish for an end to complete selflessness—that we always know we women are entitled to be full people. When some-one feels entitled and they can't get what they feel entitled to, they act for change. If you want to keep working and your company has no paid maternity leave and your company has no on-site childcare, you get mad and you make change. In the end, mothers will be able to live full lives, as women who are also mothers. Psychology and political action go together. As long as women feel guilty they won't do this—they will blame themselves and feel personally self-ish for wanting more, and instead of feeling entitled to social change they will go out and buy an $800 video camera hooked to their computer and watch the kid with the nanny. That option keeps us depoliticized.

I ask Fox what her utopia would look like, and she doesn't skip a beat, telling me that if women had better options, fewer mothers would quit their jobs entirely. If more mothers were ensconced in work they loved and in jobs that were truly flexible, then staying at home would be a different kind of decision, one to make if you really want to be with your kids, not because you've run out of options. A utopia for Fox would be having meaningful work *and* time to be an engaged parent. "This would make it less necessary to choose the patriarchal family as the best option," she says.

If the default positions are either a motherhood that blocks out work or work that blots out active motherhood, how else might we think about the situation? Might we acknowledge that some parents absolutely want to be home with their kids, and they should do that, while others end up at home and don't exactly wish to be there full-time? Fox wants workplaces to stop forcing out women who in fact want to combine motherhood and work in more sane ways. She places a political activist's demand for changed workplaces alongside a poet's respect for what we women do with our lives. In her vision, women who really want to be full-time mothers will receive the message that they are valued. Women who want to keep working, but perhaps not full-time, will have the opportunity to do so, and feel their labor is valued at home and at work, too.

Jean O'Barr, an important mentor of mine, used to say that when you're in a no-win situation, you have to stand way back and figure out the terms. Usually, no one's winning because the terms are all wrong. In the case of the Mommy Wars, it's hard to say who's winning. The winds blow this way and that, depending on the latest media missive and how long it's had to fade from our collective memories. The census numbers shift and change, but the only thing we know for certain is that no mother *can* win because the terms are all wrong.

If war is about winning (otherwise, it's not war, but occupation), what would winning the Mommy Wars mean? Posing this question, which is ridiculous, helps us see just how insane the Mommy Wars are.

If the at-home mothers win, what happens? Do they get to make all the working moms pen resignation letters? Bake cookies? Chaperone the third-grade lunchroom every Tuesday? It's absolutely silly in print, but what else might "winning" the Mommy Wars mean? If the working moms win, what happens then? Do the at-home moms pick up the working mothers' dry cleaning for a month? Cook dinner and deliver it to the working moms' houses? Watch their kids after school and relieve them of after-school care costs? Put their own kids in daycare and go to work themselves, but at punishing, menial jobs, for really low wages and no benefits? See what I mean—it's ludicrous. The current Mommy Wars have no end plan; they continue to sow discord and enmity for no helpful reason other than keeping us mamas down. The Mommy Wars I would rather see would have mothers, fathers, and parents braving patriarchal family life and the hyperproductive workplace to forge a brand-new future in which we can be parents and workers without such conflict between the two roles.

That said, I'm not exactly thrilled that we use war metaphors for talking about the future of family life, motherhood, and how we get from here to there. I'm tired of war talk and its divisions of "self" and "enemy." We've had enough war in recent years to learn its lessons. "There is no way to peace, but peace is the way," the Society of Friends banner outside my daughter's little school reminds me. We can lead by rhetoric and anger; we can also lead, powerfully, by example. We can call the Mommy Wars over.

Several months back I met Letty Cottin Pogrebin, founding editor of Ms. magazine. I was ranting to her about forces in state legislatures that are trying to roll back the number of months for which a low-income mother can receive TANF support (Temporary Assistance for Needy Families, the Clinton-era welfare-reform successor to Aid to Families with Dependent Children). Republican legislators in New Hampshire want to cut back the number of months public support is available for poor mothers. The support itself is minimal, and the legislators are now discussing decreasing the time span of this minimal support by 25 percent—from the current two years to eighteen months.

As it happened, Pogrebin had just returned from a fellowship that took her to Scandinavian countries. Now compare this: In Sweden, mothers who leave the workforce receive 85 percent of their wages for up to one year. In Finland, mothers receive one year's paid leave plus two additional years, if they wish, of unpaid leave with guaranteed job security when they return. Parents are given their choice of funded childcare or the equivalent allowance for use at home. In both countries, fathers also receive paid leave, though not for as long a period, and mothers have the legal right to part-time work when they return to the workplace. In Denmark, mothers are given fourteen weeks paid maternity leave. After that, mothers and fathers can divide up another thirty-two weeks of leave any way they like. When parents go back to work, on-site childcare is common, and the law protects nursing breaks. "Yes," Pogrebin said, shaking her head and nodding too. "The petty things that we have to argue for in this country are unimaginable there."

In contrast to the largely personal attacks that filter through the Mommy Wars discussions, imagine an angry debate with real content. One side passionately argues that the federal government should provide grants or tax breaks for childcare costs and fund childcare centers with infirmaries and prepared-food counters so hungry parents can purchase healthy dinners while they pick up their kids so that everyone's night is easier. The other side argues no, and lists large and small businesses that are ready to change workplace assumptions to include the unpaid labors of care and nurturing in how employees are compensated, promoted, and retained, and that will give careful attention to the history of bias against mothers. Imagine that debate, one of substance.

We would be debating whether we think public, governmental, or cultural workplace-driven shifts is the best option for change. Now that would be a real debate, and one that fits the historic tensions of a country that de facto believes in the power of private enterprise and the marketplace, and in the power of government, albeit in complex and often contradictory ways. No matter how angry or impassioned, such a debate would be more engaging, more helpful, and more humane than another tired story of a bunch of idealized stay-at-home mothers who love their kids and team up against a posse of working moms who putatively don't. In their constant restaging, the Mommy Wars avoid opening up a real conversation about where we're going from here—and how we're going to get there.

CHAPTER 2.

The Parent Problem

When my daughter was born in 1998, I quit my job to take care of her. This wasn't my life plan. I definitely wasn't relaxing on the porch swing and thinking, "Hey, let's re-create the traditional patriarchal family, right here between our very own walls. I can get pregnant, forswear my ten years of higher education and several advanced degrees, quit my job as a newly tenured professor, and send my husband out into the world as our sole breadwinner." No, that's not the way it happened. I never thought life would or should turn out this way, with me curving out of the working world and into the daytime life of a stay-at-home mom, and my husband, Rob, shouldering the majority of the economic burden. Then again, I'd never thought through life with a child in my arms, and I'd never really stopped to think about the different values of women's work. I'd worked like a maniac for fifteen years to get ahead, published two books, gotten tenure at my university. It was a surprise to turn up pregnant. What I did next, though, was enter a land without a map, a crazy, risky maternal and domestic dreamscape that nonetheless gave me more love and joy and happiness than I'd ever encountered.

There were other sides, too, that were much harder to account for. It's quite difficult, we know, to care for a small baby, and to experience the stunning isolation of new motherhood. All of a sudden you're out of the mainstream, away from the people you've known, and alone for hours each day. As it turns out, it's hard even to place yourself in this new life situation, to find yourself in a social trend apart from the superficial, false, and harmful pretend-trends given us by marketing professionals and the media. True-life stories about mothers and about parenting are honest and hopeful. In the face of the media hype, they're the best starting point we've got.

I ended up a stay-at-home mom because my work life had been too complex to continue. I lived in one city, Atlanta, and I worked at a university in northern Florida. My commute was a seven-hour trip by car or a forty-five-minute flight. This journey I repeated each week, rushing through the Monday-morning dawn to the airport and retracing my steps three days later past Ben & Jerry's, Au Bon Pain, and Seattle's Best Coffee on my way home from the C terminal. Life was harried, and Rob and I would at times meet up in the airport, share a drink, and hand over the car keys and parking location in the time between one of us landing and the other taking off.

When my daughter was born I quit my job as a professor. If commuting was insane but glamorous before I had a child, it turned ridiculous once she arrived. Resignation letter penned and sent, I left the male-dominated university world and entered a surprising new community of women and children, which I enjoyed despite being shocked that it could still exist. At the time, my story was novel. In 1998, friends and colleagues still lent raised eyebrows to a woman who quit her job for kids. By now, my move has become commonplace among certain working women, and the benefits, challenges, and losses of that move are a matter of great debate.

As I settled into the months and years of motherhood, I became increasingly concerned that the work/family conundrum came packaged in such all-or-nothing terms. Months into my daughter's young life, the "What have I done?" voices returned at fever pitch. My joyful devotion to being home with my daughter did not seem to quiet them, as I'd hoped they might, and this surprised me. The voices were my private Greek chorus. To an imagined audience outside my home they continually announced the tragedy of my life. When I heard them I despaired of ever seeing my name on a doorplate again, of ever again hearing an eager student call me "Professor Peskowitz," of ever again being sought out for wisdom, knowledge, or guidance. I didn't want to "do it all" in any manic '70s wonder-woman kind of way. Neither did I want to give it all up. I could deal with the ins and outs, the ups and downs, of life with a baby. Only the Greek chorus could unnerve me.

A week after we passed around the cake to celebrate my daughter's first birthday, I started a part-time job. I was continuing my career as a university professor, but on radically new terms. An old friend had called to tell me that there might be some courses I could teach at her university, just three miles from my home, and indeed there were. At each turn after quitting my job, my on-ramps back into the workplace were old friends—always women, some with children, some without—who tossed me a rope and pulled me back in.

I called the new department chair and we began a series of discussions to sort out what part-time work would mean. I still expected to be treated well; that had almost always been my experience in the work world, and it still hadn't dawned on me how much I had given up. He approached me like just another adjunct to be hired at the lowest wages possible. The full-time load was four courses per year, he told me. But the part-time load was three. We debated whether the definition of part-time work was two or three courses each year. My math told me that if full-time work was four courses, then part-time work was two. Three sounded suspiciously close to full-time, only at pittance pay. We didn't actually resolve the issue but he hired me anyway. The man who would hire me told me with empathy that I would be doing the "donkey work." That was how he described the part-time track. It's how he justified its distressing combination of pay and labor.

"Don't worry," he said. "My wife does it too."

I wasn't sure I wanted to go back to work. I was still enjoying my time at home. My daughter was about to burst into walking and I thought that would be pretty cool. I was captivated by her, I enjoyed the company of other moms at the playground, and I had just found a new playgroup. Despite the hard work, I enjoyed life as a stay-at-home mom.

Why did I go back to work, then, if I was so ambivalent? It was partially desire and partially fear: yes, ambivalence at its best. I told myself we needed the money, but in truth, we would have been almost okay without it. I told myself, and working friends pressed this point, that life at home didn't last forever and that keeping my résumé up would help me find better work later on. That made sense to me; after all, I hadn't planned on pitching out my whole career.

My neighbor Mary Thomas told me she would love to watch Samira for the few hours I needed to be on campus. One of the courses would meet in the late afternoon when Rob could be home. Still, I wasn't sure I wanted the job; I remembered well how demanding teaching could be and how much time it took to prepare. The Greek chorus reminded me that I wasn't sure that I didn't want it. And so I accepted the offer and returned to work. Perhaps it was the entitlement of my generation, perhaps the perspicacity of my temperament. I was still not willing to believe that I had traveled so far backward down the professional ladder, although this was precisely what I had done. Samira was about to walk when my part-time job began.

Truth be told, I didn't much enjoy my job, and I constantly wanted to quit. It is hard to move in between worlds. The hours and energy of my profession have few boundaries, and I really didn't have the energy to do it all even at those reduced hours. As predicted, the work took much more time than I planned for or was paid for. My journals from the time are filled with notes about exhaustion. Late nights would find me holding my eyes open to prep for class the next day. There were more positive sides, too—the graduate students I trained, the young women and men whose educations and careers I helped along, the intellectual vibrancy of my seminars, and, yes, the small paycheck that cushioned us. When, several years later, my husband lost his job, my boss stepped in graciously and humanely. She found me another class to teach, so that I could reach the minimum hours necessary to receive health insurance for myself and my family.

Though I didn't always enjoy my part-time job, it kept us going when our family went through a tough few months, and during the nine months before Rob found a new full-time job and we left Atlanta. And honestly, there were some hours and days when I did feel like I had the perfect balance, that I was the lucky one, the exceptional mom who could do it all in a new vein. Usually, that feeling would swell my head just before the unexpected happened and it all caved in—say, when my daughter had a fever and my husband was in Los Angeles for three days and the babysitter had the flu and I had to scramble to figure out what to do. Often I wished I had the guts to fully stay at home, to not hedge my bets. Of course, I knew women who had done just that, and usually the five-year résumé gap meant the end of their old career. Not always, and I loved to hear stories from mothers who'd taken time off and then had great career luck afterward. But the opposite had happened enough to help me understand my own choices and fears.

I stayed at that part-time job teaching a course each semester for three years, and during each I was paid a different wage. I started low, scooped high the next year—with benefits, even—and then plunged to low depths the year after, in accordance with the university's fiscal fortunes and my perceived value. I continued to work part-time till my daughter started kindergarten. By then, I had left Atlanta and moved north to Philadelphia, nearer to family and to where I'd grown up. There, I continued to teach one class each semester; when I added that to my work as a writer, the total edged nearer to full-time. I earned little, but my schedule was flexible, and I could rely on my husband's job for our health benefits. I had made what I now recognize as the classic mother trade-off—trading salary and benefits for flexibility and control. I was able to pick my daughter up at the schoolyard each afternoon at three, so long as I worked like hell during the school day and checked into the late shift at my desk each night when my daughter's heavy eyes fell closed.

In my years of motherhood, I've been a stay-at-home mother, a mother who has worked minimal part-time hours, and a mother who has worked long hours each day from home. When I think about motherhood and work, it's from all these positions and all these experiences.

When I first became a mother, I thought my decision was just about me. Personal. Private. I had no idea that stay-at-home moms were already being lauded as the new status symbol of the middle- and upper-middle-class family. Because media articles commonly write about at-home mothers by discussing lawyers and MBAs, I also didn't know then that many at-home mothers are quite poor.

A new friend, Libby, had introduced me to the book that saved her, *What's a Smart Woman Like You Doing at Home?*, and it quickly became the bible of my bedside table. Libby was older than I and a mother of three. She had worked as an engineer. When she told me this I quickly tallied her age and when she had gone to school and just how few women engineers there are and how hard it must have been. Later she worked at her children's school. Her hours and days off matched theirs. She told me her story: Her male-dominated workplace had no interest in accommodating her as a mother. She quit when they wouldn't find her a place to pump milk in privacy.

Smart Woman is filled with stories of stay-at-home mothers who aren't antifeminist or old-fashioned retrogrades. They are women who have a vision of life with more time for kids and who didn't find workplaces that would accommodate this fairly. How odd to watch a decision made out of my own prediction of soulful exhaustion quickly becoming a national style trend, and then find myself pulled against my will into media-driven battle imagery of stay-at-home moms and career mothers viewing one another with animosity. Depending on how the winds blow, one group is valorized and the other diminished. No mother can win.

Probably I was just tired that Sunday—November 15, 1998—or plain overwhelmed by life with an infant. Perhaps that was the date when my poor colicky baby cried for twelve hours straight, despite the love and creativity of two increasingly anxious parents who drove the gas gauge to empty trying to lull her into calm. That's the date when the *New York Times Magazine* announced that for affluent New York metro-area eight-year-old girls, an at-home mom is the cat's meow.

Maybe I wasn't entirely interested in reading the short articles about status symbols of the day, a list that included babies for gay men; caring for relatives abroad of Arab American families; and everything desired by the nouveau riche. Perhaps these cosmopolitan trends didn't catch my eye. My new family was happy enough in our modest Craftsman cottage. A pizza place, a Cuban joint, and a tattoo and piercing parlor were just up the street. The local gallery featured art made from recycled barn wood. A new lesbian owned ice-cream and coffee shop had just opened, and Mr. Lee's corner store sold everything from upscale teas and fine wine to lottery tickets, cheap bacon, and chitlins—and accepted both WIC vouchers and American Express.

As it turned out, the *New York Times* was rather late to the stump; the *Wall Street Journal* had announced the at-home trend to its more conservative readership a half decade before. From my perspective, the news was that in liberal and progressive families more mothers were staying home with their kids. The old calculus in which conservative mothers stay home while liberal mothers go to work had shifted, and I wanted to know all the reasons why. In any case, I didn't find my way back to this early applause for stay-at-home motherhood till years afterward when teasing out our current state of motherhood became my intellectual and impassioned obsession, and when I was no longer entirely a stay-at-home mom.

I wasn't interested in being a cultural prize, however, and neither did my husband find my new stay-at-home-mother status a boon to his masculine ego. He was glad that our daughter would be well cared for. His mom had been home with her kids so this new life of ours felt weird and familiar at the same time. He was nervous about the pressure of bringing in our family's only paycheck. He shared my sense of cultural confusion.

Quitting my full-time job contradicted everything I always knew was right and true in the world. My own mother had worked when my brother and I were young, and I always admired her tenacity and feminist commitments. My life, too, had been committed to the public sphere. I taught, I wrote, I spoke. I had come into adulthood as a daughter of feminism and the daughter of a feminist mom. I felt, well, entitled to any life or job or career I wanted. To leave my job for motherhood went against everything I thought life should be.

At first I thought, like many women, that identity was the problem. It was that feminism perhaps had left us with too rigid a notion of what women should do, that the feminism of our girlhoods needed to grow to incorporate motherhood. I would hear other new moms explain this, that motherhood and feminism are opposites, and that was the problem. But that's wrong. Feminism is always growing and changing, to be sure, and it has its bumps and bruises, but in itself, at core, it isn't really the problem. The problem is that our society and its work structures are more rigidly sexist than I, entitled feminist daughter, had believed them to be.

Motherhood itself didn't bother me: I had fallen deeply in love with my baby, and I found the details of caring for a tiny human enthralling and new. The conflict came because for the first time in my life I didn't want to have to do it all. I had spent years working maniacally. I was deeply tired. Rob is great and he does a decent share of the chores, but I know firsthand the second shift that mothers do. After only a few years I felt the exhaustion of having to come up with dinner each night only to look down at my daughter and calculate how many years till she would graduate high school and leave the house, when I would no longer have to cook up a main dish and a vegetable each night. When I considered returning to my full-time job, it was the fear of being too tired that washed over me. My wish not to be tired was stronger than my wish to continue at the rewards and prestige of being a professor.

As a feminist daughter, I had just smashed into two limits: first, the end of an identity built so thoroughly around work and public success, and second, the limits of our society's toleration of our liberation; we can be liberated as women but not yet, entirely, as mothers. What I didn't know then is that quitting a job because it's too demanding isn't the end of the story, and it should never be. At the time, I was caught between brazen happiness that I could be with my little girl and the sense that I was hampered and couldn't do it all. I felt like a private failure, even though I knew better. What I learned over the years is that the failure is actually a public one: a social, structural failure to account for the time it takes to parent, time that still falls more heavily on women's shoulders than on men's, and time that in important ways doesn't count, isn't counted, even though it's crucial and necessary and we can't raise kids without it.

I was stunned, quite honestly, that simultaneous commitments to do work and raise a family seemed so hard to maintain. We women are independent, aren't we? We get what we want, right? There's no more discrimination, right? We daughters of feminism can get a bit breezy about these gains, and about how hard it was to gain them. At a dinner a few months back I sat next to a young woman in her twenties, and when we talked, she enthusiastically told me how much she hoped that my slightly older generation would figure out the problems of work and motherhood so that hers could go about their way untouched. She was encouraging of me and sure that my friends and I could pave the way for her. I admire her pluck, I do. Often I feel like the fence between generations; born in 1964, the cusp between the baby boom and Generation X and all that comes after, I'm young enough to have missed the boomer mentality, but old enough to remember life before postfeminism. Many younger women are criticized for not having feminist consciousness, for believing the hype that life is good for us gals. But at the same time, I've learned much from the sense of entitlement that women younger than me bring to the table. I found myself buoyed along by this young woman's sense that we *can* make it better, even though I had to tell her it wasn't going to be that easy.

Scratch the surface and there's the glass ceiling. Peer into the company accounts and there's the persistent gender wage gap. Look at who's taking family leave, or why our public life seems so devoid of fortysomething women, and why it's still mostly men running for office or men running the TV news, and it's pretty clear that we aren't as postfeminist as we'd like to be.

After my child was born, the mythologies of liberated female life came tumbling down. The first crumbling block was finding out that no maternity leave was available for me. At my university, secretaries received maternity leave—it was assumed they were female—but professors didn't; the assumption, still, was that professors were men—and men who didn't want family leave. I was removed from the editorial board of a prestigious journal because, in the editor's words, "you're teaching part-time, but do you have a *real* job?" No one believed that one could lead a part-time professional life. When I asked that there be childcare at national professional conferences, I was told that the membership had voted against it (I never remembered such a ballot). It took many people yelling and causing a public scene to get some childcare installed.

I learned quickly that the gains for women in the past decades have not meant a similar gain for mothers. While more fathers are choosing full-time parenting than ever before, childraising remains mothers' work, and in many families it's the mother's salary that is balanced against daycare costs; it's the mom, not the dad, who's the first called when the nanny's sick or the child's sick. The gap between men's and women's earnings is 10 to 15 percent larger for mothers than for women without children; in fact, the wage gap between mothers and nonmothers is larger than that between men and women.[1] Finding myself trapped in a life careening back five decades to a mythology of white motherhood in the 1950s, I resisted the impulse to camp it up with ironic vintage aprons and instead went looking for answers.

We talk about the glass ceiling and the mommy track so regularly that these phrases seem passé, yesterday's news. It took months of research to hear the phrase that put the pieces together: "the maternal wall." While Joan Williams, professor of law at American University and director of the school's Program on WorkLife Law, didn't invent the phrase, she has given it new life in describing what happens to mothers in the workplace. The glass ceiling, where you can see the leadership roles and the upstairs executive suites but you just can't get there, comes paired with a sister concept of what stops women at work: the maternal wall, the stiff and unbending barriers to workers who are mothers. The phrase "maternal wall" helps us see what we all face individually as something broader and more generally shared among women. As Monique, an environmental engineer and working mother of two kids, says, "Everybody's had a brush with this."

Although I thought that Rob and I were making decisions stretched out in conversation on the old black-striped couch in our living room in the privacy of our home, it turns out that unbeknownst to us, I and the other new moms I knew were part of a national trend. According to the U.S. Bureau of the Census, 1998 marked the first year since 1976 in which the number of women in the workplace declined. That's important. American women have always worked. The Bureau of Labor Statistics has collected information about working women since 1948, when nearly one-third of all women in America worked.

It wasn't till 1976 that women's participation in the workforce inched near 50 percent. That's thirteen years after President Kennedy's Commission on the Status of Women produced its landmark report, *American Women*, and Betty Friedan published *The Feminine Mystique*; a decade after feminism sent shockwaves through American society. The waning years of the early-'70s recession and inflation sent more people, women and mothers included, scurrying for work, both to recover from the years of inflation and to keep up with all the new consumer items starting to hit the shelves (and the marketing blitz that accompanied them). In 1976, 31 percent of mothers *with infants* were part of the labor force (and note that the government's term "infants" means children up to two years old). Echoing our general sense of women in the workplace, the number of mothers with infants climbed in the workforce each year until by 1998 more than 50 percent of mothers with infants worked for wages. Working mothers with infants reached a high point in 1998—58 percent. Ever since, we've been slowly letting the rope out; in 2000, we were back at 55 percent, where we held steady in 2002.[2]

Reacting to these census reports of mothers leaving the workplace, newspaper and magazine articles all across America trumpeted a new trend and tried to give it meaning. They claimed a new traditionalism, a resurgence of old-fashioned motherly feeling.

By 2000, I started to see articles in the popular press about "the new stay-at-home moms" and the crises of mothers in professional careers. It's hard to remember a time before these think pieces about women leaving their jobs for motherhood. It's as if we all simultaneously took a breath and started to see what was going on. Every commentator, it seemed, had a kid who was born around 1998 or after. When my daughter was two, the playgrounds in my neighborhood were filled with other two-year-olds. Anecdotally, some people started to talk about a new baby boom.

Officially, though, and this is important, the United States saw no actual increase in the birth rate in the years before the millennium turned. Just the opposite. From 1990 to 2000, pregnancy rates for U.S. women actually fell 10 percent. In 1990, a peak year, 11.5 percent of women in America had a baby; by the year 2000, that rate had dropped to 10.4 percent.[3] As I thumbed through census reports, I learned also that women who looked like me were having more babies than ever— women who were over thirty, who were white, well-educated professionals. There was no new baby boom, not even the tiniest ricochet of the echo baby boom that filled the nation's elementary schools in the mid-1980s, and whose kids are the new bulge on our college campuses. My family was not part of a nationwide boom—it only seemed that way in certain neighborhoods. We were part of an explosion into parenting by a certain class of women and men in their thirties and forties.

If I thought that my decision to quit work was personal and private, I was both right and wrong. It was up to me. No one told me to quit. No one even pressured me outright to quit. I never asked, but most likely my university, my department, and my boss regretted my decision. They had invested five years of mentoring, research grants, and teaching prizes, they had just committed to employing me for life; they had no interest in losing me just because I'd become pregnant. In fact, many colleagues considered my decision insane and filled my ears with stories about how they had kept working and their kids had turned out just fine.

But their lives were not mine. I wanted a social context to understand myself in, some explanatory frameworks for motherhood, the care of children, and paid work. What I discovered is that it's hard to find good information and statistics about motherhood. My research trail of phone calls and emails and Internet searches led me to advocacy organizations, D.C. think tanks, and academics' offices.

A recent survey by Phyllis Moen, director of the Cornell Employment and Family Careers Institute, puts my experience and the experiences of many mothers, fathers, and families into a broader context. It shows the larger trends at stake. Her 2002 study analyzed one thousand families of married middle-class workers in order to learn how couples cope with all the conflicting demands on their time.[4] The biggest surprise in the study is just how many families have reverted to what she calls the "Neo-traditional" model of family life, in which the husband is the breadwinner and the wife either stays home with the kids full-time or works part-time. The Cornell study found that 40 percent of its families were in this category. This number doesn't account for all the people who aren't married and have children or who can't marry according to the law but still raise children together. Still, it's helpful.

Parents are at odds with the workplace, and mothers are bearing the brunt of this mismatch. According to Moen, "The taken-for-granted rules of the game about work time and nonwork time—such as the notions of a weekend, two-week vacations, sick days, a five-day workweek and a standardized retirement—are out of step with the new workforce. Today's workforce consists of women and men from a wide range of cultural backgrounds, of workers without homemakers to manage their childcare and eldercare responsibilities, and of people of all ages and life stages. Employers need to provide true flexibility to workers of both genders so that people who take time out to care for their family do not experience career setback when they return to the workforce." To back this up, Moen's study offers real statistical numbers for what families do with their time. Then she breaks those numbers down by the ages of the children. Thirty-nine percent of families with preschool-age children fall into the "Neo-traditional" category, as do, interestingly, 43 percent of families with grade-school children. Most of us think that the majority of women who leave their jobs for kids do so right away but the numbers don't back this up. Many women stay at work when their children are little and leave their jobs when more children are born. Often women can manage to work full-time with one child, but the second or third child arrives and that's the straw that breaks the camel's back.

According to the Moen/Cornell study, the 40 percent of families that are now Neo-traditional are not in this category out of ideological desire to replicate the mythic gender roles of the 1950s but because today's workplace makes it increasingly difficult for two people who are really committed to their jobs to also raise a family. Some people do it, but it's really hard, and we all need to admit that—both to offer greater support and admiration for those who make it work, and to stop trying to demonize and demean people who quit their jobs to parent. We need to recognize how much labor it takes so we can support all the decisions people make.

Twenty-one percent of the families in the study fell into the "High Commitment" category. In these families, both partners work high-intensity jobs that demand more than forty-five hours per week. Seventeen percent of families compose the "Alternative Commitment" group, in which both parents work part-time or work from home or have some kind of creative arrangement. Thirteen percent form a category called "Dual Moderates" in which both parents work but have regular working hours with no overtime; they work forty-five hours a week or less.

Moen found that mothers were the breadwinners in 11 percent of the study's families. These mothers worked forty-five hours a week or more while the fathers stayed home with the kids or worked part-time hours. These are the gender reverse of the Neo-traditional families, and the study calls their group the "Crossover Commitment" families. If we add the Neo-traditionals to the Crossovers, we end with 51 percent of families in which only one parent works full-time for wages. That contradicts the usual assumptions about parents and how much they work.[5]

One aspect of the Cornell study in particular helped me make sense of the situation that most confused me when I took a leave of absence from my job: playgrounds filled with women who once held high-powered, high-intensity jobs, the women you never would think would quit to stay home. I remember a conversation with a neighbor who worked in middle management at a local medical corporation. Twelve weeks after her baby was born, she went back to work. But she was able to do it: She left at 5:00 PM each day, she didn't travel, and there was never any reason to get on her laptop late at night. According to the Cornell study, "'High Commitment' working couples are in fact the most likely to transform into 'Neo-traditional' ones when their first child is born." The decisions come from the extreme time crunch that these families experience. It's actually much easier to keep working once your children arrive if you have a job with old-fashioned full-time hours, the real nine-to-five jobs, and if your job doesn't also come with a time-busting hour-plus commute. The answer to why so many well-educated and hardworking women end up quitting their jobs when they become mothers is that in high-commitment jobs, women experience the time crunch of work and family most acutely. These professional jobs are also least likely to have part-time options; they force us into all-or-nothing situations.

Moen also points out that families make choices about care based on the economics of paychecks and on a sense of future advancement. Statistically, men earn more than women, and unlike women, men don't face glass ceiling restrictions—at least if they're white men, anyway. When faced with giving up one job or another, families tend to hold on to the higher-paying job with better advancement opportunities. In part, the underlying economics explain why child-free High Commitment couples are the most likely to turn into Neo-traditional families when the baby arrives. It seems counterintuitive, though, when you think about it in terms of independent and high-achieving women making individual choices about their lives. Hence, the current media portrayal of lawyers and professors and corporate women packing up their desks, as if giving up a job were just a whimsical lifestyle choice for the affluent, akin to buying a luxury car. The strangeness of it all makes more sense when you set your eyes on the underlying economics of time and family life, and the gendered terms of who earns more money or for whom it is socially acceptable to care for a family.

When social debates force mothers into false categories, w lose any ability to envision helpful policy for women and families. And more personally, we lose all ability to see our own experience if we fall through the cracks, so that mothers who work part-time have no name to call themselves. In real life, where, as mother of three boys Mary Grum is fond of saying, "people care about their families and try to raise their kids right," life is more complex and less divided into distinct groups and either/or choices. At the playgrounds where I spent so much of my daughter's early years, nearly all the daytime park moms identified themselves as stay-at-home moms. However, many of them also did some kind of paid work in the outside community.

At the playground, one stay-at-home mom was a social worker. I hesitate to use the phrase "former social worker" because, in fact, some of her professional life continued on a smaller, more controllable scale. Once she'd directed a large nursing home. Now she led Internet-based support groups for the caregivers of Alzheimer's patients one evening a week from her home. Another mom at the park was a flight attendant; we'd follow the trail of when she had to take a flight, or find someone to cover for her, in order to keep her job status, to protect her seniority and her chances of returning to more work in the future. Another playground stay-at-home mom sold real estate; several times I offered to watch her girls while she went to a property closing. "The attorneys get mad when I bring them," she joked. Still another playground mom was a nurse. Every Tuesday she did a shift at the hospital. One woman was a minister at a Methodist church a few neighborhoods away. She worked full-time, then part-time, and then quit as she and her husband, a teacher, decided to relocate to Wales, where he grew up. We all talked about parenting and work in ways that were quite organic and natural, as a review of all the things that crossed our minds and paths in the course of a day. We talked about the daily ins and outs of continuing parts of our careers with the same breath we used for talking about toilet training and teaching kids manners and respect.

This easiness vanishes in the public habits of talking about women, motherhood, and work. Currently there is no room in our cultural vocabulary to talk about mothering and work in any but the most oppositional and mutually exclusive terms, and as a result, all this work that women do remains invisible. The binary Mommy Wars debate misses us all. During my daughter's infant and preschool years, when someone asked me what I did, I never exactly knew how to answer. The reason wasn't a personal identity crisis. My life increasingly made sense to me. It's that the expected answers never seemed quite right. If I answered, "I'm a professor," the next questions always assumed I was doing it full-time and knew everyone at my university, which I didn't. When I said, "No, I'm just there a few hours a week," my questioner would usually look askance, as if I were cheating and claiming a job that wasn't mine, and then would backtrack. If I said I was a stay-at-home mother, well, that erased part of the richness of my life. And if I answered that I was a stay-at-home mom who's a part-time professor—well, that seemed both too cutesy and trying-to-have-it-all, and it seemed to stump people. How much does one need to work, I used to wonder, to qualify as a working mom? If I work three hours a week teaching, but do uncounted and invisible hours at home, does that count? Do I get to count the late nights of preparation? If my salary stinks and my job feels more like a well-paid hobby am I really working? Or are these names more a matter of announcing one's priority to the world?

I refused to believe that my entitled-feminist-daughter sense that I could be both mother and professor was too utopian. I looked forward to those times when I was lucky enough to be talking with another mother or father who mixed life the way I did. We could understand and we could smile and trade stories. But as a result of how hard it is to even find the words to talk about working part-time, our creative attempts to parent and work and not do one or the other all the time remain invisible from the usual ways we think about mothering, caring for our children, and paid work.

But surely this situation was not limited to the fifty women in my Atlanta neighborhood with preschool-age children. Where were the national statistics on mothers who work part-time? I knew from the women's studies courses I had taken in graduate school, and from my own experience as a feminist historian looking for women who were absent in standard histories, that women's experiences are often missing. I should have suspected. Looking back, I laugh at my naiveté, my expectation that mothers and part-time work would be well documented.

I had some older and more general numbers in hand. The Family and Home Network had already tripped over this problem in the mid-'90s. As an advocacy organization, it needed to know how to put the stories it was hearing from individual women into a national profile. One of its members, an at-home mom trained as a statistician, did a series of calculations, and came up with some figures: 25 percent of mothers are fully at home. Forty percent work full-time, and roughly 35 percent work part-time, either from an office or at home.

I wanted to see if I couldn't get some more up-to-date figures. Specifically, I wanted to tease out the patterns of numbers from scholars like Joan Williams, who points out that 63 percent of mothers in America work less than full-time. Her number combines stay-at-home mothers with those who work part-time because she's interested in the large number of women who can't come close to filling the kinds of jobs that offer stability, benefits, decent wages, and the possibility of advancement. Further, Williams adds, women make up a whopping 70 percent of the part-time workforce in the United States and accept the lower wages and benefits that accompany this kind of labor.[6]

I dialed the Bureau of Labor Statistics. Imagine my surprise when a receptionist answered on the third ring; I had expected to enter a voicemail menu nightmare. I told her what I wanted to know and she said, "Let me put you through to one of our economists." I know no one will believe that a government agency worked with efficiency, but I must report that within moments—I was on hold for less than a minute—a real live Bureau of Labor Statistics economist in Washington, D.C., took my call. "It's the 2003 charts you'll want; that's the last year we have ready. But no, the published charts don't have what you're looking for," he told me. I was intrigued. He offered to email me the unpublished tables. I asked why some charts are published and others not.

"There's really too much data to put out, even on the website, which is huge," he replied.

"Are they reliable?" I asked.

"Well, yes," he said, "the numbers are as good as we've got. It's just that you can't disaggregate too much; you can't get as accurate as we'd like. For instance, we can't break down working mothers into groups of how old their kids are, because we don't have enough in each group. So when you do that, reliability goes out the window. With these small numbers, you can get big jumps that don't really reflect the way things are."[7] Still, he patiently instructed me on how to read the "mothers" columns against the "married women who work" columns, but then warned me again that the charts were unpublished because, well, it wasn't exactly reliable to read them off each other like that. "It's probably okay, though," were his actual words. What was I to do with that?

Tables 8 and 23a appeared in my email Inbox within the hour.

Lucky for me, I ran into economist Lonnie Golden at the Hi-Way movie theater later that week. He's a professor of economics at Penn State now but for many years he staffed a cubicle at 9to5, National Association of Working Women. I told him I had the charts and he assured me he could teach me the economist's trick of fishing for numbers, of reading charts and tables against each other. But still we were stuck. Some charts measured married women who worked full-time and part-time, but not every married woman is a mother. And some lesbians have babies and work, but they weren't counted, because they weren't married. I learned that in 2002, 75 percent of women who worked, worked full-time, and the other 25 percent of women who worked, worked part-time. One-quarter of working women worked part-time, but this still couldn't tell us much about mothers. And as we know, 18 percent of women never become mothers.

We'd stumbled on a gray zone in which work and fertility were separated in the way that our government collected data about our lives, resulting in these agencies not yet asking questions nuanced enough to reveal the intricacies of women as workers and mothers. I kept thinking, "How hard can it be to find reliable and up-to-date numbers on mothers who are trying to balance competing demands by working part-time?" I couldn't have been more wrong. At times I felt like Michael Moore in *Roger & Me* on the search for the elusive CEO of General Motors to ask him to take responsibility for poverty in Flint, Michigan, the company's corporate hometown.

Work and birth, public and private. By searching for women who combine these things in balanced proportion I'd stumbled back to the age-old binary of public male and private woman in which mothers' work lives are a contradiction, a kind of oxymoron. We can't conceive of an instance in which a parent might work without working all the time.

I then dialed the U.S. Census Bureau, and followed a lead to talk with family demographer Jason Fields. Fields understood immediately what the problem was. "The answer to mothers and part-time labor is not entirely obvious," he agreed. "The problem here is that not all mothers live with their children, and that the labor force statistics are not about fertility, but about living arrangements." As the BLS had, he too directed me to the pertinent tables and showed me how to fish around between them. I dutifully, if dubiously, wrote down his directions. I would have to add the numbers of single mothers who worked to the number of married mothers who worked. But to arrive at the latter I would need to add three columns: "Both in Labor Force/Both

Employed," "Both in Labor Force/Wife Only Employed," and "Only Wife in Labor Force/Wife Employed." Scanning the data fields on my screen, I was reminded that mothers are unemployed too. Is an unemployed mom counted as a stay-at-home mother? My cousin Ally was laid off from her dot-com job several years back. She went back to work six months later. It's tempting to count her as a stay-at-home mom, but she wasn't. She counted as an unemployed mom—that is, if she had even applied for unemployment insurance. If she hadn't, then she wouldn't even be counted. She kept her kids in daycare so she wouldn't lose their spot. She intended to find a job quickly, and even though the next job was longer coming that she planned, the waiting lists for good daycares in Boston were years long and she didn't want to be stuck in the nether land of having a job and no daycare.

The more I thought, the more columns I looked at, the more I learned, the more I despaired. By the end, I had looked for help at the Bureau of Labor Statistics, the Census Bureau, and, believe it or not, the National Center for Health Statistics, which tracks birthrates and fertility and is part of the Centers for Disease Control. Initial excitement at being able to chat with government economists aside, in all cases I quickly hit a brick wall.

Stuck, I made the rounds of the various Washington, D.C., institutes that make it their business to advocate for mothers and families. Part of advocacy, of course, is research. I was buffeted back and forth until I found myself on the telephone with Misha Werschkul, a research assistant at the Institute for Women's Policy Research. She listened as I explained my problem; she said, "I think we have what you need." A few hours later, the incoming email delivered the obscurely titled report *40-hour Work Proposal Significantly Raises Mothers' Employment* by Vicky Lovell. I wasn't sure what exactly this had to do with me, but I started reading, and everything started to click into place.

The yellow, blue, and maroon pie charts on Lovell's report gave me the nuanced story about mothers' work lives I'd been searching for—nearly as many women work part-time as work full-time. Of all mothers, 39 percent work full-time year-round. Twenty-five percent do no paid work, and 37 percent work part-time or part of the year. Of course these numbers change depending on how old the children are. Mothers of infants do less full-time work (24 percent), more are home full-time (32 percent), and 44 percent—more than any other category—work part-time. More mothers of preschoolers shift back to full-time work (33 percent), but still, 31 percent are at home and 37 percent work part-time. It's when kids reach school age that the most mothers (45 percent) return to full-time jobs. Still, even with school-age kids, 20 percent of mothers never return to paid work, and more than a third (36 percent) continue to work part-time.[8]

These numbers put into national perspective what I was seeing at the local playground (and not on *Dr. Phil*). They easily challenge the either/or Mommy Wars version of motherhood and elicit the question of why our media and news organizations don't regularly report on this aspect of mothers' lives. The media seems committed to a liberal feminist model that is too quickly challenged by mothers who leave full-time work, but simultaneously doesn't want to investigate workplace issues. The world of policy think tanks and research, however, is not afraid to take women's real struggles at home and at work much more seriously, to treat our situations less dogmatically and more empathically, and to provide actual numbers that help us think beyond the circle of people we each happen to know.

Lovell's report was the first feminist excursion into mothering and part-time work I found. Still stuck in my social world of well-educated, downwardly mobile creative types, and new to the world of policy debates about motherhood and work, I didn't immediately understand that I was entering another angle, another world. Lovell's report wasn't particularly interested in the part-time struggles of women like me. The Institute had invested its time and money in documenting the work habits of women like me, women with some privilege in life, in order to advocate for a very different class of women: mothers who were on welfare, and who were being asked by the federal government to work an increasing number of hours each week in order to receive their TANF (Temporary Assistance for Needy Families) checks. The government was proposing to raise the required work hours from thirty to forty for these mothers on welfare. Whereas some feminists would emphasize the large number of mothers and women who work full-time, for this feminist argument on behalf of lower-income women, Lovell argued that in fact, most mothers of young children don't work full-time, and neither, then, should mothers on welfare be required to work full-time. Like more affluent and financially stable mothers, they should be allowed to work less and parent more if that's what they want to do. She didn't want mythologies of motherhood to get in the way of what actual women need.

Lovell's report dispels another myth of the Mommy Wars: that all stay-at-home parents are affluent. I knew anecdotally that this wasn't true. I'd already interviewed single mothers who lived in collective households and did technical writing at night so they could have low living expenses and be home with their young kids. I'd met solidly middle-class families who drove a single car so that one parent could be home. I'd met families on public assistance. Families who scrimped and saved.

Even the mothers I met from more affluent households were aware of the financial sacrifices they were making by not working full-time, yet they did so anyway. The Mommy Wars version of motherhood is counterintuitive, isn't it? If a two-lawyer family has one lawyer quit, then doesn't their salary drop by one half, or near to it, given that women's salaries are rarely exactly equal to men's? Aren't they poorer? The Mommy Wars focus on America's tonier suburbs, on elite neighborhoods in L.A., or on Manhattan's fabled Upper East Side, and their stay-at-home mothers are the wealthiest among us. But in real life, mothers who are working less than full-time are earning less, and their families have less. According to Lovell's study, the more affluent a woman is, the more likely she is to be working. Of the mothers who work full-time, 46 percent of these are middle-class or affluent. Thirty-three percent are near-poor, and only 12 percent of poor mothers work full-time.

Our different economic positions may make it harder or easier for us. My struggles are not as visceral as those of a woman who's working two low-wage jobs to pay her rent and keep a roof over her kids' heads, and who has no health insurance for them because her employers hire all their sales associates at twenty-five hours a week, thus skirting the federal guidelines for providing healthcare and other benefits.

In the end, though, motherhood is a gender issue that faces all women. The parent problem confronts all parents who want to devote themselves to labors that have been traditionally been viewed as "women's work." The social trends that since the 1960s and '70s have let more women into the workplace didn't allow us in as mothers. Women have tried different strategies. We've tried the do-it-all approach. We've tried sequencing, doing it all at different times, so to speak. In the end, though, the workplace must change to allow us in as mothers and to allow men in as fathers, so that they too can take on the shares and joys of childraising that many want. That's the challenge for our generation, and it's alternately crippling and exciting. The crisp statistical numbers can't express the ongoing playground discussions of the parent problem—where mothers and fathers push the kids on swings and struggle their way through the conundrums of childcare and careers and family financial security—with its inklings of discontent with the way things are, and its glimmers of a vision toward how they might be instead.

CHAPTER 3.

Are Mothers Really Opting Out?

I call them the Starbucks stories. For a time, all I saw were news-paper stories about stay-at-home mothers. Even more amazingly, they were all set at Starbucks. Op-eds would report on affluent stay-at-home mothers who fritter their time over four-dollar mocha confections, spending their husbands' money instead of doing real work. *New York Times* columnist Maureen Dowd famously ribbed the "retro trend" in which women desert "the fast track for a pleasant life of sitting around Starbucks gabbing with their girlfriends, baby strollers beside them, logging time at the gym to firm up for the he-man CEO at home." The piece was published as part of her advance screed against the remake of the cult film *The Stepford Wives*. Titled "Hot Zombie Love," Dowd's column uses the film's fantasy of robotic wives to lash out against stay-at-home mothers and wives. Who needs dastardly men who program their wives into cheer and obedience, directing them to shine their kitchens with the latest scrubbing products, dress in floral regalia, and resist the spread of feminist consciousness-raising; who needs to worry about old-fashioned sexism like that, when women themselves, according to Maureen Dowd, are doing such an excellent job nowadays of giving up their hard-fought privileges?[1]

Women are cooking again, she rails. They are reading missives on gardening, decorating, and arranging flowers in proper style. Oh, for the good old days of '70s feminism when real women ate out and never ever stepped into the kitchen, classic symbol of oppression that it is. Stay-at-home moms? It's the return of the Feminine Mystique, and where's Betty Friedan when we need her?

"Trading Briefcases for Strollers," reads the caption of the next Tuesday's letters to the editor, where mothers have written in. Melissa Janoski of Pennsylvania is a former journalist, a staff reporter for the *Scranton Times Tribune*. She's aghast at the column's stereotypes and intent on debunking them. Not all stay-at-home mothers are married to titans of industry. Not all spend their mornings at the gym followed by a leisurely afternoon coffee. Stay-at-home moms are not lazy, and contra the attack, they are not necessarily feminism retrograde. Janoski feels attacked by the column, and she's explicit about the work that at-home mothers do. She also makes the point that motherhood debates are so clearly about our differing conceptions of feminism.

"As a stay-at-home mother and a feminist," she writes, "I was horrified. My life as a stay-at-home mom is pleasant because it gives me more time to relish my toddler son and to personally guide him through his days. It leaves little time for Starbucks or the gym. I often work harder now than when I was a newspaper reporter. But for me, what I am doing now is more important and rewarding. I respect that many parents make other choices. Mine is right for me. And freedom of choice is what feminism is all about."[2]

It's interesting to ask just what the phrase "freedom of choice is what feminism is all about" means. After all, "feminism" is one of the most overused and misunderstood words in our language. In the classical repertoire, stay-at-home mothers are the antithesis of feminism's dream. To find full-time mothers who stay home under the banner of feminism is to witness a sea change, a significant moment in gender culture, and to find ourselves facing something momentous that doesn't always make sense.

Over the past few years, I've heard innumerable stories from mothers who are working full-time, from women who are working part-time and parenting part-time, and from women who have quit their jobs or education to raise their kids. It's the latter, of course, who are presenting the biggest surprise, to society and often to themselves. The last feminist movement made sure we had greater opportunities in education and at work. Yet as we know, a new millennium begins and a full quarter of women with children are home with their kids, and another 37 percent are working part-time or only part of a year.

These mothers and these numbers challenge our usual perception of how we modern women comport ourselves. In response, some commentators have taken to chastising these mothers—they're no longer good role models, they're antifeminist, they're taking off all women's shoes and sending all of us back to the kitchen. These stories, especially the ones about lawyers and MBAs—the feminist icons who entered these powerful professions once so restricted to men—are a flash point because they bring us face to face with issues about feminism and its limits that I think, as a society, we would rather not face. We are arguing about motherhood, but we are actually arguing about the legacy of feminism and what it has meant for our lives.

This issue has been particularly hard generationally. Women who came of age in the '60s and '70s and remember feminist battles—and a time when the culture really did seem to be shifting toward more equality for women—fought hard to get where they are. Some were running from the tedium of housework, others from the tedium of boring, low-paying jobs, but all were running toward greater independence and life possibility. They were pioneers in their professions, demanding advancement and fair wages for women. When I quit my job, several older female colleagues took me aside and castigated me. It's hard for them to watch younger women take opportunities for granted, and treat them, in their eyes, so cavalierly. From the perspective of us younger women, we're asked to do too much. Work hours and expectations have increased in the past thirty years.

We know that feminism made life easier, in some regards, and for some of us, but that our society hasn't let in enough feminism to actually help us much as mothers. The powerful acts of opening up better jobs for women weren't accompanied by other powerful acts of social change that would have fully supported us in these new positions. Fathers and married men didn't take up dramatically new roles with regard to housecleaning and childraising; our workplaces haven't changed to accommodate parents and their childcare needs. I didn't see my dropping out of the full-time workplace as ideological, as solving any problems other than the immediate one of how to make life right now better for me and my family. Quitting doesn't solve the big problem; it offers relief, and makes us really mad when we think about it. In that regard, it shows us clearly the crisis we are in.

I do know that mothers aren't done when we quit our jobs or lower our working hours. No, we're in a process. We've begun something that must result in change, in more possibilities to combine parenting and work, in more jobs that truly allow this to happen. We must continue to expand women's place at work in a way that makes room for us to be mothers too, and that places this back-and-forth between home and work as a central option in work life. For now, though, arguments between women about how we mother must be decoded. They're about something much, much more—about deep cultural assumptions, ingrained managerial habits, economics, and other issues that belong not in the style section but on the front page.

The truths of contemporary motherhood are complicated, and we can let ourselves talk about them in public. Far from being Stepforded into quitting work and turning domestic and maternal, many women are in fact making their decisions to parent as a feminist critique of society, as feminists who don't want to give up mothering, and as women who see how the all-or-nothing demands of the workplace push women against a wall. They do this on their own, not because men want it, and often in spite of "How can you do this?" criticism from family and friends. Some men don't want the women in their lives to quit their jobs. A Father's Day article quotes a man commenting about his wife's decision to leave her job as a lawyer: "How can I say, 'No, don't stay home. Work, make money'? I sound like a jerk. I can't win," he says, ending with "It's a classic case of bait and switch."[3] Some men want their wives or partners to continue bringing home a paycheck. They don't want to give up anything material when kids come along, but neither do they always want to share in the day-to-day responsibilities of care. Parents in lesbian and gay families, too, often seek to work less and spend more time with their kids. It seems to me that we're all in a quandary over our changing notions of how much money we need, how much time we want to devote to work, and the models of these balances inherited from a just slightly older generation.

Before October 2003, well-educated mothers who left fancy professional jobs were merely quitting. After October 26 brought the publication of Lisa Belkin's "Opt-Out Revolution" in the *New York Times Magazine*, these women were "opting out," and the phrase quickly caught on.[4] The article featured stay-at-home mothers in two cities, Atlanta and San Francisco, and since Belkin's entrée to these women's lives was a shared Princeton degree, many of them had Ivy League pedigrees. A number of them were lawyers and MBAs, and all had quit high-powered jobs in law, business, TV, and journalism. Belkin's article tried to capture the hugely complex topic of why mothers quit jobs instead of working. She talked even about her own decision to leave a full-time job as a reporter for a part-time job writing a column from home, and at the end she interviewed experts on the question of how women return to careers after they've interrupted them for childraising, with the answer: they don't. The piece ended by questioning whether this trend is the end of feminism or its new challenge.

The article made a big splash, and "opting out" quickly became part of the national vocabulary to describe mothers who left full-time jobs.[5]

The first set of letters to the editor about "Opt-Out Revolution" appeared two weeks later (the day before the *Dr. Phil* show aired). The magazine received an unprecedented number of letters to the editor in response and published several weeks of them—a rarity. By the third week, the letters section included not just letters responding to the article, but letters that responded to other letters. The *Times* was allowing its readers to have a public conversation not just with its writer but with each other, one of the few sustained conversations among *Times* readers I've ever seen. Responses weren't limited to the few chosen for publication in the magazine itself. The *Times'* online response section grew to include over a thousand posts with Belkin herself responding to critics. "Opt-Out Revolution" was the most emailed *New York Times Magazine* article in *Times* history; friends would send it round with commentary, asking others what they thought. Something broke—a wall that had surrounded mothers talking about work and family life. Working-mom lunch and break talk and at-home-mom playground talk became public.

I had heard prepublication inklings of this story, and when I lazily pulled apart the *New York Times* sections that weekend I found it. The cover image is a glossy photo of a white woman seated cross-legged on the floor, a baby on her lap. Her hair is dark and long, and she is tastefully dressed in a white button-down shirt, properly mussed, with black pants, some bracelets on her left wrist, and a ring on the fourth finger of each hand. The baby is wide eyed and perfect and wears those toddler overalls that make you wish your child would never grow up. The woman's right hand rests on her baby's head, listlessly, sweetly. She is posed in a room painted entirely in coral peach. Behind the mother and child rises a ladder, the kind made, say, for bunk beds, where the edges and all surfaces are sanded smooth. The ladder ascends to the top of the page, beneath and past the magazine's logo at the top, ending where none of us can see. Floor, walls, even ladder are painted the same shade. One woman to represent all mothers, laid out against a single color. The effect is of an isolation chamber. The woman is posed so her head is tilted and her eyes look upward and off to the left, vacant, doe-eyed. Her expression is Madonna-esque, and almost mirrors those ubiquitous Byzantine icons of the Blessed Virgin Mary except this woman seems a bit wistful, whereas the Virgin Mary stands or sits straight. The Virgin Mary faces forward, her eyes address us directly, but not this mother.

I wondered about the photographer who must have positioned the woman in just this way, and I wondered about the designer who picked out the room, the ladder, and the color. A major national magazine finally recognizes this new trend in the world of motherhood and creates this cover image. What were they thinking? Here it was, a major national story about women who had made choices similar to mine and to those of many of my friends. I should have been thrilled, but instead, I felt ill.

Just below the image of the woman and her child, white words, upon which the pair sit, form a question: "Q: Why Don't More Women Get to the Top?" The response follows in black: "A: They Choose Not To." In white again: "Abandoning the Climb and Heading Home." Fighting words sufficient to get most of us to open the magazine instead of reaching over to the book reviews or the front page. "They Choose Not To," of course, is the line that got all our ganders going. How about "A: Workplaces don't accommodate motherhood"? Or even "A: Workplaces are too rigid and so ambivalent about women's success that they don't really want to be flexible and help out mothers, who still bear the majority of childcare responsibility because fathers still don't bear enough of it"?

Our national news magazines rarely attend to issues facing women and mothers in this country. Though fearing that they may not have gotten this story exactly right, I turned to the contents page to find

"Opt-Out Revolution," page forty-two, highlighted in red. The description reads "Many high-powered women today don't ever hit the glass ceiling, choosing to leave the workplace for motherhood. Is this the failure of one movement, or the beginning of another?" The sidebar adds: "While the absence of women in positions of power was once chiefly a result of sexism, the fact that women still don't rule the world is now increasingly a result of a deliberate choice."

Throughout the fall of 2003 we saw the airing of motherhood issues in public for the first time in a long time. Like the *Dr. Phil* show, many of the articles that season were on their own less than helpful. They raised some issues and ignored others, and most continued to present only the lives of affluent white women, and the thinnest high-end sliver of affluent white women at that. When mothers' quandaries are presented as affecting only wealthy women, it's hard to gain empathy for the problem that affects all women. On the upside, each time a TV station or national newspaper or magazine presented an opinion piece on motherhood and its trends, readers wrote back and talked back. They penned letters to the editor; they cell-phoned in en masse to radio talk shows, for instance, when Lisa Belkin did the radio show rounds. Those of us locked in the usual isolation of motherhood, and those of us aching to hear the politics of motherhood discussed in public, got the release we needed.

"We can't stop talking about it in my office," said Amy, a mother of two boys who works full-time running an organization that raises scholarship money for low-income, at-risk high school kids. We were chatting at a neighborhood Halloween party. Forty or so kids bounced around in their costumes, rip-roared through mac and cheese, and left behind a teetering stack of depleted juice boxes. "Opt-Out Revolution" was all anyone wanted to talk about that night. The letters to the *New York Times Magazine* editor followed soon after.

"Lisa Belkin's article and the letters in response made me queasy," writes Karen Watts from Cortlandt Manor, New York. "What an agonizing quandary: whether to be a high-powered ladder climber or an at-home parent with a full complement of support and resources. This is a feminist dilemma? Just a reminder: most people can't opt out and later reenter the work force when they've gotten that parenting thing out of their systems. Real life just doesn't allow for those kinds of luxurious choices. We live, we work, we raise our children—and all at once, imagine that."

In contrast to this honest, poignant description of maternal desire and class privilege, the *Times* posted a letter from Debora Lichtenberg of Pelham, Massachusetts, who calls women "whiners," which in American political life is the ultimate tarring accusation. Real Americans, after all, buckle up and stay in control. Whining suggests that one is pretending to be a victim.

There were letters like the one from Dena Harris, a physician in New York. She's sure that it's only women in law and business—those profiled by Belkin—who give up their jobs: "In my experience, most women who have entered other fields, like medicine, education, academia, the arts, science, etc., have not given up working. They seem to have more genuine passion for what they do and have found ways to combine raising a family with continuing to work."

While I feel empathy with this last perspective, it denies that there's any bigger problem. *If only women made better decisions about their professions.* Some want to believe that there is no general problem out there. *Yes, corporate women have these troubles, but that's because the corporate world is soulless and doesn't require any passion.* But some corporate lawyers are in fact passionate about what they do. *Women in passion-requiring fields, like medicine, the arts, and academia, don't leave because they have more passion invested in their jobs.* Well, tell that to the New York mother I met, a ballerina who stopped dancing after her children were born; to the emergency room doctor who quit after her second child arrived because the shifts were too long and the work too draining. Or to many new MDs who train in radiology or dermatology because these fields alone have manageable hours and expectations. Tell the line about passion, and the story that only corporate women have these struggles, to the many female professors I know, a passionate bunch, who left their jobs, or who couldn't find hours in the day to attend to their kids and do all the work demanded for tenure, or who were demoted to less prestigious and lower-paying positions. Passion goes only so far, and not far enough to explain the problem.

There are other ways, too, to blame women. Judith Lorber, of New York, found Belkin's article depressing. She denies that the "pull of motherhood" is at issue and thinks the women are just dissatisfied with what a career entails; work is life, too, as much as children are. If only these women—"golden girls" she calls them—who are now quitting would have fought harder to stay in. Perhaps "they thought it would all fall in their laps, and they wouldn't have to be able to have to compete. . . . Perhaps they weren't taught the old-fashioned feminist lessons of how to fight informal discrimination against women. Perhaps they got tired of trying to enlist their spouses in a genuine shared parenting arrangement? How much of these well-educated women's lives is devoted to parenting? How many are organizing something, doing voluntary charity work, or consulting for pay?"

This letter oddly blames these women for failing a feminist standard, yet never admits that when so much of the work of raising children falls on women's shoulders, we're not able to compete from an even playing field. Her letter does note that there's discrimination in the workplace, but she calls it informal, and something that can be fought against if one just follows old-fashioned feminist lessons. Really? I want to ask: Are the answers this easy? And why is it so impossible to imagine that some women and men really want to be with their kids?

Other readers look at the problem with breadth. Amy Hackney Blackwell, a reader from Greenville, South Carolina, writes that she had recently read Betty Friedan's *The Feminine Mystique* with empathy, and that she "found her description of the symptoms of hopelessness and depression suffered by desperate housewives strikingly familiar. I myself had felt all of those things, but as an associate in a law firm, where every day I sat at my desk and billed my time on tasks to enrich the partners while someone else cared for my new baby. The choice was clear: I left four years ago and have never looked back. The opt-out revolution isn't about motherhood; it's about quality of life and rejection of a system in which long hours have been confused with quality work. I suspect that if the United States had shorter workweeks and six or eight weeks of guaranteed vacation like some European countries, many more women would happily stay on the job." This answer is big and it's political and it points to the workplace.

And as if to end the discussion on a more positive and forward-thinking conclusion, the next week's letters section added one final comment. Writes Jenny Brandemuehl of Mountain View, California:

> Lisa Belkin's article and your November 23 letters [are] a great snapshot of the differences of experience and history among women of diverse generations. I'm 40, the same age as the women in Belkin's article. When I graduated from Wellesley in 1985, we took full advantage of the career opportunities that feminists fought hard for. I think our generation of career women was caught unprepared for the stresses of juggling demanding jobs in dual-career families.
>
> I traded a successful career at Hewlett-Packard for flexible hours to be with my kids by starting my own business. A few years ago, I was asked to speak on a panel about flexible work arrangements at Stanford Business School. The students asked great questions. I realized then that women today in their twenties enjoy the benefit of thinking more realistically about their careers and life choices than my generation ever did.

I can empathize with the desire to neaten up an extraordinarily messy situation. I admire those women and men who felt strongly enough about these issues to write in repeatedly and in great numbers to the newspaper that comes closest to being a weather vane of our public discussions. With all due respect, though, the solution isn't just found in women thinking more realistically about their careers. All of our thinking, as solid and realistic as it might be, won't add up to changing a situation—for mothers, work, creativity, and independence—shaped predominantly by social policies, cultural inheritance, and workplaces that are still dominated by men, by traditional male-centered ideals that don't take into account the social good of hands-on childraising and that are ruled by the fantasy that real workers work full-time. I would have felt more reassured if I thought that elite Stanford students were seeing how the structures of work are still pitted against workers who want to parent, and were brainstorming on real, specific ways to demand and create managerial change, not just thinking about life as a series of choices over which we have total control, sure that with proper advance planning and organization, the whole big problem goes away.

Those who want to see the mother-work problem as easily solvable tend to offer solutions that rely on an individual woman's choice: If only the lawyers had been artists, there would be no problem. Translated into its most basic assumption, this kind of answer says: These mothers only have problems because they made bad choices. It's their fault. Society's off the hook. An argument that starts off sounding supportive turns out to have a regressive and retrograde touch. In these letters, I understand feminist worries and big-picture fears that the last generation of advances for women and our opportunities are paper thin, fragile, and easily lost to a changing cultural landscape. I see women skipping over stones to say that the workplace is not bad, and that women can always leave a non-family-friendly environment for a better one; the choice is ours. I read women wanting to feel like we are in control.

Sometimes when I read politically charged language it feels disembodied, unreal, ideological, but somehow not intimate. This is not how these positions should be understood. Readers write things like this: "Why put years of money and effort and study and sometimes hardship and struggle into getting an advanced degree just to become a house-wife? You might as well throw your diploma in the garbage or hold a match to it. Unbelievable . . . " or "What about all those qualified, ded-icated applicants who lost their places in professional schools to these whining moms? I say go back to finding those intelligent, driven women without silver spoons in their mouths. We fought so hard in the early '70s to become recognized by top programs and change the admis-sion policies. If we're not careful, the subtle tide of hiring men over women for higher salaries will continue, and employers will be making the right decision." Their harshness, I think, houses very real fears voiced by women who have been working long enough to know the possibilities of advancement, the struggles women face to achieve, and the subtle discriminations that persist. I want to believe these are not meant as lording-it-over-you cants of political correctness; that would be making the mistake of assuming that working women have more power than most do. I want to read these words generously. The words are harsh because the feelings are raw and real, and because working women, when we scratch the surface, feel like we have less collective power than we need.

And the women who've left jobs to be with their kids also have feminist worries. Karen Blinder Akerhielm of Greenville, South Carolina, was among the first batch of letter writers. A stay-at-home mom with a PhD in economics from Yale, she writes that although she should relate to the women in the article, she can't. She can't pat herself on the back and rationalize that she is smarter for having quit. There are too many questions that haunt: "What kind of role model am I being for my children, especially my daughter? What happens in a few years when I wish to re-enter the work force? Is it really a 'choice' to stay home or rather a lack of options from which to choose?"

What will my daughters think? Am I a good role model? Where will my life and career be in five years when I want to return? Have I indeed wasted my education? For any woman on the older edge of childbearing age, feminism is the cultural landscape in which we were raised. That doesn't mean all our families were feminist, nor that there was a utopia, but that certain mainstream versions of feminism eventually came to set the stage for what we thought life would be. Questions like "What can I be when I grow up?" spread wildly past the usual female answers of nurse, teacher, saleslady, secretary, or domestic maid to include the range of professions. A decade later, sports opened up for girls, and it's a sign of my age that I still get a thrill from watching girls' soccer and basketball even though I know that full equity hasn't been reached. For many, these changes become old hat. We don't have to talk about them or argue about them. We just live within them and take them for granted. The backlash, the crisis felt by many mothers who want to keep working on their own terms, might be at the forefront of feminism's next challenge. The traditional bent of our society is able to accommodate a relatively tame version of feminism, and, can we say, is scared enough by this version and considers it quite radical. It's ironic, then, that mothers—seemingly the most traditional of women—are pushing us ahead, pushing us to think again about basic institutions like work and family.

In the *Times* letters I recognize exhaustion, fatigue, and the relentlessness of childraising and daily life, and from within all this, women who can still convey quiet passions, just below the radar of social politics: I wish I had been able to take off work to be with my children, several women write poignantly, expressing the sadness of families who couldn't afford it or who couldn't imagine a way to make it happen.

"You ran eight letters on Lisa Belkin's article," notes a letter from Shoshanna Malett of Forest Hills, New York, referring to the first Sunday of responses. "No one addressed the issue of choice, or lack thereof. As a federal employee, I am entitled to unpaid maternity leave. It broke my heart to return to work when my son was five months old. My husband and I are scrambling to find a way for me to spend as much time as possible with the daughter we are expecting in a few months. I pray that we can, but it isn't looking good. How I wish I were one of the women in Belkin's article." What comes off as Muffy-bashing in one letter— " . . . a feel-good piece for the Muffy set. . . . We know all those frou-frou Sunday Magazine ads . . . aren't targeted at single moms from the outer boroughs and the Great Unwashed beyond"—reads as a quiet longing for a life of less work in another.

I spot some boisterous visions, too, that see past the current focus on hyperproductivity and increasingly long work hours, visions beyond twelve-hour workdays: desires for a better quality of life, shorter work weeks, and more vacation time; all those policy changes that everyone says are fine for Scandinavia and France but will never happen in cowboy America, where each man cares for himself alone and his horse. There are structural critiques offered by readers who think that while individual women have some control over their lives, the key issues are in the generalized and usually unstated principles of the workplace. Women, they write, have changed in the thirty years since feminism's heyday, and now workplaces and other institutions also need to change, and that is where the focus should be. The issue is not what a single woman manages to do. These letters express a desire for a real revolution, real changes in the rules of the game.

I also hear loads of anger, annoyance, irritation, and rage. Some of the anger is expressed toward society and workplaces, where it should rightfully go. Some of the anger is sublimated into guilt. When I hear mothers say, "I felt guilty that I couldn't do it all," or "I feel guilty about choices I make," I can't help but understand this statement as anger thwarted, anger turned inward, an emotion coined as regret about personal decisions rather than anger at limited social options. At the end of the day and in the short term, guilt is an easier emotion to feel than real and focused anger. Turned upside down, of course, guilt—which at first seems self-effacing—actually insists that one is still in charge. "I made bad decisions, but at least I *made* decisions," guilt says. Anger would seem to be more empowering—and ultimately I believe it is—but to express anger also is to come to terms with not being in control, with not having something we wanted, with not getting what we think we deserve.

There's class anger, too: That's not just about motherhood, but about whose lives are the center of public attention, whose lives get media coverage, and about who and which families have the economic means to make more choices. One woman is attacked online for claiming that she had more choices because she got married; the attacker reminds her that autonomy in marriage only belongs to men, and that the economic protection of marriage is not the same thing as real independence. But doesn't it all just point to the complex tangle here? These are the confusing ways in which we try to make sense of what it means to have choices and options and freedoms—these elements of life that are so quintessentially American, we believe, that to express them is our national dream, even if at the same time we know them to be illusions.

My point, my fear, is that instead of coming to terms with how these dreams conflict with mothers' realities we will instead go on making up ever more complex reasons why something that affects so many women is not structural, not part of the ordinary contradictions of American social economy, but just a problem shared by a few women—privileged, white women at that—and it's really just their fault anyway because they made poor decisions. I'm afraid that real issues will be dismissed.

Debates about motherhood and work and families raise the most complicated and haunting fears. But concentrating on the fear dismisses the fact that these issues are in fact some of the biggest, broadest, and most philosophically astute questions we as human beings can be raising. Questions like "What do I want life to be, and can I accomplish this vision?" Questions like "What do children really mean, how do we care for them, raise them well, and send them on their way to the world of

adults? How do we raise children who will grow into the next generation of adults, of citizens, of members of our neighborhoods and communities and societies?" Questions like "How do I do all this and pay my
mortgage or rent too?"

Now, I didn't love the "Opt-Out" article. My friends, family, and
neighbors all remember my rants about it. Reading through all the
responses, though, I can't tell whether people were angriest at the article's writer, Lisa Belkin, for the way she framed the argument, quoted
her sources, and drew her conclusions; whether they were annoyed at
and envious of the women who were profiled; or whether they were
mad at the system of real workplace demands and at a culture that
makes the labor and time of childraising invisible. It makes a difference.
In the fall of 2003, though, I think that many of the people in the conversation were too raw, too pent-up mad to sort through questions like
that. In the letters, people everywhere are grappling with not having all
the choices they want. They're mad when they think others have more.

So if Belkin got it wrong, what does "choice" really mean? Growing up,
we girls were always told by our mothers and aunts, "Feminism gives
girls and women more choices." I constantly hear mothers of young
children say that quitting their interesting jobs to be home with their
kids was their choice. It's a defensive move, we all understand that. The
declaration of choice reacts against a history—of housewifery, motherhood, and feminism—in which women in some families were culturally
coerced into staying home, into being with their children even though
they may have preferred more integrated lives. And "choice" is true
only partially. We may choose to leave our jobs. But that's only the
smallest part of the picture. We don't choose the structures of the workplace that make it so difficult to get back in when we return, or to work
part-time and be paid fairly for it. This workplace predicament is not
our choice. Let's be clear about that.

When I hear the word "choice" in conjunction with motherhood I cringe. It's a nearly automatic response. We make it sound so cheery and upbeat when in fact life is much more complicated. Several times a year I pack up my car and my child and we head out on a four-and-a-half-hour trip to see my mom and dad; to get there I have to travel through New York City. At one point, halfway there, there's a choice of two roads I can take. The Belt, as it's known, is almost always filled with traffic. And so is the other road, known locally as the BQE. I can choose my road, but in the end, there's not much of a choice, since they're both usually jam packed. Real choice would be a new road that could take me where I want to go without endless stop-and-go traffic. Real choice would be a helicopter to lift us out of the jam and drop us thirty minutes later at my parents' house near the beach.

It's the same with the "choices" now offered in parenting and paid work. "Choice" is a concept we associate with "free agents," with people who have all the choices in the world, who are not structurally limited in any way. As much as it has been a phrase of feminist politics, choice itself is a fantasy, one that emerges from a classic American belief that we are independent, free, and autonomous; that we have choices and choose our options freely; and that, as a result, we ourselves are solely responsible for the results. This assumes that there is no structural discrimination against mothers, that we fit right into the normative model, which we don't. "Choice" has particular resonance for women; it's what we claim we have when we want to feel liberated and it's what we know we don't have in those depressing moments when we admit we're not.

What I don't like about the phrase "opted out" is that it forecloses any discussion about what "choice" means and about what kinds of options women have. I particularly don't like the statement "She's opted out" applied to every woman who is staying home with her kids or working hours other than full-time. "Opting out" assumes that women have options. "Option"—such a happy word—is embedded right in the description, only shortened, so we forget the big picture, the assumption, the claim, and we see it only as a verb. "I opted out," we say, instead of the bolder "I quit." "Opted out" answers any questions before they can be asked. "It was my choice," we say, instead of saying, "It's kind of complicated, but my workplace really didn't support me as a new mother or new father with new needs that don't fit the classic assumptions about workers." "I left," we might say in breezy tones, instead of saying, "There's an ongoing debate in our country about feminism, about gender roles and possibilities, about what women and men, mothers and fathers, can do; my family is part of that."

No one has all the answers. We're buffeted about right now, and our society has to be on the verge of some major changes. To say "I quit" still inspires the question "Why?"; it asks for a story to be told. It doesn't sidestep the problem. To say, "I was squeezed out by forces beyond the control of any individual woman or man," then, would seem beyond the pale of social nicety. That would be complaining, and we're supposed to be agents of our own freedom, not trod-upon workers who complain. But "being squeezed out" is in fact what is happening, and whereas this phrase hasn't yet hit the playground or the preschool yard or even the majority of the nation's newspapers and magazines, it's used with ease in business venues like *Fast Company* and rolls off the tongues of professors at our nation's most elite business schools.

"Opt-Out Revolution" introduced us to professional women who left their jobs for childraising. But as many have pointed out in response, the women profiled for that feature never voiced a desire to be full-time mothers. Across the board, their stories were not of opting out, but of being forced out by circumstance, of being "squeezed out," to use the phrase preferred by Harvard Business School professor Shoshana Zuboff.[6] To leave the workforce because you truly want to, because you really want to devote special time to your children's early years—well, you wouldn't sound like the women Belkin interviewed, who tell stories about working eighty hours a week to prepare legal

briefs and then being notified that the judge is taking a two-week vacation to go fishing. They tell stories about being high-visibility journalists and never seeing their children, and then being told there ar no
part-time work possibilities at the station. These women are being
structurally forced out because the parenting responsibilities they have
claimed have no place in the workplace.

So what's the downside to "choosing" to totally leave a job? Lack of
mental stimulation is one; the isolation and relentless work of caring
for little ones is another. Difficulty getting back into the workplace is
a big one, as are the wage hit and the loss of wages over one's lifetime.
Another major issue is security. If your family life stays intact, everything's okay. The risk paid off. But when it doesn't? That's when giving up a job and facing the wage hit that all mothers take makes a big
difference.

Leah has three kids. She's well educated, and after the kids were
born, she worked part-time as a psychotherapist. Her husband was a
clergyperson and he worked at a nearby congregation. His hours were
relatively flexible and he did his part in driving the kids to school and
being a hands-on dad. Leah worked a few hours a week as a therapist;
she was even trying to begin her own practice, but their family had
always moved for her husband's good jobs, and she was just getting
started again. The first time we met, Leah ruefully talked about the
trade-offs: the loss of financial security and independence because she
wanted three kids and also wanted not to have to work full-time. Still,
she seemed to be pretty happy with the balance of work and parenting
in her life; she had just been hired to teach a course at a nearby college
and was renting office space with hopes of building a new therapy practice. She wanted her house to be the one where her kids and their
friends hung out after school. That was part of her vision of a good life.
"I must really love my husband," she laughed.

Even at the time, I wondered at her words. Most mothers I've met make these decisions for their children and for themselves, and they talk about it that way. I hadn't ever encountered a woman who told me she did it for her husband. Most women I've asked talk about their decisions about work and caring for their kids as if their husbands don't play any role. What a big change from the classic housewife tales of the '50s. Middle-class white women who married in that decade tell me of the pressure they felt from their husbands to quit work.

I ran into Leah a year and a half later as we stood at the edge of the softball field watching our daughters. "You know that my husband and I are divorcing," she began and launched into the story of why: of paths going in different directions, of the debt they were in, the house she was trying to keep hold of, the work she was now looking for.

This is where the bottom drops out, where the economic independence that '70s feminists taught us about doesn't seem so old-fashioned or abstract anymore. "My overriding sense is panic," she continued more quietly. I asked whether she'd had luck finding work. "Well, I'm working in a group psychotherapy practice, maybe twelve hours a week, but it underpays," she said. "It's an HMO so I get half of nothing that the group brings in for each patient. I'm doing some freelance teaching, some spiritual direction work, and leading some support groups. I need more work, a normative, full-time day job, yet in my field now, in psychotherapy, this is no longer the norm. I realize I need advanced computer skills and a résumé reflecting much more consistent work in any arena than I've been able to do with three children and a spouse who kept moving from job to job."

Only now she was the primary parent. The children's father had lost his job and found another, lower-paying one. The kids would have health insurance from him, but she wouldn't, she told me, not sure of what to do. And neither would much child support be coming her way: On paper her advanced degrees painted her as the partner capable of bringing in a larger income. No one accounted, though, for her years out of the workforce and for the wage gap that affects all mothers. "I also feel like my choices are so limited," she said, "given the incredible needs of three kids of vastly different ages."

There is another side of choice—one that also goes undiscussed in Belkin's article—a choice in which career stays paramount. Laura Levitt has been my best friend for over ten years, and besides that, she's a published theologian and feminist scholar. We met at a conference back when we were graduate students and built our friendship over long discussions at Chinese restaurants. Now, I have a child and an interrupted career. Laura has no kids and she's a tenured professor with lots of leeway and freedom and support that she's been building over the years. She does live with her male partner, to answer everyone's usual first question, and their two large dogs, and yes, she's pretty near the end of the years that make childbearing easier.

Every so often we broach the question of children. Personally, I never ask people if they're going to have kids or if they want more kids. It seems rude, almost invasive, and they get enough flak from others. In order to continue her life of writing and teaching, Laura has chosen not to have children. This choice has been honest, reflective, and not without its own pain attached:

> There's no room in our culture to say, "I choose not to have kids."
> Yes, we choose abortions when we're younger, if we need them. But that's different than the pressure to choose not to have children. Because it's never just about choice. I hate that word and all it conveys. I didn't exactly choose not to have children. But there's also no room in our culture to have it all. I live in a culture that makes it impossible to do all the things I want to do with my life—my teaching, my writing, my contributions—if I were to have children. I look around at the women I know who are active in their careers, in their creative lives, and almost all of them don't have children. So that's where I've tossed my hat. It's a choice that's not exactly a

choice. My colleagues who have kids are always worried about losing their jobs, fearful and nervous and frantic. People with kids can't keep up the pace required for success these days. Men can do it. Their wives follow them and support them. The wives do more of the childcare. Or their wives have jobs that are subordinate. It's not supposed to be that way, but it is.

"Choice" is a complicated concept. We often claim we are "choosing" options that actually are not truly open choices. Popular feminism has been defined as giving women choices. Some feminist thinkers have argued to the contrary: Women don't actually have all the choices they want and need. However, the peppier power-feminism version of the argument pervades our collective psyche. Even though some feminist spokeswomen tell us that our choices as women are limited—this is, after all, the ongoing injustice that fuels feminism—other feminist spokeswomen tell us, "No, women have choices, we just need to step out and take them." What's a woman do to? Whom should we believe? We're stuck here in the classic problem, the classic opposition of victim and agent. Victims have no choices; something's been done to them against their will; they're caught in a structural, socioeconomic web and can't get out. Agents thrive on individual free will; nothing stops them. They envision what they want to do and do it. Agents make choices. American society is based on the idea of individual freedom and choice, and we like to see ourselves in this model. That makes it downright embarrassing, if not impossible, to admit that we didn't really have many great choices, but we made a decision anyway. What's confusing about the whole choice thing is that we both see ourselves as agents, as people who take life by the horns, and know that's not always true—and still, it is hard to find the words to convey this. Sometimes we get to choose and other times we don't. So the first part of the choice problem tells us that life will work out if only we make the right choices. This theology is reassuring. It tells us that we are in control.

The second part of the "choice" conundrum says that just making a decision—about anything, regardless of content—is feminist. Back in the early '70s, Supreme Court Justice Harry Blackmun kept substituting the phrase "this choice" for the word "abortion" when he penned his brief for the classic court decision *Roe v. Wade*. The name stuck. A belief in reproductive rights was pro-choice, and as mainstream feminism began to focus heavily on protecting reproductive rights against right-wing attack, "choice" was seen as a synonym for "feminism." I remember as a girl in the '70s being told by my mother, "Feminism is all about having choices." And it is. There's something about the weird reception of feminism in our society, though, that contorts all of this. As Summer Wood writes in *Bitch* magazine, "'It's my choice' becomes synonymous with 'It's a feminist thing to do.'"[7] We end up with a syllogism: Whatever I want to do is my choice; feminism is about choice; therefore, whatever I want to do is feminist. What's funny, awkward, and unsettling to me is how feminism is both reviled and desired. Ignored when it's unpopular or nerdy or embarrassing, but invoked when helpful.

"Out there, people always second-guess you and tell you how you could have done life differently," Laura says, and launches into the common advice people give about finding the "convenient" time to have children. But the language of "convenience" misses the issue—that children take time, and all the conveniently timed pregnancies and scheduled C-sections don't change that, they can't solve the problem.

It's one question to think about when I could have "conveniently" had kids—in graduate school? After high school, like my friends from Dover, Delaware, who have grown kids now and are all getting divorced? At the start of my career? A few years from now, when I'm 49? But that doesn't solve the real problem, we know. It's about what kind of mothering you want to do. That it takes time to raise a family right. And it takes time to do your career right, time and focus, and for some careers and their demands, there's not really enough time in the day.

Some people go for the kids; I went for my job. It's hard to share when you really love what you do.

Laura mentions a friend of ours, a working mother with two children who dared admit that sometimes, actually, she wished she didn't have kids—sometimes she wishes she could just do her work. "These aren't really choices," Laura adds, "not really. The sadness is that I like kids. Last year I was invited to speak at a college in Massachusetts. They toured me around and I saw that they had an on-site daycare. It's beautiful. Parents walk over during the day to see their kids. I couldn't help but think that if my job, if my workplace, supported parents and kids like that, I could have imagined having children."

I don't want to simplify the really intimate and complicated reasons we each do what we do. I know in my own case that to reduce my story about work and parenting to a single political fighting point would be to strip away some of what makes it human, and to be alive is confusing and contradictory. We don't have all the choices we need, and still we manage to make the decisions we make. But that shouldn't be conflated with a belief that we have uninhibited choice. Life has its random events, its magic, and its moments when the universe falls into place. The complexity of decisions about mothering and work is that at times that which is as spiritually and psychically moving as motherhood also comes entangled and fraught, caught in a history of sexism and oppression so that it becomes hard to say straightforwardly that we love our kids and want to spend more time with them. We must own our choices and desires, and take the routes through life that come our way.

But we shouldn't misread the situation. We have many choices, those daily decisions we make. We shouldn't confuse a bunch of decisions we make with real "choice" that we don't have as women and mothers. It's only really a "choice" if you have more control over the consequences. And with the current workplace and its expectations, and with an economic system where you have to fall pretty hard and far to find the safety net, mothers and fathers don't yet have control over the consequences of taking time to parent.

The problem with the "Women are opting out" explanation is that it treats quitting like a personal choice. It is, but it's a personal choice made in response to a limited set of workplace options, and a culture that has a constricted imagination of work and family. Personal choice within a social context is a different thing altogether and the phrase "opting out" can't ever capture this part of it.

One rainy afternoon I listen to a friend, Celeste, talk about how she's ready to leave her job in the arts. She has one child. She's pregnant with another. She loves her job, it's relatively flexible, her office is at home, and her child's daycare is nearby. Her boss even agreed to an 80 percent schedule, with Mondays off. It's one of those deals that other mothers talk about, using it as an example of what can go right in the work and family mix. She never thought she would quit. Still, the job demands many hours—more than full-time. Management doesn't give it enough support to make it a viable part-time job, so instead she is left, like many part-time working mothers, with a full-time job merely masquerading as part-time—and with part-time pay. "I want time with the new baby," she says. "And I want to spend time with my daughter before the new baby arrives. Mostly, I want a part-time job that really is a part-time job."

It's not that there will be many good work choices for her when she's ready to return. There won't be. She's already watched enough friends and relatives to know. She tells me her story and I feel a pit in my stomach. There's good ahead, too: the chance to shift career gears, a positive vision of work and family to keep her going. But all the personal positivity and belief in the future can't make the heaviness of her lack of real options go away. This is not opting out—not when she tried hard and asked for work appropriate to her schedule, and her managers didn't try hard enough to create a viable part-time job, one with space for her family. As I listen to her story, all the emotion about my own journey into motherhood and out of full-time work comes unraveled and turns bare. It's one thing to muster some bravado, quit my job, and reassure myself life will all be okay later. It's quite another to watch someone else do it, to see the rigidity of someone else's workplace, especially someone I thought had it all. I am incredibly sad that this talented woman has so few options. "I guess I'm lucky," she told me, "in that I can afford to stay home for a while because of my husband's salary. But that's never what I wanted to do—depend on his making money."

Too often, when women in professional life are faced with these stark decisions, people point to them, as if to say, "But it's a choice, a privilege, to stay home." In other words, "Stop complaining." This misses the point: We need better options for ourselves, not just options that have to do with the luck of partnering up with someone bringing home a decent salary. Wasn't that the advice given to girls in the 1950s? Marry a man with money? We should have come further than that by now. Our society was supposed to have changed dramatically. But has it? Can it until we solve the work and family problem? A woman shouldn't have to give up a job and career entirely for want of some time off, a year or two, or even more. She shouldn't lose wages for the rest of her life because she dared to take a few years off for her family. That's what we're talking about: a few years off, a few less hours of work each day. What can this mean in the context of careers and work lives that begin in our twenties and last till we turn sixty-five?

The popularity of the opt-out explanation can't account for what's really happening. Words like "choice" and "options" substitute for a much richer and complex human tangle of desire and circumstance, consequence and limitation; of foibles and regretted decisions, and happiness and fierce love and relentless commitment. The numbers of mothers who leave their jobs or who work part-time are in fact resisting a system that they feel makes them work too hard. They are finding lives that feel sane and spiritually satisfying to them (even with the losses they experience), lives that can't yet be understood in the terms that our culture provides, and which get unutterably entwined in the complexities of our expectations of gender, parenting, and women's and men's roles. Many of these mothers also know how much work it takes to raise kids well and keep a home life running relatively sanely. If they live with men, they still don't have enough help from their male partners in doing this. Far from retreating to a retrograde past, they are resisting the huge amount of labor our society asks mothers to do. As we start talking about a debate over feminism and motherhood that has been staged as if it's entirely a problem between women, we must remember the big picture, which is that mothers bear a much greater burden of work than fathers. Because feminist criticism is part of what can't be spoken these days, the role of men at home, and of male-centered notions of the workplace, usually remains all too invisible to the conversation about parenting.

We live our lives with grace, with eloquence, bumbling through one day, ballooning above it all the next. Mothers are making decisions about work and family that are pushing us all to think again about feminism and our future. Feminism was never meant to be a claim of triumph, a pronouncement that women have all the choices we want and that we can amble happily among them. No, it was a critique stating that women—and, we can emphasize, *mothers*—don't yet have all the choices and options we need.

CHAPTER 4.

Mothers in the Middle

To get in the door to Laura S. and Rick's December holiday party, your arms had to be weighed down with a muscle-building bag of wrapped presents for the homeless kids at the People's Emergency Center. By the time Rob and I arrived with Samira and several of her friends shuttled over from a birthday party, walked through the door, and pulled off our wet shoes and winter coats, the party was in full swing. Warm crab dip and crackers were set on one table, a tower of homemade chocolate truffles on another, and cider was on the stove. The tall tree was dwarfed by large bags and festive boxes—toys and gadgets that people had brought—that would eventually take three minivan-loads to haul away. Laura S. is the type who thinks big, who sees how the ordinary events of the holidays are linked to something bigger than having a good time, that these are moments of value and times to express values. Family and neighborhood life are canvases, more than what they seem. Laura feels passionately and actively about improving our world; knowing where the injustices are, she insists on being part of the solution, not the problem. She also feels strongly about spending time with her two girls.

I knew she had been working part-time and had recently changed jobs. I asked to interview her because I knew that part of what mother-hood means is not a single decision to work or be at home, but an ongoing journey through different arrangements. "Sequencing" is what it used to be called: taking time off for kids and then returning to work. Many mothers, though, find that their experience of work and family looks more like a jumble than like a nice, neat sequence. "We know that most mothers are on a carousel in and out of the workplace," says Janet Jakobsen, director of the Barnard Center for Research on Women. Change and interrupted work become part of life for many mothers.

When her first daughter, Zoe, was born, Laura had worked for a trade organization that represents community development financial institutions (CDFIs), the small banks, credit unions, and other finance institutions committed to community revitalization that operate in low-income communities. When you drive through poor neighborhoods and see new housing or a new grocery store, chances are that a CDFI, not the major downtown banks, is taking the risk to fund it.

"I worked thirty-two hours a week, but of course it always bled into more," Laura explained. As director of policy, Laura developed policy strategy. She organized the group's 150 members so that they could conduct public advocacy on their own behalf. And she did lobbying work on Capitol Hill to protect and increase the money the federal government gives to community development organizations. She loved what she did. She profoundly believes in working on behalf of people with less, and this fundamental work in supporting lenders who support low-income neighborhoods was right up her alley.

"After Zoe was born they gave me three months of paid maternity leave, which is generous by today's standards," she told me. "I went back to work full-time, but when Emma was born two years later I went down to three days a week. Then I was promoted, and I moved up to four days, against my better judgment." Laura was clear that she wanted part-time work. When she talked, there wasn't a doubt in her mind that her life would always combine family life and work in manageable portions. We never even spoke about it—it was assumed, natural, even as the stories themselves retold how fragile this equilibrium can be. "I wanted a better work/life balance," she said. "I wanted to be more engaged in my daughters' lives so that I could go with Zoe to hang out in her pre-K classroom and really participate in her classroom experience. Last year on Wednesdays I stayed longer in Zoe's kindergarten. It's to make life more relaxed. For two days a week Emma, my youngest daughter, gets to be at home, to be more creative, to wander around the house and follow her imagination. I wanted her to have that. I love spending time with my girls. It's really fun for me; I think it's important if parents can afford it, to be there in your kids' lives. That's more important than making a lot of money."

Managing a part-time job was harder than she thought: "I wanted less, they wanted more. And honestly, the job needed more hours. There were options. I promoted a job share, but my boss didn't want to go there. And so I left. A new job fell in my lap. It happened quickly, and I was hired on the spot to work three days a week. That job really was three days a week. I was there for eight years."

One of the problems in her field is that in her case, employers who liked her and admired her work let her work part-time. It was always done as a special dispensation. There was never a rethinking of the job itself, a careful, management-focused sense of how to reorganize expectations so that the work would fit the hours Laura could devote to it. In each case, Laura was really working a full-time job part-time. It was always set up to be frustrating. When will managers and directors begin to think creatively about how to divide work tasks and responsibilities into segments that fit the energy and time employees have? I asked Laura what she really wanted. Her reply: "Honestly, I feel caught in the middle. I need a part-time job that really is part-time."

Thirty-seven percent of us mothers, and a staggering 44 percent of those with infants, work part-time. Women make up 70 percent of the part-time workforce, and mothers make up a large percentage of this. Laura had had her share of struggling with part-time jobs that really weren't, and she'd been on her own active carousel in and out of those jobs. I asked Laura if Rick ever thought about changing his work life to spend more time with the kids. "I think if we could find a way to financially manage it he would do it in a heartbeat," she replied. "He jokes about me getting the corporate job and he being the househusband. We have one of the most equal partnerships of the people I know. He cooks more than me. He cleans. He wants to engage the girls as much as I do. He's more introverted than me so he also likes time alone, whereas my energy comes from socializing." In the end, though, it was his full-time benefits they relied on. Until benefits are allotted more regularly to part-time workers, very few families will be able to share parenting work more equally, and the work/life balance of fathers will continue to depend on the labor that mothers do.

As it turned out, Laura was about to leave her new job, the one that had fallen into her lap so easily. The three-day-a-week arrangement was no longer working out, and her boss was particularly difficult to work with. She was working twenty hours a week and managing two other people. The executive director had taken her twenty-hour-a-week job and reclassified it as a full-time position. The salary was kept the same. And to justify the wage drop, she'd turned it into a lower-level position. Laura had argued for a severance package and decided it was time to move on: "I'm taking some time to reflect, a mini-sabbatical to figure out what good part-time work would be. As I grow, I have a changing expectation of what work does and what it gives us. I need to work; we couldn't afford for me not to, not on Rick's nonprofit salary. But the questions remain: Do I just want to work to make money? Should my passion for policy and politics be done as a volunteer? In the '90s, workplaces were much more employee friendly. That's changed. What do I do now?"

Like Laura, Deb feels passionately about community. At college, Deb majored in elementary education. She worked at inner-city schools and saw early education as linked with issues of social justice: "I worked for almost nothing but it changed the way I saw the world." She applied to graduate school with a passion and a sense of calling. And like Laura, Deb too has moved in and out of jobs since her kids were born. "I expected that when I got married and had kids I would stay home, and that I would really love that," Deb said, and that's pretty much what happened, at least at the start. When she and Dave married, Deb was teaching again in inner-city communities. They were members of a very conservative church that reinforced and exaggerated much of what her family had taught her about how husbands go out to work and mothers should be home with their kids. Sure enough, after their wedding Deb quit her job. She and Dave wanted to have a child soon, and she still needed to finish her MA thesis. Later that year their son Josh was born. The MA thesis was turned in eighteen months later.

"By the time I actually married and had a child, I hated being home full-time," she told me. "But to admit that was too threatening. I kept thinking, 'I'm a kid person. I'm trained in early education. I should love this.' I also had a sense that I'm a Christian woman and this is the Christian woman thing to do. It was very threatening to deal with this. How could I deal with the discontent? I saw three friends divorce over issues like these, when the woman wanted a stronger role. It was really threatening to me."

The Mommy Wars vision suggests that mothers stay defined by a single commitment to being at work or being at home. And when you've got a fussy two-year-old at midafternoon or a tired, tantrumy three-year-old at 6:15, you may *feel* stuck in your life's rut forever. It turns out not to be so. Many mothers and some fathers are on that carousel that brings them back and forth, round and again, between work and home.

When Josh was still little, Deb took a job tutoring at an after-school program for ten hours a week. To make it work, she traded babysitting with a friend so that for ten hours, two afternoons a week, each of them could work their $10-an-hour jobs. Deb kept moving up, and almost before she knew it, she was codirecting the tutoring program. Then she took a part-time job at a parent-infant center and then two months later she was asked to start a new childcare program at a homeless shelter.

"I don't want to work full-time," she told the director who asked her to take on the start-up. "Just start it. You love starting things," was the director's response. A year and a half later, the program was licensed and the childcare center was up and running, serving the infants and toddlers and preschoolers of homeless women who were working or in job training. It enriched the kids while giving the mothers the ability to begin to provide for their families. Deb worked at the center about thirty hours a week. That counts as part-time in our society, but it's a lot if you're a parent with a small child and household responsibilities. On days when she knew there was low enrollment, she brought Josh along. It's not easy to run a daycare center, and serving homeless kids and their moms meant lots of turnover and even more pressure on her teachers. Tired, stressed, and pregnant again, Deb resigned. She and her husband had bought a new house. They were moving to a neighborhood on the other side of town and the house would need lots of rehabbing and someone to keep an eye on it. "By that time," Deb confided, "I had worked through my perception of myself. I'd been in therapy. I knew I didn't like working full-time and I knew I didn't want to be home full-time. I was okay with it and knowing that freed me up; I had a total blast being home with Devin. That was a wonderful phase in my life, during that pregnancy and Devin's first year. I knew I wanted to be a professional, and I was okay that there were parts of parenting I didn't like."

Deb told me that she spent that year feeling out what was next: "I read and read and read. I thought I wanted to start a PhD program in urban studies. I went to the annual National Association for the Education of Young Children conferences to see what was happening in my field, to get the big picture. I took a small part-time job nearby at the Mennonite historical trust. It interested me for three weeks. Here's the economics: They paid me thirteen dollars an hour and I paid a babysitter ten dollars an hour, so at the end of the week I had about fifty dollars. That's barely break-even. Plus my mother-in-law used to come and watch Devin for a few hours a week; she still did that, but now I was at work. I lost even those few hours of time to be out and about by myself. For fifty dollars a week."

Some time after we spoke, I ran into Deb on the playground after school. It was a warm day despite the season. She was all dressed up. I had to ask. Usually when a playground mom sports new outfits and heels she's found her way back to work. Sure enough, that's what had happened. There'd been a job advertised for director of a neighborhood childcare program. Deb hadn't responded for five weeks but the job had stayed open. She had never been a full director of a program before. It would be a big step up in responsibility from her previous jobs and with more prestige and a larger salary than she was used to. She was excited as she told me, "I needed to take a jump. I thought hard about this one. The program was a mess. It would take tons of work." She really wanted a part-time job but when she looked around, all the leadership positions were full-time, except, perhaps, for the ones far out in the very affluent suburbs and those weren't the kids she wanted to serve: "I needed a challenge. I didn't want to work full-time. I knew what the personal losses would be. But I took it."

Deb had moved in and out of the workplace, in and out of full-time childraising. At first, Dave too had believed Deb should be at home. It was what their church preached and what members of their congregation seemed to do. But his own mother had worked: After staying home with him a few years, she'd returned to work as a teacher, a librarian, and then as a church organist, which is a powerful position in the African American church. Deb's struggles were not with her husband, but with her images of what she wanted her family to be; with her belief that the kids should have unstructured time in their lives—outside of school, beyond daycare—to explore and just exist; and, above all, with her sense of her own talents and what she wanted to give to the world. "Parenting is hard no matter what choices you've made about work," she told me. "I struggle with my own privilege to make a choice. We need a vision that supports our kids, supports their teachers, and supports all parents."

A year and a half after our playground conversation, Deb and I were sitting together, quietly savoring sweet potato fries in her favorite lunch spot, when she announced, "I resigned last Thursday. The board hasn't told anyone yet; I'll stay till they find a new director. I've given them lots of time. But I've resigned. I've really done it."

I was shocked. I'd thought her story would be different. I'd thought Deb was the on-ramp success story, the poster woman who took time off and ended up with a big career jump and higher responsibility at the end anyway. "Directing this program is a big step for me professionally," she said. "I love being part of the early childhood leadership community. There's so much going on right now looking at kids and parents and staff together. I see this as all connected.

"The reality is, though," she continued, "that it takes 90 percent of me to do my job well and 10 percent is not enough to have left for everything else and everyone else in my life. It's not enough. I want more than that left over when I come home.

"I've been meeting with other directors," Deb told me. "I've been asking them, 'How do you do it? What can I change? How can I do my job differently so I can stay, so I can survive?' One friend has been doing this job for twenty years. Her answer was that she's single and childless, and so are most of the long-term daycare directors she knows. That's how she's been able to do it. When stuff comes up, she can stay till eight. When stuff comes up for me, I still have to be home to get the 3:45 camp bus. I can't do my job well and still limit it to forty hours a week." As Deb was wondering why she couldn't be successful, she was learning that the other directors didn't have kids—and young kids, at that. They weren't experiencing that pull between working extra hours and attending to their families. She felt both frustrated that the job entailed so much work and relieved that someone had finally demystified the situation for her. She's a hardworking, talented woman. She knew it couldn't have been her personal failing, and finally she'd learned part of the truth. Successful directors are unencumbered by family responsibilities. They are, in other words, and as we're about to find out, ideal workers.

I sit in a café near Samira's preschool. With fifteen minutes till her pickup, I'm grading student papers. Next to me are two women, clearly friends. A nearly three-year-old girl sits with them, arranging her colored pencils into a rainbow. She is the daughter of the younger woman, the one wearing mom clothes. The conversation turns to the mother's quandary over returning to work. Their family can no longer afford for her not to work, she tells her companion, and she's trying to figure out what to do.

She wants part-time work, but she's skeptical. In her corporate setting, part-time easily becomes forty hours a week. "Too many companies take advantage of women," she tells her friend. "They get hired to work part-time but they end up working full-time and getting paid for half." She knows. Her time will be crunched. If in reality she will be working a forty-hour week, she'll need the salary of a full-time job in order to pay the babysitter to watch her kids, and, if she can swing it, a housekeeper to clean. She finishes, "I might as well go back full-time and have the money to pay other people to do the things I won't have time to do."

A letter to the editor of the New York Times joins her complaint: "I see the $70,000 full-time jobs and I see the $20,000 part-time jobs. Where are the $35,000 a year part-time jobs?"

Lucia Herndon, a columnist for the *Philadelphia Inquirer*, wrote a column that began with her perplexity over a conversation with her daughter and her daughter's twentysomething friends, who would stay home with kids if they found a partner who would support them. They were college-educated. They knew they could support themselves. But they wanted the option to stay home with the kids. Herndon describes herself as a fiftyish woman; to her, the younger women's position "sounded strangely old-fashioned. I find myself on the older side of the generation gap." When she asked her readers about their experiences, they answered loud and clear: We want part-time work options. Responds one reader: "Perhaps full-time work is not the ideal for everyone, especially when full-time often ends up being forty-plus hours a week. Maybe women and men should look at ways to work part-time in order to have professional challenges and responsibilities as well as sanity in their lives." Writes another: "Can society embrace more part-time work for moms? Can we be more supportive with each other? Can husbands pitch in more? Our generation has tried to have it all, and maybe your daughter and her friends are perceptive enough to see that it is impossible."[1]

Although large numbers of mothers choose part-time work, it's not a perfect solution in part because most part-time jobs are low paying, come without benefits, and are relatively low level, and because many managers do not know how to conceive and manage part-time jobs well. Mothers—and fathers—want flexible jobs and many want part-time work, but the workplace doesn't seem to deliver either. In search of answers to this conundrum, I called Joan Williams, a lawyer who teaches at the Washington College of Law at American University. Her book *Unbending Gender: Why Family and Work Conflict and What to Do About It* is an excellent guide to why we are in such a bind. Williams leaps past the specific details of the different professions and gets right to the heart of the matter: the cultural beliefs that undergird our workplaces. She introduces us to the pervasive notion of the "ideal worker" that structures our workplaces.[2]

The fact that 37 percent of mothers are combining parenting and part-time work stems in part from society's definition of full-time workers. In Williams's analysis, the ideal worker has no commitments and responsibilities outside of the workplace. There are no kids to care for, dinners to make, basic errands to run. Someone else is doing all this labor for the ideal worker. As a result, the worker's attention is, and can be, devoted only to work. One consequence is that only full-time workers count as "real" workers.

The ideal worker can be old or young but is essentially childless, and has no elderly parents to care for. The ideal worker, or breadwinner, is supported by the domestic caregiver. If there are children, someone else takes them to school and packs their lunches and makes sure their homework's done. If there are household chores, someone else ticks them off the list. Someone at home relieves the worker of these duties. Someone else keeps the home clean, watches the kids, prepares dinner, and does the myriad tasks that keep a family together. This expectation for workers holds for most decent jobs, whether blue-collar jobs that pay decently or white-collar professional-track positions. The breadwinner must be free to earn the bread. The fact that the breadwinner's child is sick and has a doctor's appointment cannot be allowed to stop production.

How many professional women of a slightly older generation have long sighed to each other, "I need a wife," as they worked their jobs and made sure the house ran too? There's good reason for their sighs, and it's built right in to the structure of our workplaces and their out-of-touch expectations for what we workers are supposed to do.

Ideal worker and domestic caregiver. This system of opposites accounts for why it is hard to transform part-time work into a valued option. Despite the fact that many people feel they are working too hard, and despite the fact that many families do not conform to the old worker-and-caregiver model, as a society we continue in the same habits. If the breadwinner model stays intact for workers, as work hours increase it will predictably produce what it needs, the domestic caregiver, whenever there's enough money for the family to make this happen.

You wouldn't think it would be so hard to organize part-time work for women who are mothers, for men who are fathers, for anyone wanting to live life more sanely. People in the business world are smart enough to conceptualize incredibly complicated financial products. They are smart enough to imagine nebulous and multilayered partnerships that move money around the earth, to be hidden behind invisible firewalls on obscure but electronically connected Pacific islands. They are smart enough to move crops and commodities from the largest city ports to the smallest country towns. They are savvy enough to manipulate global markets and energy futures, manage mutual funds, conduct international operations in several languages, and oversee risky and intricate conglomerates with intellectual commitment and creativity. Couldn't some of this energy be harnessed to create a system that incorporates people who wish to work part-time and be paid fairly for their labor and talents?

Blue-collar workplaces are remarkably inflexible and startlingly unfeeling toward the families of those who work there. The white-collar professions can be slightly more flexible day to day—and lawyers and professors and doctors can leave without asking permission—but they are punishing in other ways and can be very unforgiving of those who step off track, of those who move through at different paces and with different values. The organization of most workplaces remains relatively rigid despite trends toward flextime, telecommuting, and alternate tracks. Cultural habits are remarkably difficult to alter.

Some people are trying to change all that. When I spoke with Joan Williams, I was seeking those elusive numbers on mothers and part-time work, and I, of course, had been thinking about part-time work in terms of twenty-hour-per-week jobs. Williams didn't have this info; it wasn't what interested her.

"People usually talk about 'mothers in the workplace,'" Williams began, "as if it includes everyone. That's not a helpful description. A lot of mothers in the workforce can't fit the model of what is valued because they can't work full-time. And because they can't conform to the pattern of work, mothers in the workplace are getting completely screwed."

When I posed the question I had still been thinking in terms of lifestyle, about whether it fit more easily for new mothers to work ten or twenty hours a week rather than working four days, rather than easing so close to the full-time line. According to Williams, that was the wrong question. By her analysis, 63 percent of mothers (of nonadult children) aged twenty-five to forty-four work less than full-time. Since 82 percent of women in America eventually become mothers, that's a shocking number of women who, by definition, can't compete for fair wages, benefits, and advancement.

Every so often I meet someone I admire, and I think, I want to be on her team. Joan Williams is one of those people. She's figured out a vision and she knows how to make it happen. Her analysis of the workplace also makes clear that the same issues face stay-at-home mothers, part-time working mothers, and mothers who work full-time. The very structure and assumptions of the workplace discriminate against us all. Williams sees all the issues facing mothers as peas in a pod, and she's going after the cultural sensibilities that make work life hard for mothers: "Long term, in the United States, we need to open a conversation about working hours," she told me, "about true flexibility, part-time equity, proportional benefits, and about advancement through part-time work." Williams's Program on WorkLife Law at American University is starting that conversation. Her first partners are labor unions: "Without union support we can't do anything," she said. "You can't have new legislation unless there's union support, and traditionally, the unions have been apprehensive about job flexibility. They've seen lots of good jobs turn into bad jobs. Full-time jobs with benefits turn into part-time jobs without security and healthcare. They feel it's likely to turn into flexibility for the employer and not for the employee."

On Capitol Hill, legislators, like the rest of us, read the media coverage of work and family issues that so predominantly focuses on affluent women. Their response, often, is to say, "This problem is only about rich women; we can only make legislation for ordinary working people." And thus, union support for something that has been framed entirely as a "women's issue" or a "mothers' issue" is crucial. To start this conversation about flexibility and part-time work with the unions who represent working-class men and women, Williams commissioned a report on labor arbitrations related to family care, called *Work/Family Conflict, Union Style*.

Williams sent me the report. I thought it would be boring. I started reading it one night, late, and was riveted. I kept to it through bleary eyes, like I would a good novel or mystery. The report studies workplace disputes that are resolved by an arbitrator. The disputes usually involve an employer who has disapproved of something a worker did and moved to suspend or fire him or her. The workers appeal, they take their grievances to the union, and the union asks for mediation. (Workers without unions don't have this protection and if fired or suspended they have to find an attorney willing to take the case and sue, or, most likely, they have to just try to find a new job.) The arbitrations on work and family issues touch both mothers and fathers in the workplace. One surprise is just how often the workplace problems of fathers stem directly from work/family conflict.[3]

At Rochester Psychiatric Center, a single mother with a five-year-old and a fourteen-month-old was fired because she refused to accept overtime. Overtime hours were mandatory, and workers were usually told of their overtime assignments just a few hours before their regular shift was to end. The mother explained that she couldn't find childcare on such short notice. She offered some alternatives: perhaps working a few overtime hours but not the whole eight-hour overtime shift or perhaps bringing her kids to work so they could sleep while she worked. Her suggestions were rejected. She was first cited for misconduct, then suspended once, then again; the third time, her boss fired her. The arbitrator found in her favor, saying, "No person should be forced to choose between his children or his livelihood," and noting that "her efforts to be a good parent . . . have created her problems at work." She was fined one dollar and given her job back. She was told to give her employer thirty days' notice of three days each month that she could work full overtime shifts.

Jefferson Smurfit Corporation suspended the father of a three-year-old boy for three days because he couldn't work overtime. He had gotten an emergency call from his wife saying that their son was ill at the same time that his supervisor had told him to stay for four hours of overtime because someone else had called in sick. His coworkers wouldn't or couldn't fill in for him. He tried to tell his supervisor that he was sick, but was told he would then have to take a fitness exam to prove it. Twenty minutes into the overtime shift, his wife called again. Their son was feverish and needed medicine, but she couldn't get it because he had taken their only car to work that morning. The supervisor finally agreed that the man could leave work, but warned him to return with evidence and documentation. The Wal-Mart receipt he brought the next day was deemed unacceptable, since it showed he made the purchase just after the overtime shift would have ended. The supervisor suspended the worker for three days saying he could have worked the full shift and then gone for the medicine. The arbitrator ruled that the supervisor was technically correct, but that the worker's reason for leaving was not fraudulent and he had a clean employment record. The suspension was removed and replaced by a written warning. The company was ordered to compensate the worker for the three days of lost pay.

The report is filled with cases like this: home lives where a wife is sick, where a son has a serious heart condition. A father who drives the airport shuttle bus for Budget Rent A Car requests family and medical leave but doesn't dot the i's and cross the t's on the documentation required to substantiate it (he writes that his son is "ill" but doesn't describe the cardiac severity). A mechanic father rejects overtime because he has to pick up his daughter from school. A worker at the Social Security Administration is denied emergency leave after both her regular and her backup babysitters cancel, leaving her with no option save leaving her kids home alone. A long-term worker at Tenneco Packaging and a single parent of a mentally and physically disabled child, a woman who normally works sixty hours a week, is fired for taking time from work to care for her son and not furnishing the right proof.

This is where the long haul that might eventually lead to legislation for flexible, part-time workplaces starts: with the time-consuming collection of what ordinary workers need, with the understanding that family does matter—in the extreme cases of fevers and congenital heart problems and in the ordinary cases of kids needing to be picked up from school each day. It starts with casting a net wide, with cultivating political partners and explaining point by point how family responsibilities are important, how they aren't extraneous to the paid work we do, and how workplaces need to recognize this, even if it makes managing how many employees show up for the shifts a bit harder for the supervisors in charge. It is the humane thing to do. This is where mothers' and fathers' lives are connected, where everyone should be paying attention to incipient efforts to protect motherhood no matter the economic class or professional location of the mothers involved.

At a Fortune 500 company in L.A., a newly pregnant woman is counseled by other women to hide the evidence as long as possible. I was shocked at this story, though I shouldn't have been. She hides her pregnancy as long as she can and then quits in exasperation. This is the maternal wall, the series of offenses that derail pregnant women and mothers at work. It's the exact experience a Florida woman, now in her sixties, told me about life in "the old days." She knew that as soon as her belly showed, she would be fired from her job as a counselor to college students. How far have we come?

Back v. Hastings on Hudson Union Free School District is a case we should all be watching, and Joan Williams, of American University, herself is following it with a trained legal eye. Elana Back is a school psychologist. She had worked for three years at Hillside Elementary School and during that time had her first child, taken three months of maternity leave, received superior reviews, and been assured that after her three years of probation were up she would certainly receive tenure and job security. In her third year, though, as alleged in her court case, her supervisor, the director of personnel services, asked her how she was going to space her children, asked her not to get pregnant until the supervisor retired, and advised her to "wait until [her son] was in kindergarten" before bearing another child. The supervisor allegedly suggested she should "maybe . . . reconsider whether she could be a mother and do this job." The personnel director and the principal allegedly told her that "they were concerned she would only work until 3:15 after she received tenure, and couldn't see how it would be possible for her to do her job and raise children." In spring 2001, they recommended that the school district not grant her tenure. It was her first poor review ever, and she was accused of being "inconsistent, defensive, and difficult to supervise."[4] Back then received a letter from the school superintendent telling her that her three-year probation was being terminated, and that in effect, she was fired.

When this case was first brought to trial in October 2001, the judge granted summary judgment, which means he favored the defendants (the school district and Back's supervisors) and decided that the case was too weak to send to a jury. If you're like me, you're shocked at this point. You're saying, *This is insane; of course Back should not have been fired.* I know five women who've dealt with a similar situation. The law, however, doesn't yet reflect what mothers already know or what should

be changed. Another wrinkle in this case is that the alleged discrimination took place between women. This is important because much of
the law that protects women at work assumes that men are in power. It
frames discrimination in the terms of sexual harassment, assumes that
only men harass other women.

This becomes a problem because most workplaces remain gender-
segregated. Williams told me during our conversation that more than
70 percent of women in the workforce work with and for other women.
Thus, 70 percent of working women are unable to sue for discrimination on maternal grounds, since they can't point to men who have been
treated differently, and since they can't point to men who have
harassed them. A vast number of women and mothers in the workplace
are unprotected.

"People always said that you can't litigate in the jobs that most
women have, because most women work with other women," Williams
explained to me. To counter this, Williams and Nancy Segal published
a landmark article in the *Harvard Women's Law Journal*, "Beyond the
Maternal Wall: Relief for Family Caregivers Who Are Discriminated
Against on the Job." "We all know about the glass ceiling," the article
begins. "But many women never get near it; they are stopped long
before by the maternal wall." The maternal wall is not just about
women, but also about any fathers who play a traditional sex role, that
of family caretaker. The cases that Williams and Segal cite reflect both
fathers and mothers who were penalized for caregiving.[5]

In doing this, Williams and others are also providing some of the
new legal theory that makes it possible to fight maternal wall discrimination in the courts; it's been impossible up until now. The discrimination is one of those things that women know is happening but that
the law hasn't yet caught up with. Williams has been building a network of attorneys that gathers cases where women workers have successfully sued their employers on family issues, and makes this case law
available and easily accessible. "The business case for family-friendly

workplaces has been made," she told me. "But without the potential for legal liability, we haven't seen things change very fast. Employers often say to me, 'We would love to give people family-friendly policies, but we can't because we might get sued' (say, for offering different policies for different workers). Our response is to turn around and say to employers, 'You may as well have family-friendly policy, because if you don't, attorneys will sue you, and here's the case law to help.'"

And sue they have. Williams and Segal found more than twenty successful cases based on both federal and state statutes. Several of these resulted in large award settlements. Three million dollars in one case, $495,000 in another. These large sums were overturned when the companies appealed, but the trials and appeals themselves are expensive. Williams and Segal envision that things will change only when it costs employers too much to discriminate: "This new potential for liability will become an integral part of the business case for creating workplaces that are truly responsive to family caregivers' needs," they wrote. To help lawyers help their clients, they've identified ten legal foundations and theories on which successful work/family cases have been argued.

Back's lawyer, Christopher Watkins, appealed using the new legal foundations that Williams and Segal wrote about. And it worked. A three-judge panel of the U.S. Court of Appeals, Second Circuit, ruled unanimously that part of her case could go forward. To be sure, the case has not yet been won; it has only been given a second chance to go to court. And it's shocking to see how slowly the law changes: The case was first heard in October 2001 and it was April 2004 before a ruling on the appeal was handed down.

Joan Williams is highly critical of what she calls the "women's choice" model in which women are caught in the middle of work expectations they did not create. The popular claim is that mothers choose on their own to leave work, perhaps out of biological drive or psychological dreams or social pressures to be full-time parents. These explanations, however, ignore the workplace assumptions about ideal workers and ignore the fact that many mothers, and some fathers, can't possibly fit this expectation for basic success. They have other loves and responsibilities in their lives, and they can't and don't want to pretend them away to fit an expectation that was never constructed with them in mind.

This perspective turns the "opting out" stories into what they more often are: stories about women and men who don't have work conditions that also support them as parents, and who, as a result, move in and out of jobs, lose wages and seniority, and work at bad part-time jobs because time-wise that's the best short-term option. Williams insisted in our conversation that the solution is not psychological—it's not limited to a mother coming to terms with her life, as the magazines and memoirs claim. Instead, she pushes us till we consider the problem from this other angle: "Will this clash be internalized as a psychological problem of women's hard choices or will the clash be understood as a structural problem, fueling demand for institutional change?"

CHAPTER 5.

We Need Some Relief

Molly and I are huddled around her kitchen table; it's gray and drizzly outside. Our kids, three years old already, are playing in the next room. We're past the old days of juggling infants and breast-feeding and getting a few words in between cries. Now we can trade stories for so long that the tea in the pot turns cool, and as it does, the day-to-day trials of parenting lead to larger questions about how to live good and rewarding lives, about what we think being a good mother means, and what it means to have other life callings besides parenting.

Molly's been through quite a lot since we first met back when the girls were barely six weeks old. We found each other in a church-basement baby massage class we'd each signed up for not because we thought we needed lessons in how to massage our tots, but because it's so hard to meet other new moms. Then, I was on long-term leave from my university job and Molly had just finished business school. In her final year she had realized that she was pregnant. At elite business schools, pregnant women are nearly unheard of. It was even more startling for Molly herself. She'd always been the "smart girl." She knew she wanted children, but it had never crossed her mind that having them would derail her professionally. As she says, just before taking a sip of tea, "I'd read all the books about breaking the glass ceiling, but I remained blissfully unaware of 'sequencing,' of doing kids and career but not all at the same time. I had no clue what it's really like out there."

Molly had already worked at consulting firms for several years and had a great reputation in communications when she returned to school for her MBA. Graduation was topped off with a fabulous offer, an almost too-good-to-be-true job with a great signing bonus. All involved agreed she could delay the usual September start (when she was giving birth). They even offered her four months of paid maternity leave. By February, Molly was on the job and Aurora's framed photo topped her office desk. Her half sister moved to town to live nearby and care for the baby while Molly worked.

With indubitable spirit, Molly gave it a go. She believed in attachment parenting, so each night Aurora slept in Molly's bed and was breastfed on and off through the night. When the company sent her for weeklong trainings in New York or on four-day client visits to Chicago, Molly packed up the baby and her half sister, buying their tickets with money from her own paycheck. It worked for a time. By summer, though, Molly was battling serious depression and looking at the edge of a breakdown. She needed some work relief, desperately. Seeing no other options, she filed for an unpaid leave of absence and started to get back pieces of her life. Still, whenever she remembered her promise to return six months later, her stomach ached and the gloom returned. She couldn't imagine going back. Her husband had thrown himself into a 24/7 dotcom project and didn't help much with childcare, and her boss made no concessions on her work responsibilities. Part-time work was not a possibility. The top accounting and consulting firm that had considered her valuable enough to recruit didn't consider her maternal responsibilities and desires important enough to accommodate so that she could continue working for them. Rather than work with her, rather than shift policy and rethink working hours for parents of young children, the company wrote off the loss of its signing bonus and her four-month maternity leave. That March, her leave of absence about to end, Molly quit.

Sometimes when we're talking about work and our professions, it's still hard to believe we are stay-at-home moms, or that we've downshifted and are working only part-time. Molly never planned to be a stay-at-home mom. Sure, she was an attachment parenting devotee, but to her, that never meant she wouldn't work away from the home. For her, work and intensive parenting weren't opposites. She had her attachment parenting mothers' listserv, her virtual playground, for support. Molly fell into full-time motherhood backward. "I left my job because I was too unhappy to continue, not because I wanted to be home with my child," she says. "But suddenly I found myself home full-time. I had always looked down my nose at women who stayed home with their kids. And all of a sudden, there I was." She did sporadic projects at first. Fields like communications lend themselves to freelance work from home. She wrote business plans for emerging dotcoms. She freelance edited and did skills coaching for management executives.

About a year later, the economy turned sour and work was harder to find. A big client went broke and didn't pay. Without reliable income she couldn't afford a babysitter; working now meant staying up all night while her daughter slept. It was too much. Molly didn't feel like splitting herself anymore, and the all-nighters left her too tired. "I worked a grand total of two days last year. I don't think I qualify as a working mom anymore," she jokes. The funny flourish masks the pain. She wanted to work, and despite her good intentions, work wasn't willing to work for her. "After all these years of going back and forth and being anxious about it," she finishes, "Ari and I finally made an explicit choice that I wasn't going to look for work right now, that we are going to do this intentionally. Sometimes, though, outside the world of kiddom, I still feel the need to name-drop my MBA and my old management consulting credentials—I worked for McKinsey & Company—in the first thirty seconds of conversation. I still can't say I'm just hanging with the kidlets for the time being, that I'm one of *those* women."

Molly's glad to have the conversation, the chance to talk about how it wasn't supposed to be this way. Are we nothing more than a hipper, more multicultural update of Betty Friedan's 1950s housewives? What happened to our careers? Our paychecks? Our culturally shared dream in which male and female parents would share equally in childrearing labors and around-the-house chores? We tend to take the blame on ourselves, as if we've failed. We don't always have the frameworks that we need to explain what's going on, and the public reporting on motherhood doesn't help. It's harder to think about who and what is to blame—especially when the answer is so simultaneously simple, on the one hand, and on the other, entangled and complex.

Molly's not the only tired mother around who needs some relief. One day, in between teaching my class at the university and heading back to pick Samira up from preschool, I stop in to see my friend Amy. Amy is a poet, a writer, an editor, and the mother of two girls. She's also one of the wise women in my life. I tell her how tired I'm getting. She sits back in her chair and then leans forward to share her secret. "Yes. The fatigue," she says simply. "You've discovered it. There's an incredible fatigue that sets in, year after year. It only gets worse." Her eldest daughter just finished kindergarten; the younger one's still in preschool. I take her warning seriously.

A few years later, I've whisked Amy away from her family for a 9:00 AM Saturday breakfast. She's telling me that she's going down, once again, to part-time work. In her seven years as a mother she's moved rather quickly in and out of full-time and part-time employment; life has been a constant renegotiation of time. "It's all just too much," she says. "I need some relief."

I start to notice mothers' fatigue everywhere I go. One afternoon I drop my daughter off at Nana's house for a few hours, so granddaughter and grandmother can visit. They play ball in the hallway outside Nana's apartment. They make paper cutouts, dance to the *Lion King* CD, have a snack, and cuddle together on the couch with a book. In the meantime, I run some errands, pick up some groceries, and stand in line at the post office. Mothers are everywhere, with two-year-olds in strollers, infants in chest carriers, preschoolers running and jumping alongside. One adorable mother and daughter pair holds hands as they walk. Without my own daughter nearby, I look at other mothers' faces, not just at their kids. The mothers: Some are messy and disheveled. Some wear shorts and crisp polo shirts. Some wear Kmart. Some sport great glasses and a hip look. Others have donned glamour outfits. All— even the latter and even through perfectly applied makeup—look tired, bone-deep tired.

When I see mothers, I see tired women. And I know that we women are not trained to take our tiredness seriously, to count our labor, to let ourselves feel it and to feel that it matters. We even twist it around and brag about how tired we are, as a badge of our value and worth, as if to say, "Hardworking moms are tired, and that's a good thing." That's the way things are. What would it mean to see fatigue not just as a personal condition, but as a more widespread, political issue facing mothers, an issue about time and expectations and giving value and credence to the labor it takes not just to produce children, but to raise them, and raise them well?

Felicia Kornbluh is a historian of women and welfare and she teaches at Duke University. Now, it may seem odd to bring a historian of welfare into a discussion of motherhood and work, but that's mostly because the public debate, the public face of motherhood, has been crafted so predominantly as one of white and affluent and educated women, and because we assume that welfare is about poor, uneducated women of color. Both images are incorrect. It turns out that in the end, debates that include the history of welfare—with its assumptions about what it means to mother—have an awful lot to do with how more affluent women manage their family lives.

Kornbluh tells a story about Theresa Funiciello, a former welfare recipient who led a welfare rights group in New York City during the

1980s. Funiciello also wrote a memoir, *Tyranny of Kindness,* in which she was quite critical of how welfare social workers treat women. In the memoir, Funiciello recalls that during the 1980s, "poor women kept saying we need more money and a better way to make rational choices about the care of our children. We did not say we needed more work. Everyone else said that." Poor women were saying something similar to some women who had more money and more types of choices in their lives: We want a release from working for money so we can care for our children, at least in their earliest years.

Phrases like "release from work" or "relief from work" sound odd to our ears. Since, say, 1970 the normative sense of womanhood and the national paradigm of motherhood—in many neighborhoods, and in the urban communities that most affect public opinion, in any case—have shifted from the expectation that women will leave the paid workforce to care for children to the expectation that all adults should work for pay. As Kornbluh notes, "[T]he cultural presumption [has] largely switched from mothers' removal from the labor force, to their continued participation in it."[1]

This shift has had profound effects on the welfare system—the 1996 Welfare Reform Act signed by President Clinton sent welfare recipients, mothers with children, out to work thirty hours a week since that was by then seen as the new cultural norm for mothers. The shift has had profound effects on expectations for middle-class women as well: We now routinely expect that mothers stay in the workforce. The cultural surprise of the past few years has been to hear the numbers of mothers who refuse to work for pay while their children are young, who refuse to work full-time, refuse to do *double duty.* In the Mommy Wars version of events, these women are running toward home to be hands-on, hyper mothers. That, I argue, obscures what's really going on here. Yes, some mothers, and some fathers, absolutely want to be with their children. But it's a rigid workplace, and too high a demand on our hours and energy sends us out of the workplace and into the home. Many mothers leave paid work, at least for a while, because they are exhausted and need relief. We just call them stay-at-home moms, though, and we forget why some of them are there.

Welfare programs in this country were started to help mothers who didn't have boyfriends or husbands who could help them economically. The state stepped in and in 1935 created Aid to Families with Dependent Children. As Kornbluh describes, this resulted from "decades of activism by women who claimed that the capacity to raise children made mothers valuable as citizens and worthy of financial aid." If the history of welfare has been marred by what recipients have described as the way that the system actually blocks their efforts to be good parents, it is still worth thinking about the original impetus of maternalism because it is the social question that has not been solved by all the decades of programs and social change that followed. Maternalism as policy recognizes the actual work that women do as mothers and compensates them for it, in a roundabout way, when these mothers and their children are not supported by the kids' father(s) or by their families. Encapsulated in this are both the positive and the negative. The positive argument, still pushed by mothers' advocates, says that we must honestly recognize and value the work that mothers do as mothers, and protect their right to do it, and support them in their maternal labor. This perspective often clashes with a critique that finds maternalism to be culturally frightening; some people fear that maternalism can easily slip into the assumption that all women are maternal, that all women need protection and support, and that women are domestic creatures rightfully excluded from fair and lucrative "men's" jobs, the ones with better wages, more interesting work, and the possibility of public power.

In 1996, welfare reform recognized the shift in working norms for women belatedly—and, some would argue, punitively—by moving 180 degrees from the initial conception that the work of mothering was valuable to a conception that pushed women who needed state assis-

tance into minimum-wage and mostly dead-end jobs, and then gave
them an extra subsidy to place the kids in childcare. They were considered most valuable not as active mothers, but as workers—and even
then, not worth much.

Debates about motherhood usually assume that mothers are middle-class and white, and that they share a certain sense of white,
middle-class motherhood. This story traces back to the 1950s, when
many mothers were stationed at home and advances through the '60s
and '70s with women's move into the workplace. They assume a certain
politics in which conservative women want to stay at home with their
kids and liberal women go to work. One side effect of thinking about
the history of poor women, and about the history of African American
women, is that we see that women in America have different assumptions and stories about women and work.

Some families from my daughter's school are at a birthday party. I'm
on the couch with one of the moms and we're talking about, what else,
how we balance the demands of work and life and kids and all the other
things we value. Like me, she has one child, and her son and Samira
have been in the same class since pre-K. This woman is a high school
teacher, English is her field, and she's telling me about how many
teachers at her school leave their jobs each year. She teaches out in the
suburbs, but in what are now called the near suburbs: not the affluent
exurban suburbs that we're told are the new American dream, but those
more ordinary, working-class suburbs where people are not wealthy.
The desks in her classroom are filled with kids from immigrant families.

She talks to me about her colleagues with exasperation in her
voice. "They go to school and then they teach for only a few years.
Their husbands are plumbers or electricians or contractors and they
make $80,000 a year; then the minute the baby comes along, the wife
quits her teaching job to be a stay-at-home mom. That's what they do;
that's what all their friends do. White women will do this—they'll quit
the jobs they trained for," she tells me. "We African American women

work. We don't wait around for someone else to take care of us. That's not our history."

Other black women have told me the same story—that in the face of their history, they must work. I also know that historically it's not exactly true, and that some black women take other directions. As with white women, race doesn't exactly or predictably tell us what to do.

Mocha Moms was founded in 1997 with a newsletter to women of color who were taking time away from careers to raise their kids. The group started small—the first batch went to a hundred mothers across the nation. The two women behind the Mocha Moms newsletter, Jolene Ivey and Karla Chutz, soon teamed up with a third, Cheli English-Figaro, to create a national organization. Its goal is to support at-home mothers of color, mothers who because of social racism are easily uncomfortable with white mothers and marginal to a community that may feel that real black women don't stay home with their kids. Its vision of motherhood and membership is open-armed: "We will never pass judgment," its website promises, "on mothers who choose to make or are forced to make different decisions for their families." Many of its members are full-time moms; others work part-time or freelance or do night shifts or run a small business from home—the usual options that mothers and fathers take when they want to work but desire more control of their time.[2]

Mocha Moms plans to build a network of home businesses so that work-at-home mothers can network and connect and support each other. The organization is nonpartisan, it's not religious, and it doesn't care whether Mocha Moms send their kids to private school, public school, charter schools, or home schools—it wants to support women who support and nurture their families, and it wants to remind women to take care of themselves, mind, body, and spirit. "Self-care is absent in the lives of many at-home mothers," reads pillar number six of the group's platform, "but it is crucial to maintaining a sense of well-being and balance." The local chapters sponsor weekly informal meetings, because although most people take for granted adult talk, it's often missing from at-home mothers' daily lives. Monthly potlucks are moms only, no kids, and often feature speakers on financial planning, on how to operate a home-based business, and on educational options for kids.

In an African American context, perhaps this debate between work and relief from work seems clearer. "Black women in our country have inherited a different framework for thinking about work and family life," Christina Greene, a professor of Afro-American studies at the University of Wisconsin at Madison, said to me in conversation. Most of the reigning notions of feminism come from white women and from the middle class. We know this, but what it means specifically is worth considering. Feminism assumed that women in the period after World War II followed the cultural dicta that told them to give up their high-paying blue-collar wartime jobs to the soldiers now returning home. This is the classic Rosie the Riveter tale. The '50s, then, were a time when families left the cities, moved to the newly built suburbs, and all the men went to work and all the women had three babies and stayed home to take care of them. This is the starting point for influential books like Betty Friedan's *The Feminine Mystique*: that mothers live in suburbs where men work for pay and women keep the house clean and carpool the kids.

Black families didn't all see things the same way. Yes, there were some affluent black families in which mothers didn't work; there were also some professionally trained black mothers in the '40s and '50s who kept working at career jobs, kids and all. By and large, black women didn't have the same experience of being pushed back home in the 1950s. Even black members of the middle class had less money than similar white families since black men earned comparably less than white men. Black women's experience was to have always worked, often as domestics, and often raising other people's children. "If White women tired of the pedestal," writes Cecelie S. Berry, author of *Rise Up Single: Black Women Writers on Motherhood*, "Black women longed for respite from the double yoke of being breadwinner and nurturer. If White women felt men were expendable [as income providers], most Black women—regardless of their socioeconomic or educational level—continued to feel that a man, particularly a 'do right' man, was a luxury worth almost any price."[3]

When the feminist movement arose in the early 1960s, some black women brought this history to the table. They had been working very hard, and what they wanted most immediately was some relief from work. Working-class women, too, shared this perspective. But their experiences were not as mythological, as larger-than-life metaphorical as the middle-class housewife's, and at the end of the day, with the beginning of an organized feminist movement, it was the interests of the latter group that won.

Perhaps the early feminists were too utopian in their belief that men would start sharing childcare equally with women. The social pattern that allotted childraising and domestic responsibilities to mothers was one they were unable to truly shift with much success. There was too much backlash too soon. More mothers went back to work, and most mothers kept on doing most of the childcare and the housekeeping, too. Currently, of heterosexually married working moms, 70 percent have more responsibility for routine childcare than the men they live with. When the kids are sick and both parents work, 70 percent of mothers take time off compared to 30 percent of dads.[4] Childcare defaults to mothers, and while we love our children and want to spend time with them, mothers shouldn't have to bear all this extra work. Why the difference in these numbers? Why don't fathers take off more days when their kids are sick? Why do more mothers than fathers ultimately consider their paid jobs expendable? To all the contemporary answers given I want to add another: We inherit ancient habits that divide up men's work and women's work. After all the social change of the last half century, we're still struggling with this. We can't let go of the long-standing idea that men work and women raise children.

Yet the historical moment that strikes my curiosity returns us to the crossroads of the early 1960s and to those working-class women who did not have the economic privilege to be housewives and to be home with their children. I'm interested in how they were articulating what they needed as women and mothers. We need to pull these demands back into the way we understand feminism, mostly because they offer us seeds of a new and helpful vision. Precisely at the moment that some women were forming the first feminist organizations of the 1960s, these other women were voicing their own visions of policies that would improve their lives. Prime among these was the desire to be relieved of work during children's early years. What women already in the workplace knew was that it is no fun to try and work eight or ten or twelve hours a day while your children are young. It's no fun when they are little and you must leave them with relatives or caretakers for long stretches. It's no fun when you see them only in the early morning and late at night. It's no fun when they are older and you must get them to school and worry about whether they're well occupied afterward until you return home. These working-class working women already knew what it would take more affluent women decades to figure out.

Their voices and their wisdom were unfortunately ignored. Feminism as a social change movement took off in very different directions. Many of these working-class women dropped out of the feminist movement. This exacerbated the absence of their perspectives and voices. We needed both of these things. We needed access to work and we needed relief from it. We argued for only one.

Can we imagine the history of work and family life in the last few decades had working-class women been able to promote their needs? Perhaps relief from work, with financial compensation or tax relief or protection of job seniority, might have become an additional component of women's demands on the workplace. If these kinds of labor issues had emerged alongside the others, perhaps real restructuring of life and work might have occurred earlier. Perhaps I am the one who is too utopian now; feminist demands themselves were hard enough to achieve—where is the political will, the nuance, and the PR to explain that mothers and fathers need both better work and relief from work, in different measures, to best raise their kids? How poignant that in the most recent plight of mothering it is the older, middle-class mothers— the women who gained the most from liberal feminism and the professional advancements it offered—who are now most vocal in wanting the same relief from work that was spurned in their names forty years before. In any case, this small piece of a strategy difference from forty years ago can offer us some visions for the future, now, as working women across class lines realize the importance of real relief from work, paired with easier, more flexible on-ramps and reentry.

Even Betty Friedan, whose work did so much to rally an emerging 1960s women's movement, understood the particular and demanding labor of caring for young children. I'm never sure how many people actually read *The Feminine Mystique*. Everybody knew about it. Newspapers reviewed it. People across America talked about it. Many people purchased it and still do. But read it, cover to cover? The woman everyone cites may have written the book that no one really read. When I queried my mother's friends who had young children in the '60s, when the book was published, I found few who could remember having opened its covers. "My book group read it," recalled one, but that was in the mid-'70s, more than ten years after the book's initial publication. She didn't think she made it through the whole book, maybe not past the first chapter. She did remember enjoying the consciousness-raising conversation.

Friedan, in the early '60s, was trying, in her words, "to fit together the puzzle of women's retreat to home." It was clear to her that Occupation: Housewife, as she called it, was popular among both women and men (the latter of whom, she argued, were able to assure that they would be cared for, and to keep women from competing with them in the workplace). It was also clear to Friedan that many women felt empty, alienated, and depressed by the single dimension of their maternal and wifely lives. This, in her words, was the problem without a name.[5]

Friedan's final chapter in the book carries the title "A New Life Plan for Women." She has already walked us through a history of American women in which women of different classes were encouraged to work, expected to work, and then persuaded to abstain from work. She has already introduced us to the way that media and women's magazines helped accomplish this. She has explained why corporations and advertisers wanted women at home where they would consume more products on behalf of their families (this may sound familiar . . .). She has introduced us to many female doctors and engineers, teachers and journalists, so that we know that throughout the 1940s and 1950s some women were resisting the feminine mystique and pursuing advanced careers despite the obstacles placed in their way. On the downside, she has shown clearly the way that these women were mostly prevented from pursuing both a domestic life and a professional life, how drastic an either/or scenario they faced.

In these final pages Friedan offers her readers one last vision: the whole woman who is aware of her desires, wants to have children, and also needs a life of the mind. The new life plan incorporates all of this. Friedan does not believe that mothers are stupid. She does not want us to go uneducated. She wants women to keep up some study through the childbearing years. She is concerned for the minds of mothering women, for their creativity, for the things that make them other than mothers, better mothers, happier mothers. She wants to make sure that mothers have time for their own interests. She's not just talking about cake decorating or flower arranging. Now, my hunch is that Friedan's not against indulging every so often in *Wallpaper* or *Martha Stewart Living*; she just wants to make sure mothers—and all women—are reading something more meaty besides.

That's important. But there's a paragraph, one sweet, small, paragraph toward the end of *The Feminine Mystique* that offers the sense of fluidity that so many of us crave. Friedan offers a vision in which women claim "lifelong commitments to an art or science, to politics or profession. Such a commitment is not tied to a specific job or locality. It permits year-to-year variation—a full-time paid job in one community, part-time in another, exercise of the professional skill in serious volunteer work or a period of study during pregnancy or early motherhood when a full-time job is not feasible."[6]

She knows how overwhelming those first years of parenting can be. Even in a book that sends us into the paid workforce, that helps inspire the smashing of career barriers everywhere, she wants to look out for those early years, preserving our desire to be home with the youngest of our children. This feminist mother, this mother of feminism, knew the difference, the specialness, of those years. She couldn't solve the economics of it, but she does find room for raising young children within the vision of work. It's not quite the stark directive of either/or we're told to expect from feminism.

This piece of Friedan's vision is one worth remembering. What strikes me is its flexibility, its acknowledgment that practical devotions to work and to children vary. Here we have an old map that navigates us between the extremes of either working full-time or being solely home with our children. Even white middle-class feminists who wanted schools and better workplaces opened to women understood that mothers, and especially the parents of young children, also need relief.

Parents of young children face an enormous increase in the work they do; this needs to be recognized as difficult and needs to be relieved in some way. It's not a question of style and social status, but about more tedious things, like how many hours in a day should we have to work, and just how tired do mothers and fathers have to be? I think often of this debate, so unknown in our popular culture, so poignant and so important. I think of how the winds ended up blowing in one direction—a good direction, that of opening up educational opportunity and workplace advancement to women. It's never a one-or-the-other choice. Building now on the opportunities we've gained, and protecting them, we can also demand relief from work, relief that recognizes how much labor women currently do beyond their paid jobs, the extra work that comes along with kids.

"Relief from work" captures some of what mothers want. And it helps us reframe the current debates away from whether working moms or stay-at-home moms are better at raising their kids (and where are all the dads here? Why do our public debates veer from asking about gender role change, from suggesting that fathers parent more actively?). It helps by putting "work" back into the equation. Work has a way of turning invisible, especially work that doesn't have a price tag and a salary attached. When mothers are asked what they want, often the answer is part-time work. We phrase it in terms of how much work we want to do, when often, the real answer would come phrased as how much work we want relief from doing.

The mothers who are part of the 63 percent who work less then full-time are aware of the fatigue of being asked to do full-time work and to carry the majority of domestic work too. Some can articulate it and others cannot. The mainstream Mommy Wars discourse makes it hard to see the real work issues involved. But by their actions—quitting jobs or leaving full-time employment—mothers are demanding relief from all this work. They have been willing, though not happy, to sacrifice income for this relief, and they have been willing to sacrifice their personal advancement and their family's future earnings. It's this simple fact that needs recognition so we can move ahead to ways of better supporting parents and families. It's about a principled refusal to do all that extra work, mixed with an alternative vision of what matters in life.

Mothers aren't asking for such all-or-nothing choices as many are given. They're often not asking to take sides in ideological debates about motherhood. That's why the surprise of politically progressive mothers staying home with their kids hasn't made sense. Instead of continuing to use this older framework, I want us to consider that what most of those 63 percent of mothers who work less than full-time want is some relief from work, especially when their children are young. We need to be able to phrase it this way, to ask for relief, to say that in families where mothers carry so much of the domestic and childraising labor and they work, they might need some relief. Without this alternate view, mothers who leave work to devote time to the work of unpaid childraising will be immediately thrust into a politicized world of being a "working mom" or a "stay-at-home mom" and having to somehow take sides. But parenting, motherhood, should never be about sides. Parenting is about care, about modeling a good life and solid values for our kids. Molly, for example, wasn't looking to find herself on an ideological battlefield. She wasn't trying to be a supermom or a hyper mom or even the best mom on her block. She was just really tired, exhausted. She was trying to make it through the day. That's something many mothers and fathers can recognize. She needed a break. She needed more support. She needed some relief from work. She should have been able to get it without having to chuck out her career. It should have been a rightful expectation, not a privilege that, unfortunately, she didn't have.

"What do mothers want?" we're often asked. The classic answer of sexist society was that we wanted to be home with our kids, taking care of the hearth (or, if we were poor, taking care of someone else's hearth). The mainstream feminist answer was that we wanted better educations, to work for pay and be paid fairly for our work, and the chance to contribute actively to public life. That's a good answer, and we need that answer. But big questions like "What do mothers want?" have several answers, because not all mothers want the same thing and because we have different answers throughout our lives.

So here's a new answer to those who ask, "What do mothers want?": We want lots of things. We want fair work and wages, and we want some relief from work, too. We want access to all the well-paid full-time work we desire, in the fields we want to work in, and at fair wages that equal those of men. We want flexibility for all parents, male and female, when it comes to caring for children, for the littlest ones who need so much time and attention and who keep us up all night, and for the older ones, too, who still need our care, and often at unpredictable times. We want good part-time work options, with fair wages, benefits, and security and advancement. We want it recognized that kids' preschool years are special, and that daycare is important, crucially important, but it's not the entire answer. We want policies that both improve daycare options and support caring for one's own children at home. And we want unpaid childraising and domestic labor to be valued, for men and for women. We want this unpaid labor to no longer be devalued as "women's work," but to be seen as important work without which little of life as we know it would be possible.

There. That's what we want. And if it seems like a lot, it's not. It's actually the bare minimum. But it's long overdue and about time.

CHAPTER 6.

What Do You Do with Your Time?

Years ago I read a novel by Kim Chernin called *My Life as a Boy*. As I remember it, the conceit of the book was a young woman who was able to act with the confidence, say, of an imagined adolescent boy. Able to walk out a door without looking back. Able to leave behind the fears and anxieties and frustrations of womanhood—and the history of gender roles that can leave us scared and shy of their boundaries—and have confidence in what she did.

My Life as a Boy came back to me recently. If the usual timbre of motherhood and fatherhood is defensive—and, yes, filled with the fear that there are no right ways to do it—what will it mean to shift to a more self-assured stance, one that doesn't easily apologize for what actually are basic and understandable positions? When I argue in the previous chapter that relief from work is what we need, I very much mean to replace those other explanations we use, of false choice or opting out or the Mommy Wars model. We no longer need to worry about whether one can be a feminist and a mother at the same time; we know that's a false opposition, that the real issue is how much labor mothers are doing. In fact, recognizing the labor of motherhood, whether combined with paid work in any combination or on its own, will be the key point for a new feminism. Instead of walking through our lives as parents worrying where the next round of judgment or hardship is going to come from, we can walk through life with more assuredness in what we're doing.

Just ahead are stories from at-home moms whom I specifically asked what they love about what they do. And I've asked some fathers who have made similar choices in life to talk about that. I wanted parents to be able to talk about what they loved. For example, Peter Lighte lives in London, with his partner, Julian, and their two daughters, Hattie and Tillie, who as we speak are hanging in the most intriguing upside-down positions on the swingset nearby. "Why is it so hard for some people to realize that others actually like parenting?" Peter asks, "that some of us want to do it?" Often, it's easier to talk about the negatives: about losing a job, about being squeezed out, or about having a breakdown when it all became too much. But coupled with that, there are positive desires to parent. To hear those desires is to explain the impetus behind some choices—that family time and home time can be both rewarding and important.

Further, if my dream is to inhabit a world in which parenting doesn't have a gender, and in which childraising's sometimes-partner—housework—isn't equated with the old-fashioned notion of women's work, then stay-at-home dads, by their very presence, go a long way in breaking down the most intimate family gender roles we inherit. In fact, their banner is that by raising the kids, an at-home father may be supporting a woman's desire to work, and thus contributing to a vision where homemaking and childcare will no longer be the default definition of "women's work."

Roseanne lives in Van Nuys, California, just outside L.A. For the first three years of her son's life, she was a writer and producer for the TV show *Touched by an Angel*. She worked full-time, living in Van Nuys, and her job included two- and three-week stints to the show's filming site in Arizona. During those years, her husband supported her job by being the stay-at-home dad, carrying full responsibility for cooking and household chores. He was a computer guy, and worked in the evenings; but it was his willingness to be home that made her job, with its demanding schedule, possible. He often brought their baby in to see her at lunchtime, and would set up housekeeping in Arizona while she filmed. If My *Life as a Boy* impressed itself upon me, these men's lives, in effect, are "My Life as a Girl." Both formulations break down our usual ideas about gender and parenting. And both show what a buoyant and self-assured parenting life might look like beyond the usual expectations and constrictions of gendered expectations.

Welcome to TheNewHomemaker.com. "Who is the New Homemaker?" asks Lynn Siprelle, typing from her home in Portland, Oregon, while her two children hover nearby.

> She is the person who has discovered that having both partners in the work world is not "having it all." Children, elders, and the community have been sacrificed for two generations to the crazy notion that households can run themselves. Well, they can't, and never have. Working parents have struggled valiantly to "have it all," but are increasingly saying, "We've had enough"; someone has to be home. Even single parents are exploring ways to spend more time at home and less at work, or to work at home. . . .
>
> Today's homemakers must take the best from what our foremothers have to offer us—both the independent thinkers and the shy housewives—and create something new, a homemaker who knows the value of her work, respects herself, and gets respect from the rest of the world. Every person who puts his or her family's best interests first, as people have for centuries, is now a rebel, reclaiming an America that might never have been except in our minds and hearts, but that deserves to be born.

Lynn is the founder and editor of The New Homemaker, a website for parents who are home. She's an obsessive reader, she tells me, and one day back in the late '90s she was reading Mary Pipher's book *The Shelter of Each Other: Rebuilding our Families*. *Shelter* argues that we live in a family-hurting culture, and that we're surrounded by a society that glamorizes sex, drugs, and violence, and which treats children like little consumers instead of protecting them from the world. There's too much junk media and job stress, and not nearly enough family time to keep us healthy. "*The Shelter of Each Other* hit me right between the eyes," she says. "Next thing I knew, I was looking around on the Web for a site that reflected those values. All I found for homemakers was right-wing Christian fundamentalist stuff, which is fine if that's who you are, but that's not who I am. I thought: What about the rest of us? I couldn't possibly be the only non-fundamentalist-Christian homemaker in the universe."

Siprelle didn't feel like ceding the territory of family life and home-making to the right wing. As a web designer, she set about making the site she was looking for—a site that would support homemakers' work; give advice on cooking, organizing, cleaning; and also provide a sense of community. Launched in 1999, The New Homemaker is now celebrating its fifth year as an online community. On the site are everything from household tips on recycled holiday cards and nontoxic solutions to ant infestations to reviews of books like Edward H. Romney's *Living Well on Practically Nothing* and Laurie Colwin's *More Home Cooking*. Readers post questions and answer each other. If someone from Nebraska complains about the pesky problem of keeping raccoons out of the trash, a reader from California offers suggestions.

The site is not about the so-called new momism, a hyper-perfect fantasy of motherhood that Susan Douglas and Meredith Michaels denounce in their book, *The Mommy Myth*, but about things much more mundane, and more important. What are the real family issues? I ask Lynn, and responses come quickly to her tongue. Family wages, for one: so that families can make it on one income, so there's support for stay-at-home parents. There are social issues, too: Stay-at-home parents need to stand up and say, "I am worth something; I'm not here because I don't have anything better to do. I do have a brain." At-home parents like Lynn have a different vision, a political one for its being focused on the home and coming from the home, and counter to much of American life. These parents stand up to the corporatization and commodification of everyday life. "Especially the commodification. Everything's getting a price tag," Lynn says. "If there's anything that homemaking stands for, it's that life does not carry a price tag.

"People have such odd reactions to The New Homemaker," Lynn continues. They assume that because the site advocates homemaking she's antifeminist and pregnant and barefoot. Lynn thinks that's bullshit: "It's not patriarchal family redux. That says that you think that traditional women's work is not worth as much as men's work. You're telling me that cooking, cleaning, and taking care of children is worthless, and that the only work of worth is running a corporation or being a lawyer or flying a fighter jet or whatever the traditional guy things are when you think of 'important' stuff. Excuse me, but what I do is ten times more important than what any CEO does. Ten times more important. There is no more important job in this world than taking care of a household. We're the ones who get things done. We don't run the show, but we get things done."

Who cleans the messes of daily life? This is the critical issue, because it leads so quickly to all others. Women in our country have risked quite a lot through the past forty years to be relieved of traditional "women's work," of cleaning house and preparing dinner each night. Yet, in feminism's "stalled revolution," women who live with men still do more of the housework. The result: Domesticity has gone underground. We can talk about household and decorating tips; in fact, we can't get away from home repair shows and room makeovers and magazines filled with new ideas for interior design and organizing our stuff. We just can't talk about the actual work of domesticity, the time it takes, what's fun and what's tedious and what's life draining, save in hushed tones to each other. Many mothers have lots of extra work, but it remains invisible and mute so we don't have to think deeply about its role in our society and its cost in our lives. It's supposed to be invisible work that someone else does. How mortifying to admit to cleaning one's own floors, to organizing one's supply closet; to seek out advice on how to do these things with more ease and better efficiency.

Once household labor and the effort it takes to raise children went underground, we had to stop counting. We made fun of those earnest 1970s feminist stories about charts that mapped out the equal domestic contributions of male and female partners. We stopped paying attention, but that didn't make the issue go away; it just made it harder to talk about.

It's important to separate childrearing from housework. They have long been twinned, but they are not the same. Many new moms are quite clear that they wish to be active mothers and not housewives. Susan is a fortyish mother who left her job in international public health after she adopted her now eighteen-month-old daughter. Once she had a child, it was hard to keep up a job that included several long trips each year to Southeast Asia. She tells me in no uncertain terms that she is a mother and loves it, but does not enjoy the domestic chores that ride shotgun with the ordinary messes little kids make. "I'm a mother, not a housekeeper," she declares. Many women and men who have great fun finger painting with the kids, playing in mud puddles on a rainy day, baking cookies, and visiting the local fire station on a whim are less than thrilled with the cleanup and tidying that comes with the territory. Many of us who adore parenting would not similarly rave about the tedium of dish cleaning, floor sweeping, and grocery shopping, those continual tasks never done that always need repeating (as important as anything there is—imagine life without clean clothes, with constantly dirty dishes, or mildewy bathtubs and bathroom sinks covered in slithery, dried-up toothpaste residue and soap scum) and nonetheless add up to so little. This labor never seems to "count" as real work. Even after years of writing about the value of ordinary housework, I find it hard to take seriously. I still find myself frustrated and self-hating because I've "wasted" an hour or so folding clothes, putting magazines and bills and toys and empty water glasses back in their places, unpacking the dishwasher yet again, and drawing up a grocery list that will take an hour to shop and unpack, and will need to be repeated just a few days later.

My old friend Tim Tyson is now a professor of African American history at the University of Wisconsin. Back when we were graduate students together and teaching, I stopped by his classroom one evening as he was finishing and we were set to head out for a beer. He gathered his books, said goodbye to the students still hanging about, and then moved the trash can from under the desk at the far side of the room to over near the door, making life just a tad easier for the janitor who would be cleaning up later that night. "Every day when I leave the classroom," he said to me, "I think, 'By the grace of God I'm at the front, teaching, and not the person cleaning up after.'" I thought about this when, for the first time, I moved away from the front of the action and became the one who cleaned up after. For years I swept and brushed and swirled. Rob vacuumed, and did a share of the daily chores, and always got the trash out in time for Tuesday pickup. But I was so aware of the presence of domestic work—unpaid, invisible, yet time-consuming—in my life. My mother thought I was crazy. "Hire someone," she said. "You're the parent. Just because you're not working doesn't mean you have to do all the housework."

Many years later, my family had left Atlanta and settled in Philadelphia, closer to our extended families. My daughter started pre-K full-day and I started to work more hours, teaching and writing—but I still crammed all this into six daytime hours and the late-night shift so

I could pick her up at school and hang out at the playground with the other parents, talking while the kids played. Old habits are hard to break, and I've always loved the parent camaraderie at the playground. Still, there was more money coming into our budget. My neighbor Ellen—a single mom who works long hours—had just found someone to clean her house, and on her advice I hired him too. Bill stopped by my house once every other week to clean. To organize. To take everything off the kitchen counters and wipe them down. To vacuum under the couch and keep the dust at bay. And before he left a day's work, Bill would clip flowers and greens from the yard and make sure every tabletop and windowsill got a vaseful. For a few hours at my house, Bill did the "women's work." He spent a few hours with scrub brush in hand. When he was done, everything sparkled. In our gender swap, he was better at "women's work" than I was, and he got paid for it, which I didn't. When I watched him work, I became aware of how much I must have been doing before.

We love those clean sheets and home-cooked meals. As for the domestic labor of blanket straightening and pillow fluffing, of grocery shopping, chopping vegetables, reading recipes, setting the table, and cleaning the dishes afterward, well, that's too boring to talk about, let alone do. Vacuuming the floors, cleaning the bathrooms—no, no, no. We won't even talk about doing the laundry.

It's women's work. In our house, now, it's men's work too.

The reality is, we need to be able to talk honestly about domestic life and its details. In the apparent triviality of who keeps the grocery list and who swishes away the icky stuff from the bathroom sink rests the major gender and work distinction of Western civilization: Domestic equals private equals women, combined with its putative opposite, work equals public equals men. I'm here to say that if we are to solve our frustrations with family life and mothering and paid work, we must go directly to this elemental distinction and change it, for real this time.

꙳

Parenting can bring frustration, but it also brings joy, which is more than we can usually claim for housework. Anita and I are at the self-service car wash on DeKalb Avenue. My daughter and Anita's two girls are roaming free inside Anita's fire-engine-red minivan. For months I've been wanting to ask Anita how she decided to be a stay-at-home mom. Turns out she's glad to be asked.

"After Kalei was born," she tells me, "I realized that kids are a full-time commitment. Life is not about juggling and about being great at everything. My daughters now are my main focus."

The water spray has stopped but the kids are still having fun. Anita leans against the car: tall, lean, and confident. "My goal is to give the girls a good foundation. To let them have a healthy and well-balanced childhood. With me at home they get different kinds of experiences. We can have an impromptu picnic in the middle of the day, go look at the leaves change, learn how to ride a bike, or dig for worms and make mud pies in the backyard. We're calm. I think my girls are doing really well. I think I'm doing really well.

"One last thing I'm thinking about," Anita says, "Is that it's a very humbling experience. Childraising is not about you. If you're brought up to be independent, it is hard to let all that go, and sit back, and raise a happy child. I feel like I've made a conscious decision. What makes me happy is knowing that the girls are happy and that they are okay. If I have a bad day because someone pooped on the floor or threw up on me, so be it. What can you do? What can you do? You get a wipe and clean it up. The whole thing is very humbling."

Before her daughter was born, Lisa was an international entrepreneur. She lived for many years in China and in Vietnam, where she ran an international machine import business. For nearly two years after Grace arrived, Lisa didn't work. "I think Grace is the better for it," she tells me, in her fast-talking, mince-no-words style. "This 'quality time' thing is crap. I think quantity time is important. Just being there for four hours playing with them, reading the paper, putting together dinner, being in the same room or in the next room while they watch TV, all for the thirty seconds they will really need you. They know the difference." She wishes she could have continued to be home with Grace. I understand this; they are a very intense mother-daughter pair. But Lisa is recently divorced. Her ex-husband pays minimal child support and no alimony, and work is a necessity. "Believe me, I love to work," she says, "but I didn't go back to work for self-actualization. I went back because I had to support my kid. I made a decision to work at home, and when it came down to it, I gave up twice the salary I could have made to do so. It's counterintuitive. I prayed for a job at home where I could build a home for my daughter. A home-home, not just the physical building we live in, but the home that I make for her because I'm there all day, because she can pop down and see me in my office, because I can be with her after preschool and before her nap, and work all night after she's in bed if I have to."

When Lisa and I talk the conversation is usually peppered with references to the glamorous things she used to do—her lengthy stays in Hong Kong and Beijing, fun times she spent in Italian cities, her life as an expat American in Saigon. Was it a sacrifice, I ask her?

"No, no, no," she says. "You've got to flip it around, reframe it. It's not a sacrifice; it's not a loss. I have Grace in my life. She changes everything. It's a bigger picture, an investment, an opportunity. I love Grace. What do we really need, anyway? With kids and work, you have to know your own answers. I know it's unfashionable to say, but we do become ourselves through our children. You lose yourself for a time, and then you put yourself together and you come out someone else. I'm a better person than I used to be."

Of course it's been scary to talk about the desire to have kids and the desire to be with them. After all, what are the cultural options available for voicing this desire? Because of how hard women have fought to be taken seriously at work (and often, how much fighting we still have left to do in order to accomplish this, children or no), it's terrifying to talk about a desire for children. But Lisa and Anita are progressive women who are voicing these desires. They're fully aware of what they give up to follow their specific visions of family life; they're mad about that, and both of them—I can vouch for this!—are avid feminists who are very capable of voicing exactly what is wrong with the current system. But both have also moved beyond a sense of fear. They work hard at what they do, but they're optimistic and poised in being who they are.

It can help if we look at men who are able to voice these desires. At-home dads are daring to do something new—they are nontraditional men, men creating new traditions, and one price they pay is fending off everyone's comments of discomfort: Who wears the pants in your family? You're Mr. Mom and that's a nice Mommy Wagon you drive. What does your wife think about you not working? When are you going back to your real job?

On a website devoted to at-home dads, a father, Edward Shaw, checks in about day 6,635 of being a stay-at-home dad. That's almost nineteen years, during which he's been the primary caretaker for three children—years in which he was home, in which he learned how to be a contractor so he could control his time, years in which he left work at 2:30 to be with his kids after school. Years during which he divorced, and received primary custody (with child support) of his three kids, and still made sure they had a home life. Years in which, despite the divorce, the children's mother came to dinner each night, so the kids would still have a family life that included her. Shaw—a former high school athlete, an honors college graduate, and an independent businessman—writes: "Home remains the center of my life. It is my nest. It is my fort. I am proud of it and of my children. Through an age when most of my generation invested in their careers and the market, I invested in my heart."[1]

When I listen to stay-at-home dads, I hear a straightforward senti-mentality, something that sometimes is missing from mothers' accounts. They're just not as tortured as some mothers are. For so many reasons, we mothers are largely defensive. We keep explaining and jus-tifying and rationalizing why we do what we do. Frustrations about work and parenting and the history of gender weigh us down. Fears that clas-sic discrimination against women will conquer us make it even harder; many women don't feel comfortable giving voice to these critiques, as if to say them in words makes the problem real. After all, in risking a jump out of the workplace, or into fewer hours, we're betting quite a lot on the hope that sexism isn't quite as bad as we think it might be.

But listen to Shaw, this at-home father of nearly nineteen years, this man who is concerned that four out of ten dads aren't with their kids every day:

> Love your children and tell them you love them. Hug them. Laugh with them. Play with them. Listen to their dreams. Appreciate them, for their youth passes oh so quickly. It will not be all fun, games, and joy. There will be broken bones and hearts along the way. Just be there to help them.
>
> Turn off the TV. Play a board game or cards. Take your kids for a walk. Know that no matter how much experience you have, there will always be something new with which to deal. Parenting is a job. But make it your calling. Make your family number 1.
>
> Do something for yourself during their quiet time. Read, write, play a musical instrument. Stay busy and continue to grow within yourself, not from without.

This is what at-home parenting without the Mommy Wars, with-out gendered expectations, looks like. It's quite different from what many mothers end up experiencing, and a helpful reminder for those who are doing this absolutely from love.

♪

Damien Bryan used to be a highly paid, well-connected salesman. He backed out of his driveway Monday mornings, headed to the airport, then wined and dined and sold outdoor sports products all week. Late on Thursday night, he would stagger back home, tired. This life made sense before his son, Hamish, was born. But once a child was in the picture it seemed a bit insane, and way too hard. It was difficult for Damien's wife, Brenda, and it pressed strongly on him, too, to leave a business rhythm behind and slot himself into life at home with a new baby. Just as he was relaxing into it on Sunday evenings, he would find himself preparing for the onslaught of Monday morning. At work Damien was responsible for the entire Australian side of Kathmandu stores, the Aussie version of our REI. Four hundred people worked in his operation. He was opening new stores, flying between cities to keep everything working. So with life at work on one fast-paced track and life at home on another, he resigned.

Needless to say, people around him were shocked. But his wife's career was starting to gear up, and his decision made sense to him: "It was tough. I was thirty. I had full autonomy, flew around the nation, made big decisions. I had the trust of my boss. And I like my business. I like business. I like selling, I like talking to people and getting things done. It was a dream job in that sense, but it came with baggage. I didn't have kids to not see them."

When he quit, people told him he would never again get a job like the one he had left. "I was worried about it pragmatically," he says. "Then, I figured that someone with my background and experience is always employable. I wasn't too scared about the unknown. I've always been unorthodox." And he is. Damien never went to college. He had other things to do, and though he's smart and was good at school, it just didn't appeal to him. In fact, he never even finished high school. He wanted to work with his hands, to apprentice and become a tradesperson, and that's what he did. He spent four years learning and working as an electrician.

Life at home with Hamish was a different world. Days were slow; father and son hung out. Damien did some renovations around the house. And as Hamish grew and went to preschool a few mornings a week, Damien started to look for a job that wouldn't take him away from home.

As it turned out, his friends' advice was for naught. He answered an ad for a retail manager for a new store opening in Canberra, Australia, where he lived. The salary was significant, a big jump up from his last job. He applied just to get the interview experience and then it took off from there: "They emailed right back and asked if we could meet that day at noon. I told them I couldn't, that I was home and my son was napping, and how about 1:30? And later that day I spent an hour talking with the CEO on a park bench." It was stressful and high pressure, but the hours were nine to five and he had a company car. Hamish was already in preschool three days a week; Damien took Wednesdays off, and his wife's job as a researcher was flexible, so the boy's schedule stayed the same. Their second child, Anna, was born.

Damien tells me all this as we sit in the upstairs family room of the house his family now rents in Germantown, Pennsylvania. It's a huge Victorian, in a neighborhood that has seen its better days, and there's paint peeling in the back foyer where we enter.

His wife was considering a position in the United States. When her offer came through, Damien resigned, and they packed up to move for a few years. It's complicated, though, he says. He didn't just quit because they were moving. His job was great, but he was getting tired. His decision took place on many levels: He was tired of working a high-powered job; there was an adventure to be had; his wife's career would be primary for the moment; and there were now two young children to be cared for during a move halfway around the world and then settled in afterward.

So here we are at his table. Steaming coffee mixed with whole milk fills the cups. Earlier in the day Damien had stopped by the local bakery to pick up some pastries for us and the treats fill several plates, disappearing as we talk. "Work is such a blokey world," he says, pausing to make sure I understand what "bloke" means. Anna has just woken from her nap. She sprawls sleepily across Damien's chest and slowly reenters the world. She reminds me of my long toddler afternoons with Samira: the tranquility that glides into a home when a child falls asleep; minutes that open longer, like tulips in the sun, till they close, the child wakes, and there we are in the sweet, slow warmth of the half-awake.

"Most women, when they find out I'm home with my kids, say 'Good for you!'" Damien continues. "At the fruit and vegetable shop down the street the older ladies go gaga, and often they watch me to make sure I'm doing it right." The matronly women sometimes ask him if they might hold Anna while he shops. They assume that as a man he can't really do both at the same time. Damien does all the grocery shopping and prepares the family meals, so shopping with child in hand is as natural to him as it is to all the mothers who do exactly the same thing. The older ladies in the neighborhood can't exactly believe that he's the father spending dedicated time with his kids. They ask if the mother is sick. Most men react first with some jealousy, and then immediately move on to tell him they could never do it. But Damien likes life the way it is. He gets to pick Hamish up at school at three and hang out with the other parents at the playground. He even signed on to be the president of the school's parents' association. "Most people of our generation can't remember our fathers being home. Mine ran a small business and was always at work. I hope it all adds up for my kids, that as they grow some part of them is anchored in the fact that when they were young we traveled, and that Dad was around."

Ours is not a forgiving society. We've made certain ways of being in the workplace seem natural and normal, claiming they are the most productive, even if they aren't. "Face time" trumps all, so that the cult of being there makes it difficult to be an active parent and an active worker and not be exhausted and drained at the end of the day. You can't be a company man or woman and leave at 4:30, flextime, job sharing, and telecommuting aside. Yet Damien reminds me of other ways of living—ways that resist this fear and this culture of competition, ways that are sure that life is long and that a little pluck and courage and following of one's heart go a long way.

When I talk with dads who have made these choices, what comes out front and center is the love they have for their kids, and a desire, so simply expressed, to spend more time with them. It's all so straightforward. Of course someone would want to spend more time with his or her kids, career sacrifice, afternoon tedium, and all. The genderedness of it disappears—for the moment, anyway. It's easier to see the desire as such.

Tom Weeks was once a member of the Seattle City Council. He left the council to take a high-level job with Seattle Public Schools. Two years later he left that job, turning in his office keys when there were too many stresses at home. "Basically, it wasn't working," he told me. "I didn't feel like I was doing justice to my marriage or my parenting. I'm not judging other couples with demanding jobs, but with the two of us, it just plain wasn't working. We weren't doing the quality parenting we wanted, we weren't attending to our marriage. You want some time in your life for reflection, when it's not out of control and busy every single minute."

His wife, Deb Oyer, is a doctor; she runs Aurora Medical Services, which provides reproductive healthcare to women. After the kids were born, she worked part-time, and by Tom's account, she enjoyed her time with infant care more than he would have. As the kids grew, he really wanted to be with them. Deb was more excited professionally about what she was doing at the moment than was Tom. Deb's salary made it possible for their family to live comfortably with only one parent at work. So in February 1998, when his kids were five and nine, Tom quit and stayed home.

Now that his kids are older, he has more time during the day for volunteer work. He sits on the board at his children's school, and he chairs a citizens' initiative on mass transit. In his daytime hours he bridges the good works of activists and city government. Because he is not paid for his work, he can call his own hours; he leaves midafternoon to pick his kids up from school, do the grocery shopping, and coach the kids' sports teams.

Of the many parents I've interviewed, Tom has the oldest kids, and he has more free daytime hours. In many ways, Tom's the classic 1950s homemaker (except that, by his own admission, he's not so great on making dinner every night, but then who among us is?). We forget that several decades back we assumed that homemakers would also be civically active. It's an irony that in today's high-intensity, get-your-own-child-ahead culture, we've lost part of what was really inter-esting about 1950s suburban housewives: They were activists and volunteers in their communities. This is a legacy to grab on to. Tom volunteers, he coaches, he runs political initiatives. Being at home with the kids doesn't mean he's left public life.

It's not always easy. Recently Tom was at a meeting of the Greater Seattle Chamber of Commerce. The head of the chamber turned to him and said, "So, Tom, what do I tell people when they ask me what you are doing now?"

"People don't always get it," Tom tells me, "even after five years." Like many stay-at-home parents, Tom has done some paid work. He's done some consulting and taught a course or two on public policy at the University of Washington. But he hasn't seriously considered a full-time job. "Now when I get job offers," he tells me, "my kids are the loudest voices saying, 'Don't do it. We want you right here.'"

In part, what makes spending time with children so fraught for women is, ironically, the fact that our cultural history so easily assigns this role only to women. Mothers are constantly telling each other that if more men quit their jobs or went part-time to care for children, then the repercussions for women would not be so strong or severe. They are convinced that the sanctions against women who react to our culture's mixed messages (parent fully, but we will punish you if you do) have much to do with parenting's association with women, and with women's lower status. If men actively parented, parenting's status would rise with good results for the men and women who do it. If stay-at-home parenting were more gender neutral or more gender inclusive, if it were not just "a woman thing," part-time possibilities and entry back to the workplace later would be easier and life would improve for all.

The census numbers for stay-at-home dads are rising, though still small, around 180,000.[2] And in a summer 2004 poll, 40 percent of fathers said they would consider being stay-at-home dads and another 42 percent wished they could work fewer hours. All talked of how they felt pulled between work and home.[3] This spans all economic classes. When researchers at American University's Program on WorkLife Law combed through the records of union arbitrations, they found that much of the conflict in male workers' lives came from balancing work duties with childcare, as in the case of a factory worker who turns down mandatory overtime because his kids are home and he can't locate an evening babysitter for them.

Are we moving toward a new consensus in our country that values more active parenting? Might we be able to value this without a return to the patriarchal family, without expecting that the parent at home should also be the mom? The current numbers aren't enough, yet, to foster widespread social, cultural, and workplace change, but they're a good start, and one to encourage. The stories of Tom and other men who take on the work of hands-on parenting remind us that parenthood is not the sole domain of women, nor is the desire to parent. Many books and articles about mothers repeat the old idea that parenting has a gender; that children, sacrifice, life change, and parenting are some-how essential parts of being a woman. Stories from the fathers I spoke to lift us out of this pattern and help us think about parenting in a less gender-charged way.

It all sounds so joyful—desire, love for children—that it puts into context how messed up it is that we can't spend more time with our kids, that the "work" part of "work and family" is so rigid, and that for women, veering away from work and toward kids has so many unin-tended and unwanted consequences. Here, the media is complicit in sending undermining messages: the Mommy Wars—or, more accu-rately, the war against mothers—again.

Recently I read a pair of newspaper articles about stay-at-home mothers and stay-at-home fathers whose children are older and who want to return to paid work. I couldn't help but notice the different tones of the advice offered to moms and dads who want some on-ramps back into the workforce. The article on dads addresses the question of eventually returning to the workplace with a largely positive pitch: "After five years at home full-time with two children," it begins, "Martin Banks was itching to get back to the adult world of work." In order to explain the five-year gap on his résumé, Martin describes the parenting work he's done and labels it as "Temporary Retirement: Devoted five years to raising my son and daughter. Responsibilities included changing diapers, preparing nutritious meals, making boo-boos feel better." He is offered a job running the San Francisco office for a video equipment supply company, but turns it down and opens a similar business of his own instead. Being more entrepreneurial gives him a more flexible schedule so he can still pick the kids up at school. In each example of at-home dads returning to work, the article announces a positive ending. "I said I was a stay-at-home dad, and I would fit the work around my schedule," Bill White tells an interviewer for a part-time position consulting on mortgages, and he gets the job. An executive coach quoted toward the article's end offers this advice:

"If the interviewers do not appear to be receptive, do not waste time trying to enlighten them. Move on to the next company. Some industries are more open than others. You want to work for a company that considers this a badge of honor, rather than an embarrassment." The article ends with this positive statement. It reassures men that they have choice, and that their lives will work for them.[4]

Compare this to the tone offered to women, and right before Mother's Day, of all days. To celebrate mothers' contributions, the *Wall Street Journal* offered its readers "After Years Off, Women Struggle to Revive Careers."[5] The article features the work and family stories of several women. In New York, Catherine King has a Stanford MBA and has worked at Credit Suisse First Boston and Chase Manhattan Bank. She left her job as a Wall Street portfolio manager after her second child was born, and has been a stay-at-home mother for fourteen years, during which she's earned a master's in early childhood education. Now fifty, she and her husband are divorcing, and a headhunter is telling her that she has a 15 percent chance of landing a job in her former field.

A Dallas woman left her job in special education when her husband's company transferred him to Oregon. She was thirty. She wasn't certified to teach special ed in Oregon so she ended up staying home with three children. This couple, too, is divorcing. Now forty-five, she wants and needs to work, but she's no longer up to date in her old field. Even with connections through friends, she can't land an interview, even for a reception job. She ends up working as a barista at her local Starbucks for twenty-five hours a week and starting at minimum wage. She's running the espresso machine and cleaning the bathrooms but hopes to move up into management. The article ends with a quote from King stating that motherhood doesn't offer applause, and that professional women yearn for "overachieving applause." That may be true, but for the women in this article, the search is not really for the emotional reward of applause; it's for work that pays a decent salary. Since both women are divorcing, and on their own, they need some economic independence and a way to support their families. Applause seems secondary to more mundane questions like, "Will I plummet close to poverty because I raised my kids for fifteen years and now I'm fifty and a displaced homemaker and I'm facing a changed workplace, not to mention age and gender discrimination and that my husband's gone and I need a salary?" No, in this article the word "discrimination" never appears. Conflict with husbands and social expectation is absent. And fathers never seem to end up taking care of the kids or their homemaker wives after a divorce.

The *Wall Street Journal* article never questions employers about other options, though it does mention that some consulting firms offer women who leave them for motherhood some contract work, and that one firm plans a program that will allow employees to take a five-year unpaid leave, with the hope of rehiring them afterward.

On its own, the *WSJ* article shows how women are punished for the time they take to raise children. It's a clear illustration of the on-ramps problem, in which few businesses see it as worth their while to hire at-home mothers because they don't value the skills the mothers have learned during those years. In the article, though, employers are never asked to explain themselves, and there are no positive examples of mothers who, say, start a new business or find a new job. The effect is dire. One is not sure whether the intent is to scare women away from quitting their jobs in the first place or to reassure employers that if they're not hiring former homemakers, don't worry, they're with the trend, no one else is either.

Contrast this with the upbeat article about returning fathers and the different approaches to fathers and mothers who want to take time off to parent become clear. Now, neither article is a scholarly study. The writers haven't done much research beyond contacting a handful of mothers and fathers, following leads, talking with a consultant or CEO or headhunter here and there, and sampling from the nonprofit websites on work and family. These are not sociological studies but slices of a picture produced under deadline. And the differences between them aren't explained by casting the conservative, market-oriented *Wall Street Journal* against the more liberal-leaning *New York Times*. The two articles show our divergent cultural expectations for women and men. Mothers who take time off to parent are told to expect punishment and discipline and loss. Fathers who do the same are told that reentry will be relatively easy.

There's something new happening in people's visions for life with their kids and community, in their reflections on what their own childhoods were like with fathers who worked too much or mothers who worked too much. There's something new in their desire for more balance, their willingness to take the risk to make balance happen, and, dare I say it, their sense of entitlement to a new family life. This is what we now face. We don't yet have the road maps for it, but the old signposts no longer hold. Granted, we'll still need a nonsexist gender system and a revamped workplace to make space for these emerging values, and that's no small task to establish. But a too-rigid workplace and the absence of a gender-free culture can't hold us back from admitting the changes that are already happening. We just need the culture and the workplace and government policy, too, to catch up.

CHAPTER 7.

Playground Revolution

When I was first trying to give a name to what was wrong—to the new problem without a name (or, perhaps, the problem with too many names), the parent problem whose designations fall everywhere on the spectrum from the battle-ready Mommy Wars to the too-tame "work-family balance"—I remember sputtering, "Well, the problem is . . . sexism." Which, as explanations go, is helpful and right and worth remembering, but not very specific. It's hard to know who and what to blame when the problem's so big and broad. The idea of speaking out on these issues was unimaginable. It was just too hard to put it in a box, to give it a sound bite. It seemed like I could describe it either in the largest terms possible ("old-fashioned sexism redux") or in the most personal, first-person narratives. It was hard to combine my experience with a politics of parenting, an explanatory framework. From every angle, the frustration I felt—that many mothers and fathers face in wanting to work and wanting to parent and wanting more control over how to do both—would lead into every other social issue imaginable. It was overwhelming.

I started to frame the question in a different way. What were the specific problems each of us experienced and how might they be solved? Aside from a general anger at the way things are, what specifically will help the most? By tackling pieces, I brought a larger picture into place.

Personally, my largest worries were about my career and about reentering the workplace later on with hours that were manageable. My family was financially okay—we lived simply, and in the end I did receive a patched-together six months of partial sick leave that masqueraded as family leave. I wanted to know that I could continue in the field I was trained in with fair wages and control over time. I knew one or two much older women who had raised families and then managed to jump back into decent full-time jobs, and they stood as my proof that it could be done. Still, I had resigned from my job and had left with no guarantees of being able to return to the work I loved; I gave up tenure, too, the ultimate job security. So when I thought about policy change, what I wanted most was job security. I wanted my entry back into the workplace at a similar level to be *easier* than I feared it would be. When I faced the expanse of the parent problem, it helped to think specifically about what I wanted changed.

Each parent who steps away from the ideal worker track has his or her own sense of what support he or she needs, and as I started interviewing others, I realized again just how complex the parent problem is. The minute I started to research new ideas about workplace organization, I landed in the complicated field of management books and business bestsellers, American capitalism's assumptions about how workplaces must be competitive, and all the government regulations that temper employers' worst instincts. I veered into feminist economics, research on ideal workers, and into the particularity of my own profession, filled as it is with not enough good jobs for the people who want them and with little incentive to provide quality part-time work. Lots of young professors were ready to take my job if I didn't want it. What reason would my employer have for keeping it open or temporarily filled for five years till I was ready to return? What incentives would other employers need to hire me after a five-year-or-so résumé gap?

It's hard to even know where to begin to fix these issues, to know how to separate off a chunk that can be fixed. But by asking for specifically what I needed, I opened the gate to thinking more broadly about policy changes that would benefit all families. As Karen Kornbluh, director of the Work & Family Program at the New America Foundation, writes, "Families 'have trouble translating this issue into policies that might help. The structural causes are so broad.'"[1] Where do you even start? You can point at the usual emperor's quadriga of suspects: media, advertising, workplace structures, and government policy. These are easier to finger. You can add male partners and husbands, too, and the vagueness of the culture and religious traditions we inherit. Even so, these are nebulous, hard to pinpoint exactly, and often difficult to know how to change.

Many of us, for instance, want better options for part-time work with benefits, with advancement, with prorated pay. If we are lucky, a sensitive boss agrees. Even so, that boss has to deal with a whole array of federal, state, and city regulations about benefits, taxes, and Social Security deductions. There are laws and policies governing health benefits and how many hours per week one must work to qualify, and whether the benefits extend to other members of your family if you're not legally married (or able to legally marry); individual bosses may be sensitive and caring, but they don't have control over all these factors. Pension and other kinds of annuity deductions, too, are subject to very specific laws, as are pretax programs like dependent care assistance, which allows you to deduct money each month, before taxes are taken out, that can be used on childcare and school up till the end of kindergarten.

If you need reminding that our individual, family-based desires are part of a web of wider social policy, look at a recent paycheck stub. I'm perusing mine from a course I teach at a nearby college. It turns out my work is not solely related to an agreement between my employer and me. My paycheck links me to the state budget of Pennsylvania, to the despised Philadelphia wage tax, and to the Medicare program of national health insurance for people over sixty-five. The largest share by far connects me to the entire bureaucracy of the Social Security

Administration. With each paycheck I deposit, I am connected to people who collect retirement benefits or disability checks or survivor's benefits or unemployment, and to those on public assistance and welfare.

The current practices of parenting and childcare in this country stress individual, not communal, solutions. Often it's hard to see past the rhetoric of "choice"—the accusation that we "chose" to have children and thus have sole responsibility to roll with what happens next. On top of this, many parents are busy, isolated, or depressed. With the kids interrupting and needing attention, who can finish a sentence, let alone organize a piece of a revolution?

Still, there are women, men, and groups of concerned parents who are getting together to make change for the better, who are part of what we might call the playground revolution. They're taking their insights and skills and they're tending home and looking outward, too, from their small corners of the world to make things better for others. Some of them are doing so quietly, in the interstices of their private lives and work lives. They're asking for family-friendly workplaces, and getting them, and making sure they're available for others. They're finding creative solutions. They're reflecting with spouses and parenting partners about how to share domestic work and paid work and care for the kids. They're trading childcare with neighbors and friends or organizing babysitting co-ops. They're setting up websites that offer community to other parents.

They talk openly about what's wrong, and about specific ways to make family life and their own lives as mothers and women and fathers and parents a bit better. They meet with preschool directors to discuss expanding hours to accommodate working parents. Or they ask elementary school principles to schedule the winter concert in the morning so parents can go directly to work afterward, instead of at 11:30 AM, when they'd need to take off so much more of the day. Perhaps they meet with the manager of a local dance studio, empty during the day, and convince her to open the studio to a morning parent group, and advertise a drop-in playgroup so that parents at home with their kids can meet each other, can end their loneliness and isolation. On a community bulletin board recently I saw an ad placed by a mother for other moms and dads with infants who wanted a playgroup. She put "play-group" in quotation marks, and beneath it wrote, in parentheses, "for us to talk and visit." She was reaching out beyond her own home, beyond her own isolation, hoping to make friends among strangers. It's a step.

Small acts matter. They expand our consciousness; they create more visible space for family life that's integrated with work; they acknowledge the work it takes to build and nurture a family. They show other families what change is possible when people start thinking about life with their kids in tow.

Others are in positions where their ideas take on a more public and active role. We've met some of them already: Professor Joan Williams, at American University's Program on WorkLife Law, who takes her vision of workplaces without maternal walls and finds the legal basis that can make this more of a reality, who organizes other attorneys so they know the best practices and newest ideas to advocate and argue in the courtroom for their clients. When my daughter was two and I was called to jury duty, I was glad to learn that just the year before, the Atlanta chapter of Mothers & More had organized a letter-writing campaign and successfully lobbied for family-friendly jury duty. As of 2001, primary caretakers of children under four could delay serving. Facing the possibility of a jury trial and no childcare, I saw firsthand how the activism of a few women had changed the law for mothers and fathers throughout the state.[2]

Often, mothers are told to be activists, told that we have responsibility for fixing the problem. In her response to "Opt-Out Revolution," Katha Pollitt writes in the *Nation* that affluent mothers who have the economic privilege to leave the workplace should take the lead in developing a more "muscular" feminism, devoted to raising issues and to social change.[3] I agree, but through my research for this book, I've been reminded that leadership on motherhood issues is certainly not limited to affluent white women—that women of all classes and colors are taking charge of the social landscape of motherhood, even if their work remains just below the public radar. I've met many of them in the worlds of policy and advocacy groups: lobbyists and anarchists, women in conservative suits and women with purple hair, women who come to motherhood with many of the resources and privileges that life can offer, and women who become activists and leaders because they have, materially speaking, very little else in the world. I've learned to listen to both high-end lawyers and to welfare mothers, and have been humble in the presence of both. This experience was new to me and often challenged me to move out of the comfort zone of my own family and circle of friends, to witness the strength and vision that these women bring to the world.

Most Americans know people who look and act similar to them. When I started thinking about motherhood, I reflected mostly on the plight of educated and professional women like me. But in the middle of my research journey, I started an email exchange with a group called M*A*M*A, or Mothers Alliance for Militant Action, based in Manhattan's Lower East Side. They were planning an event for Mother's Day called Mamas Rising Up, a political alternative to the ubiquitous Mother's Day brunch. The origin of Mother's Day is political, after all; Julia Ward Howe envisioned a Mother's Day of "worldwide protest of women against the cruelties of war." I had read about M*A*M*A's work getting activist communities to recognize the needs of mothers and families, and had seen a stirring account of a small action they did at Eastertime in which they dressed up as Easter bunnies and protested the local Kmart's choice to sell Easter baskets stocked with toy guns. I've always been partial to creative actions, so since my family and I were planning to be in New York on the weekend of Mamas Rising Up, we arranged our day to attend the festivities that were planned for a small park on the Lower East Side off Avenue B.

Because rain threatened, the celebration was held instead at the Campos Community Center, a center in a low-income housing project. The first time I walked by the alternate site, I saw the small Mamas Rising Up sign, but pretended not to. I had no idea what the inside of a housing project looked like, and—I want to admit this—it scared me. I continued to walk, not sure what to do. I didn't know the area, I didn't know the people. I walked. A bit later, I circled back and found the front door and followed the signs. Comfort zones are good things to challenge, and if I was sincere about making sure we think about class as we think about motherhood, I was going to have to walk in that door. As it turned out, the gym inside Campos Community Center was quite lovely, everyone welcomed me, and what I saw inside inspired me to keep writing. After the short time I spent at Campos, I started seeking out poor women, welfare mothers, and former welfare recipients, convinced they had something to teach me and others with regard to family policy.

Angie is twenty-five. She has a degree in political science from the University of Montana with a minor in Native American studies. She was a year away from finishing when she became pregnant; the father was a man whom she didn't trust to parent her child.

"I didn't know what to do," she tells me. "I was in my senior year, and I was facing single motherhood. I was totally on my own. I was at school in Missoula, and my family lives over in Helena. It was complicated. I could only get welfare support if I first went after the baby's father for child support."

Angie didn't want the father in her life, and he didn't want to be part of the baby's. He had already come round to Angie's workplace with a new woman, introduced her as his fiancée, told everyone in hearing distance that the baby Angie carried was his, and then walked off, laughing. Angie didn't want to tangle with him legally, even though she could have used the money: "He was flaky, inconsistent. He told me he wouldn't marry me. He didn't come to the birth. He's never even seen the baby, and he went ahead and married that girl." She never wanted to end up in a situation where the baby's father came by and said, "I'm paying for him, now I want to see him; now I want to harass you and be part of your life."

"I couldn't get on TANF (Temporary Assistance for Needy Families) unless they went after child support, but I couldn't go that route," she says. She wanted to finish school. And she really didn't want to enter the state's welfare system with its requirement that mothers of infants work full-time and put their babies in subsidized daycare. "I was really in a bind."

Angie was resourceful enough to pick up the telephone and place a call for help. She found Mary Caferro, an organizer for WEEL and a mother of three girls and a boy, on the other end. WEEL (Working for Equality & Economic Liberation) is a grassroots economic and social justice nonprofit made up of people experiencing poverty and their supporters. WEEL is dedicated to putting poor people first and encourages leadership and opportunities to use their collective voice to effect compassionate social change. Thinking carefully about women and work and motherhood is central to what WEEL does. "Caregiving is work," Caferro says on the group's website. "Parenting my children is the most important job of my life. We as a society need to view raising children as work. . . . We will change the debate. We have to, it is about our lives."

Angie's star was shining that day because WEEL had just convinced the Early Childhood Services Bureau of Montana's Department of Public Health & Human Services to inaugurate a pilot program called At-Home Infant Care (AHIC) that offered poor women the chance to stay home with their infants and go through a parent-directed education component instead of signing up for welfare, agreeing to its work requirements, and using a daycare subsidy to make work possible.

"Mary at WEEL suggested the At-Home Infant Care program," Angie tells me. "It had just gotten started. I was able to live off that plus financial aid from school. I was taking eighteen credits, full-time, to finish. I brought my baby to class; the teachers understood. The AHIC program let me finish my college degree. It let me stay home and raise my own child."

Here's what would have happened if Angie didn't luck into the few months the pilot program for AHIC was in place. She would have gone on welfare. Most likely she would have left school, since most welfare caseworkers don't tell their clients that they can stay in school, and many states require upwards of thirty hours a week of low-grade work in order to receive a welfare check. Angie would have ended up without a college degree and with a few years of low-paying, dead-end work experience instead. Her child would have been in daycare pretty much full-time. The state would be paying her welfare stipend and sending her a voucher for an even larger amount in the form of daycare subsidy for her son.

Here's what Montana's At-Home Infant Care program provided her, instead: Angie finished her college degree. She didn't have to put her son in daycare, which in Montana is scarce. When her son was a year old she started a home daycare to make money, and she now takes care of six children. "I run a daycare so I can work and still stay home with my son," she tells me. "Finishing college allowed me opportunity, a stable chance for a career when Avery starts school. I can support us. I can give back to the community. Especially since I went on the welfare system, I want to give back. This program was a godsend. Life is about family. There was one less stress on my shoulders. I could focus on being a mother, provide a better future for myself and my son. It allowed me to be the mother I wanted to be. It gave me assurance that my son would have a future, that he would have the basics."

At-home infant care programs exist in Minnesota, Missouri, and Montana, three states out of fifty. When I learned about WEEL through the policy grapevine, I tracked down Caferro. She sat me down and made sure I understood not just the program, and not just the way that in 2003 WEEL successfully pulled the bill through Montana's legislative session, but the process itself—what it meant, and the vision and the people behind it.[4]

"What's most important here," Caferro began, "is to understand how At-Home Infant Care got started and who started it. WEEL is an organization of low-income families. We're not an 'advocacy' organization. I don't go out and advocate on behalf of low-income people. I organize low-income people so they can advocate on their own behalf because they know the real solutions." Caferro hadn't always been the organizer. She had joined WEEL as a mom on welfare. She had left an abusive relationship, and to support her kids she got a second job: "I went from working at a daycare to going home, loading up my kids, and taking them to evening daycare. I waitressed at the Brew Pub. I got off late and I would go and pick up my kids and take them home.

"I had no skills," she said. "I couldn't even write a sentence; I didn't know how to turn on a computer." People kept telling her to check into public assistance and see what was available. She resisted for a while, but she wasn't getting any child support from the kids' father: "Then I thought, 'My children are really suffering.' And so I went and applied. I thought of welfare as a child support program." Eventually, she quit her day job, went to college, waitressed at night, and got on welfare. "I knew because I had joined WEEL that I had the right to go to college," she explained, "even though my caseworker discouraged it." She was on welfare and nearly done with college when the organizer for WEEL left. Caferro applied for the job and got it. "It's really in my blood," she said.

The year was 2000 and the board members of WEEL were huddled around a conference table talking about how life could be better for low-income women with children. Most of the women at the table had once been poor enough themselves to qualify once for state assistance.

Now, with their life experience, their college degrees, their positions in the community, and, mostly, their compassion, they were brainstorming on what their next policy program would be. The staff organizer and director were taking notes when the mothers on the board told them, "We want parenting to count as work."

That's how it went, Caferro recalls. "We were planning our legislative platform for the next year, and the women on the board said, 'We need parenting to count as work.'" Simple as that.

Caferro remembers thinking, "Okay, great, that's going to fly. . . . " She and other staff members asked the board to keep telling them what they meant. The answer was both conceptual and very practical. After the Welfare Reform Act of 1996, people who received monthly state assistance needed to work thirty hours a week to receive their welfare checks. They could do a lot of things: They could watch someone else's children and have their job as a daycare worker count. But one thing they couldn't do was parent their own children and have it count as meaningful work. "The state would rather pay other people to watch your kids while you go out and do sometimes very meaningless work activities," says Caferro. "But there's no accorded value in watching your own kids." Parenting doesn't count; there's no economic value in it. Rather than value women's parenting labor, the government would rather pay double—that is, pay the woman on welfare/workfare and pay someone to watch her child. WEEL wanted that to change.

"These moms on our board said, 'We want parenting to count as work,'" Caferro recounts. "'You guys, go back, figure out how we're going to do it, and let's do it. This is what mothers need.' The staff thought, 'Oh my gosh, no way. Universal healthcare, minimum wage, anything but this!' They thought it would be impossible. But the board was adamant. They said, 'No, this is what is needed.'" None of the women on the board would benefit from a policy like this—they were all former welfare recipients, who were now self sustaining. Most had older children. One's a single mother with a college degree who works for Qwest, another is a fundraiser for the Democratic Party. Another is married with five children and has a business with her husband caring for trees. Two others had just finished college. They weren't thinking about themselves, but about what might really help poor mothers.

These women were devoted to giving low-income families the same option to be home with their babies that other, more affluent mothers have. They wanted infants to have the opportunity to bond at home with their own parents. "They said, 'just do it,'" Caferro says, "and that's how At-Home Infant Care became our number-one priority for the upcoming legislative session that would begin in January 2001."

WEEL's staff set out to research the problem. They found out that Minnesota had a similar program on the books. "We modeled ours after that," explains Caferro, "but made it into a stronger policy for families. And that's how it all got started. It's important to know that this whole thing that has just gone crazy started from women recognizing that their children deserved better, and that social policy has done a three-sixty. Welfare started out as a program for children so that children could be home with their moms. Now it's a program that takes moms away from their children. Our state is willing to pay a daycare provider to watch children while their mom goes out to work. That's twice the amount of money as at-home infant care would cost. This is bridging what really needs to happen with social policy, and we've been working our butts off ever since."

To put this in context, in a study of daycare costs for infants in cities, the National Partnership for Women & Families found that infant daycare cost more than public college tuition in every state, averaging $5,750 a year in urban areas. Further, 40 percent of the buildings used by infant daycare providers were in such poor condition that they actually jeopardized kids' health and safety.[5]

Once word got out, the Montana Department of Public Health & Human Services (HHS) came to WEEL and said, "Don't try and legislate this yet, we can work it out." Health & Human Services wanted to do a pilot program. WEEL had already written up a bill. They already had a legislative sponsor when HHS' Early Childhood Services Bureau wrote a letter saying that it would implement AHIC. Says Caferro, "HHS saw how it worked for them. They didn't necessarily think, 'Hey, this is great for moms and kids, let's do it.' No, they saw that it would save them money, and it would be a solution to the shortage of infant care, especially in rural Montana. You can tell low-income people and moms on welfare to work, but if there's no childcare, they can't do it."

AHIC began in 2002 with a $150,000 budget and it was extremely successful. It served fifty-two families, all of whom earned within 150 percent of the poverty line. For a family of two, that's $18,180 a year; for three, it's $22,890, and a family of four can qualify if they earn under $27,600 annually. The AHIC rates were limited to whatever the maximum cost was for childcare. Some of the families had more than one child; one family had triplets and received three payments. Families received $378 a month per child, and a family could still qualify for food stamps, subsidized housing, or Medicaid if they needed it.

The bureau thought the program would be too controversial in a conservative state like Montana. It thought that if too many people knew about it, flares of controversy would spark; the bureau feared criticism over returning to the initial impetus of welfare in this country (supporting mothers so they could be home with their children), the impetus that the welfare reform bill sponsored by President Clinton in 1996 had done so much to change. Although HHS had a media program set to advertise AHIC, it nixed it. WEEL got going instead. It began sending out press releases and public service ads; it did interviews and went to cable access channels and left packets of info at WIC offices. It sent flyers to all the childcare providers in the state who were more than happy to put them up.

In this alternative to the Mommy Wars, which in any case are always supposed to be limited to the affluent classes, daycare providers and advocates of at-home care worked together. "We covered all our bases," Caferro tells me. "We talked with the childcare providers and asked them how they would feel about this project. They were supportive. In Montana, people aren't bending over backward to become childcare providers for infants. There's a shortage and if a provider has infants, you can only have so many, according to the law. I was a childcare provider for years, and we have a strong network. What we found out was that in Montana, providers said, 'Go for it. This can't hurt me.' Maybe it's different in other states, but we have a shortage of providers. There's professionalism among childcare providers. AHIC is about options. It's not about competition. They're children, not a commodity or a market product."

The irony, I suppose, is that in 2002–2003, when the program was in place, a mother and child on welfare would receive around $270 per month. Because the AHIC program was set up around labor, around the actual payments that daycares would have received for caring for an infant, the AHIC check was significantly higher at $378 per month. A mother working for welfare received a smaller take-home check, but in fact, her family cost the government a great deal more, as she was also given vouchers for daycare, as much as $421 per month for an infant, as low as $340 per month for an older preschool child. The standards of payment were set around what HHS actually figured was the cost of caring for an infant. "The program really looks at it from this perspective: The parent is the primary childcare provider and should be reimbursed the same," Caferro says. "It's the total opposite of welfare. We found that a lot of two-parent families accessed it, especially in rural Montana, and Mom would be home with the baby and it would be enough to bridge the gap between total poverty and being able to stay home with the baby. One woman continued to go to college while she was doing this. Another couple, both continued to work, but they were able to cut back on hours because it gave them enough to make ends meet. There were all different kinds of situations."

The pilot program ended in 2003 due to a bureaucratic snafu. That same year, the Montana legislature was in session (it meets every other year); Gail Gutsche, a Democrat, sponsored House Bill 569 (to authorize the creation of an AHIC program), and John Bohlinger, a Republican, introduced AHIC in the state senate and the bill passed. But Montana was in steep financial decline that year, and the bill was signed into law that April by Governor Judy Martz without any mandate for funding. It's law, but there's no money yet put aside for it.

Caferro describes the process:

By 2003 [we'd] had three years to build up a solid base of support. The bill passed out of the house committee unanimously. It passed the house with a good majority. It passed out of senate committee and made it to the floor. There was some poor-bashing on the floor, some bad comments about oversexed low-income women and wouldn't this bill just encourage promiscuity, that kind of stuff. Senator Carolyn Squires responded, "Promiscuity, that doesn't come with an income level. I want to tell you, go down to the local bar where many legislators hang out, if we want to talk about promiscuity."

Some of the senators stood up and brought it right back to what it was: This is a bill about children; this is a bill about infants who otherwise would not have a chance to be home and bond with their parents. That's what this is about. One senator stood up, and she's a former welfare mom, and she just called them on it. And the bill passed. Conservatives like it. Liberals like it. The mental health community supports it, as does the medical community, the churches, and Native Americans, who make up about 40 percent of the population living in poverty. We had moms and dads come to the state house with their babies, families who had signed up for the AHIC when it was a pilot program. They met with senators personally, they lobbied, they testified to the committees. They brought their babies in their packs. I'd say the babies were the ones who got the bill passed. The babies would flirt with the legislators, with all the grandpas, who then wanted to go home and see their grandchildren.

Even in 2003, a few Republican senators told her they could make the funding happen. Human services throughout the state were being cut, though, and the WEEL board members had a different perspective on things. "When those three Republicans told me they could get it funded, I went back to talk with WEEL's members about it," Caferro explains. "On the board there's one woman with advanced-stage renal disease, and another with breast cancer, and both their programs were being eliminated. And the women said, 'You know what, let's not go for funding this time. We're looking at programs that are getting cut for the same amount that AHIC might get funded. It feels like we're taking money away from people; let's wait till next session, till things get better.' It was a conscious decision by the membership to wait till the next session. They didn't want to be taking money away from others."

"We'll return in 2005 and get it funded," promises Caferro. AHIC is already funded in Minnesota. In Missouri, it's financed by a portion of the entry fees to riverboat casinos.

Low-income mothers deserve options, true options, and the work of mothering deserves value in the welfare system that structures the lives of low-income families, whether they are on welfare or emerging off it. What about those people who think that all parents deserve extra money to care for young children? Middle-class families struggle to come up with the thousands of dollars required for daycare, not to mention the tens of thousands needed to hire an au pair or a full-time babysitter. AHIC merely starts with the families who need assistance the most. Daycare, sociologist Julie E. Press tells us, is one of the elements that makes it hardest for poor women to consistently show up for work.[6] To critics who say that welfare mothers need to go right out and gain work experience, WEEL responds that mothers will be able to work more consistently once their infants grow; that AHIC allows low-income families a chance to find some stability, to bond together as a family; and that these bonds will allow parents to be more stable and consistent in the workplace when their children are a bit older.

WEEL, too, finds itself answering questions about feminist priorities and encountering the criticism that it's reinforcing conservative and oppressive notions that women belong at home caring for kids. That's the wrong issue. WEEL is complicatedly trying to expand the options for poor women that more affluent women already have. Abstraction and ideology aside, large numbers of mothers in America do not work full-time, and low-income mothers want this possibility too. When the National Partnership for Women & Families announced that Congresswoman Rosa DeLauro, a Connecticut Democrat, had introduced a bill on At-Home Infant Care to the United States Congress, the move was described not in Mommy Wars terms, but as a boon to "working families, giving parents the chance to care for children during their essential early years of life, without risking the family's financial stability."[7]

As the National Partnership notes, in urban areas the average cost of infant childcare exceeds the average cost of public college tuition. And unlike many state welfare systems, AHIC allows mothers to attend college, and this, as in Angie's case, gives them a chance for better jobs later. And mothers can switch from AHIC back to the regular welfare system whenever they want. In any case, AHIC ends when the children reach age two, the government's definition of the end of infancy. WEEL wants a "both/and" perspective on work and childraising for women whose choices in life are remarkably limited. They want, in other words, all of a mother's work to count.

꒛

Jonathan Baird is the director of policy advocacy at New Hampshire Legal Services, the legal aid office in Claremont, New Hampshire. He's a fiftyish man, once described by *USA Today* as "a bearded lawyer with scruffy jeans," who has devoted his life to working with people who are poor and protecting their legal rights.

One of Baird's most pressing goals is to provide some opportunities for work-family balance for low-income Americans. Baird recently argued and won an important case regarding part-time workers, new mothers, and the unemployment codes. New Hampshire's cash assistance for unemployed workers only covers full-time workers—in real terms, those who work thirty-seven or more hours per week and are available to work all shifts, daytime and evening. The only exception to this rule is that single parents are exempt from having to seek third-shift work and don't have to be available to work the overnight shift. In other words, facing some hard luck and the loss of a job, an out-of-work parent might still be faced with having to accept a 3–11:00 PM evening job if it's the first offer that comes along, even though it means losing after-school and dinnertime contact with their kids.

The current definitions date back to the New Deal and the 1930s, when President Roosevelt initiated the unemployment compensation program. When they created the program, policymakers had in mind the male breadwinner who had a wife at home. It didn't matter then, as now, that many married women and mothers did work; it was just that only men's work was seen as needing protection should it disappear. Women's wages were nice, helpful even, but not considered primary, even when they were.

Since the '30s, everything has changed: economy, gender roles, the nature of work, and the jobs that are available. While the law assumes that full-time hours are the norm, many large workplaces have changed. Many employers—think Wal-Mart, for example—hire mostly part-time workers. They cut their labor costs by making sure that they don't have to pay into health insurance and other benefit programs. If only full-time workers qualify for health benefits, one way to escape soaring employer premiums is to only hire part-time help. Many sales jobs, Wal-Mart-type jobs, typically schedule salespeople for twenty-four hours a week.

In defending part-time workers, Baird had another angle to think about as well. Some people need to work part-time or they need to combine part-time jobs in order to care for their children or for elderly or sick relatives. They might work a sales shift some days, a factory shift others, and a cleaning job on the weekend because the time in between means they can be home for dinner or pick their kids up from school. They may work full-time hours or more in total, but not through a single employer, in order to have a bit more flexibility or because good full-time jobs are hard to find. New Hampshire law states that in order to collect unemployment payments, workers must be available to work a single job full-time and all shifts (single parents excepted). According to Baird and his client, a new mom who worked in a factory, this regulation isn't fair to parents of young children and especially to breastfeeding mothers, who believe the law should account for their particular situations and needs to work fewer hours or to have more flexibility.

Here was the case on the docket: A woman worker had a new baby and wanted to go back to work. She also was breastfeeding. Her shift was set up so that she had to work "straight through," so she wasn't able to pump milk. She wanted to go back to work, and she wanted to work part-time for family reasons. When she was laid off, she was denied unemployment benefits because these require that the worker be ready and able to work full-time, which she wasn't, given that she had a small baby at home and was breastfeeding. Family obligations really do preclude full-time employment for many parents who envision more than placing a three-week-old baby in full-time, poor-quality daycare that takes much of a near-minimum-wage check. Remember, poor women, too, want to be around their kids, want some relief from work, want some choices. Poor women, too, should be able to breastfeed. They too want some change from a workplace that defines work around an ideal worker with no family obligations. In this case, the woman won the hearing when she promised that she was willing to breastfeed at work, and that she would be willing to accept full-time work if she got a job.

As I enter the world of legal activists who are trying to secure greater possibilities for parents caring for their youngest children, I am struck by the minutiae to which they must attend. The array of state and federal programs is dazzling and confusing. The world of public assistance and welfare encompasses a continent of programs, each with different eligibility rules. Political campaigns are waged on slogans and broad demands. For every handmade sign that demands paid family leave, for every dinnertime conversation about how people of all classes deserve more real choices about childraising, work, and childcare, there are hundreds of tired, bleary-eyed, underpaid attorneys sorting the law, imagining new law, fighting judges and politicians and employers on a case-by-case basis as they pave the way for more structural legal change. They know all the programs, and they know the body of law developed around each one. They know the hearing officers and administrative law judges on the third-tier circuits where cases about unemployment, disability, Social Security, and TANF are heard.

Cases that can chip away at the law, that can make these regulations more responsive to family needs, are battled state to state. Each state sets its own unemployment code, and now welfare codes have been devolved to the states as well. In the old way of providing entitlement programs to people who needed them, there were codes of federal regulation. A single federal code affected all fifty states. Changes and challenges to the code were made centrally, and then affected the whole nation. Now, with a welfare reform program that sends block grants to each state, there cannot be a team of attorneys who lobby one set of politicians—say, U.S. senators, or members of the House of Representatives—or who work with the Department of Labor. Instead, each state has different regulations, its own politicians, its own judges elected or appointed to the bench. Attempts to change these programs have been made fifty times harder, and fifty times more exasperating and expensive.

The last major federal bill for families was the Family and Medical Leave Act, signed into law by Bill Clinton in 1993. The FMLA provides twelve weeks of unpaid leave for both mother and father to care for a newborn, a newly adopted child, or a seriously ill family member, or to recover from a serious health condition. Because the law faced so much resistance from the business community, it applies only to workplaces with fifty or more employees. Since 1993, there has developed a body of law wherein people can use the FMLA regulations to get time off from work, without pay, but also without penalty. Still, though touted as a major step forward—and it is—the FMLA is not a perfect answer. Currently, 41 percent of the workforce is not offered any protection by the FMLA, and two-thirds of those eligible for FMLA leave don't take it because they can't afford to. An estimated 10 percent of the families who use FMLA leave go on some kind of public assistance to make ends meet.[8] If FMLA has only a possibility of working for middle-class people, it is even harder to make it work for people with less income, for those with even greater worries about paying the next month's rent and who aren't sure where the money to cover daycare is going to come from in an already meager minimum-wage job.

Further, many low-wage employees work for small businesses that aren't covered by the FMLA. In New Hampshire, for instance, the majority of businesses look less like Wal-Mart and more like a mom-and-pop corner store with five employees; thus, most businesses aren't required to offer their workers any time off after birthing or adopting a child. Even if they could afford a few weeks without a paycheck, these workers are not guaranteed leave by law. If they are temporary workers, they have no vacation or personal-day benefits, and no job security at all.

"The FMLA passed in the mid-'90s," Baird tells me. "If United States social policy were more rational, we would be talking now about incremental steps to improve on it and expand. The U.S. is one of the

few countries without paid family leave. We are out of the global mainstream on this issue. The president and Congress have moved so far to
the right. Still, these issues are logical, and they are widely supported
by Americans. A movement can't get traction because the Congress
and most of the state houses have moved so far to the right.
Furthermore, with the move to state grants, there is no longer a way to
fight for this on a national stage. Possibilities for work and family balance for poor people have to take place locally. It's state specific. It's a
laboratory of the states."

Beneath the radar of media attention, Legal Aid attorneys have
been working hard to expand the number of people who are eligible for
unpaid family leave by making it apply to businesses with fewer than
fifty employers. They are also at work trying to institute a new legal
trend: paid family leave. Of 168 nations studied (out of 193 in the
world), the United States is one of only five countries that don't offer
paid family leave (the others are Lesotho, Papua New Guinea,
Swaziland, and Australia; the last does, however, offer fifty-two weeks
of unpaid family leave).[9]

Paid family leave sounds radical, doesn't it? In New Hampshire,
advocates convinced the governor to establish a committee to study
these issues and suggest legislation. The committee looked to other
states and recommended establishing a "Family and Disability Trust
Fund." That was in 2001. The next year, House Bill 744 was introduced. It aimed to implement the fund for family and temporary disability leave, but began by establishing a committee of legislators to
hash out the details, and of course, the funding. The bill died in the
committee and went nowhere. Advocates are still strategizing about
new and more effective strategies with the legislature to secure parental
leave. Small businesses say they can't afford family leave as it is: They
rely on their workers, and often, the business is barely squeaking by.
Paid family leave would kill small businesses, they claim. They may be
honestly buckling under the rising cost-pressure of employee health

insurance, the costs of caring for pregnant employees and their growing families, and competition from larger stores, global companies, and the Internet. Or they might be trying to protect their own profits by keeping their labor costs as low as they can.

The National Partnership for Women & Families polled Americans in 1998: Should the FMLA be expanded to cover midsize companies (that is, with twenty-five or more employees, instead of the current fifty employees)? The support was staggering: 84 percent of women said yes, as did 74 percent of men. Supporters included working mothers and at-home mothers, Democrats (87 percent in support) and Republicans (70 percent), people across ethnic and racial communities, and people of all ages. The National Partnership poll also asked about paid family leave. The response: 82 percent of women were in favor, as were 75 percent of the men.[10]

Paid family leave sounds radical and utopian until you realize that the state of California has already signed it into law, and that other states are considering similar programs. On January 1, 2004, California began collecting an additional payroll tax from all employees. Six months later, the first grants were made. The bill was sponsored by Senator Sheila Kuehl, elected in 2000 to represent State Senate District 23 in Los Angeles. Before that she had served six years in the state assembly, rising to become the first woman ever to serve as its speaker pro tempore. She's also the first openly gay or lesbian member of the California legislature. As it stands, any employee who needs to take time off work to tend to a new child, a seriously ill child, or spouse, or parent, or domestic partner—yes, this bill even includes domestic partners—can receive partial wages of about 55 percent up to the maximum amount of $728 per week. Here's how it works. The check for replaced wages comes from the state disability fund, California's temporary disability fund. California workers already contribute to the fund through an automatic payroll tax. To cover the additional use for family leave, the tax was raised by .08 percent. That costs each worker an average of twenty-seven dollars a year.[11]

California's paid family leave emerged during a unique political moment brought about by a Democratic legislature, the Democratic governorship of Gray Davis (before his recall), and a coalition of women's groups and labor unions. And it makes a big difference. Marie Crawford of San Jose was among the first parents to apply. She was thrilled to hear about the program on the nightly news and tracked down the forms so that she and two other women at her San Jose workplace could use the program. With paid family leave, she was able to take the full twelve weeks that the national FMLA provides; otherwise, she would have had to return to work much earlier.

For Christina and her family in Mill Valley, the program was an absolute blessing. Her husband was unemployed at the time of their baby's birth, and at six weeks, when Christina's disability leave ran out, her baby was still nursing through the night. "With my husband out of work," she says, "paid family leave made all the difference in the world as we made the huge adjustment to life as a family."

If you take the Golden Gate Bridge north out of San Francisco, you'll end up in California's Sixth Congressional District, represented since 1992 by Congresswoman Lynn Woolsey. Woolsey describes herself as the only former welfare mother to serve in the U.S. Congress. When her children were young, even though she was working, Woolsey accepted public assistance to make ends meet. Experiencing life as a mother, as a person living at poverty's edge, and as a parent concerned with getting a decent public education for her children and everyone's children, Woolsey, when her kids were grown, got up the gumption to run for Congress. Many terms later, she's the assistant whip and part of the House Democratic leadership.

In February 2004, Woolsey and her staff, along with twenty-nine cosponsors, proposed HR 3780, the Family and Workplace Balancing Act of 2004, a bill to improve working families' lives. The next month it was sent for consideration to the Subcommittee on Education Reform, where Woolsey is the ranking member and the top Democrat.

Woolsey strikes ahead. "We're interested in a real pro-family agenda," she says. "The Balancing Act addresses the issues families struggle with at the kitchen table." She takes on that "sane social policy" and pushes forward. The sections of her bill read like a dream list of family help. It's hard to imagine this on the floor of Congress, snaking its way through Rayburn Building staff cubicles and conferences: "a comprehensive bill that improves the lives of working families by providing paid leave for new parents, school events, and family emergencies; improving the quality and availability of child care, in-school nutrition, and after school assistance; funding voluntary universal preschool, and encouraging a family friendly work place."

So in the world according to Woolsey and twenty-nine other congressional representatives, here's what parents might expect: family leave with wage replacement after birth or adoption, to respond to a family emergency, or on days spread throughout the year so that parents and grandparents could take limited leave to be more active in their children's schools. This builds on a New Jersey proposal that lets parents take off sixteen hours a year from work—without penalty—in order to be part of their kids' educational lives. It helps all working parents be part of our school communities.

The Woolsey bill would expand childcare grants for kids under three and for kids with disabilities. It imagines scholarships for childcare providers—to increase their currently low pay, to help them improve their own educations, to make sure that the people watching kids in daycare can provide better-quality care than many kids currently get. It shouldn't cost ten thousand dollars a year to get good day-

care in our country. It shouldn't be limited to the children of the affluent. Woolsey would authorize the Housing and Urban Development
authority to provide mortgages for new daycare buildings or provide
funds to renovate old ones. The bill would also provide funds to businesses, or groups of businesses, to create on-site childcare.

The voluntary universal preschool part of the bill would authorize
the Secretary of Health and Human Services to make grants to the
states so that they could create high-quality, full-day, full-year pre-K
programs for three- and four- and five-year-old kids. Nutritious breakfasts would be given to all kids who need them, nutritional foods would
be available throughout the day, and the government would reimburse
providers for dinners served to students in after-school programs. And
speaking of after-school programs, the Woolsey bill wants funds made
available for all schools who become part of the 21st Century
Community Learning Centers after-school program.

Woolsey has vision, and she knows that the world of care for children is part of the world of schools, is part of the world of work. Only
policies that change all these things in tandem have a chance of making a meaningful difference. So title IV part A of the Balancing Act is
the Part-time and Temporary Workers Benefits Act; it makes sure that
these workers will be eligible for the same benefits as full-time employees, on a prorated basis, as long as they work more than five hundred
hours per year.

Expensive, I hear all of us saying. *Impossible. Never in our country.*
Yes, but as the congresswoman tells us, "If we can cut taxes for the rich-
est Americans; if we can preemptively go to war; and, if we can even
think about sending a man to Mars, we can give families the tools they
need to be both responsible parents and responsible employees."

The culture has changed, and we need to change with it. "We used
to be a nation of predominantly nuclear families with one breadwinner
who went to work each day and a full-time parent who minded the
domestic front," says Congresswoman Woolsey.

Today, for complex economic and cultural reasons, more than two-thirds of families have two parents—or one unmarried parent—working outside the home.

But our government hasn't been responsive enough to these changes in the American family. Amid this socioeconomic revolution, public policy remains largely stuck in an Ozzie and Harriet world. . . . It's time we have a comprehensive, holistic approach to family policies.

"Will it get passed?" Woolsey asks. "No. Do we want to start talking about this so someday people will pay attention? Yes."

If federal legislation like the Balancing Act were to become law, Legal Aid attorneys would no longer need to fight these things one at a time, case by case, state by state, each time a poor parent finds the path into their offices seeking help in navigating the system. Some institutional, structural change would have been made.

So what does change look like up close? Washington, D.C., and the imposing Capitol building seem so far away. Its offices are mysterious, and who among us can sort through the labyrinthine committee structure of the U.S. Congress? As I've learned to do throughout this project, I picked up the phone and dialed, and within a few minutes was speaking to both the senior legislative assistant and the press secretary in Congresswoman Woolsey's office. It was as much of a reminder as I needed that change happens through individual people doing their work day after day.

As it turned out, the Balancing Act didn't go too far in the 108th Congress in 2004. It's a big bill and its contents touch the concerns of many different committees. By the end of the year, in the Republican-controlled Congress, it had yet to have a hearing in all these different committees. Now, the Woolsey team is looking toward 2005's 109th congressional session, when they'll be reintroducing the bill. Perhaps they will break it into pieces. The Balancing Act provides a big-picture scenario, but it is made up of lots of specific, smaller changes, each of which can be painstakingly guided throughout the appropriate com-mittees and subcommittees of the U.S. House of Representatives. It's painstaking work to make social change, to find enough family-friendly members who will embrace paid family leave and have no trouble pro-viding all those breakfasts and dinners to schoolchildren and benefits and fair pay to part-time working parents.

To promote the message, the congresswoman's staff is talking with a coalition of organizations—groups like the National Partnership for Women & Families, Legal Momentum, the New America Foundation, the Children's Defense Fund, and Americans for Democratic Action. These organizations provide briefings on the Hill to educate representa-tives and their staffers. They educate their own members to provide some urgency and pressure. On the day I called Woolsey's office, Legal Momentum had just posted an action alert about the bill and asked its members to send letters in support. And on the phone, talking about her shock at the Knight Ridder coverage of the bill—apparently they con-sidered it silly that you might need federal money to upgrade the equip-ment at childcare centers—Woolsey's press secretary Susannah Cernojevich sounds, well, as thoughtful, and as wonderfully ordinary and real as any parent you'd meet at the playground or at your kid's school.[12]

Change is about people, whether it's in the state capitals or D.C. or our neighborhoods. Change might look like ordinary letter-writer Carol McClintock, who reads through the morning newspaper and gets mad enough at an article about Social Security that she pens a letter to the editor, published a few days afterward. Quoting the upsetting original— "One benefit that should be cut is the retirement benefit paid to spouses who have never worked or paid into the system. . . . The only people who can afford not to work are those with wealthy spouses"— she writes back:

I am a stay-at-home mother of four. I worked full-time for four years early in my marriage and saved so that when children came along, I could be at home with them. We can afford this "luxury" not because we are wealthy but because we live within our means. Many young couples with two incomes buy homes and cars based on these incomes. When they start their families, both parents have to work in order to make ends meet.

I shouldn't be denied benefits that my husband contributed to simply because I haven't worked in ten years and therefore must be well off. My husband and I prioritized. Stay-at-home caregivers should not be denied benefits on the ignorant assumption that they must not need it.[13]

From the world of TANF, low-income mothers, cramped Legal Aid offices, and visionary legislation for educating daycare workers, Carol's middle-class world is ordinary luxury, with its long-lived stability and modesty of style. Often in the public discussion and rhetoric of motherhood, the needs of a middle-class homemaker like Carol are pitted against the needs of, say, a Kmart employee. The experience, or stereotype, of each is twisted to devalue the needs of both. Class difference is used to split a wedge between women. Both these women's positions and needs are important, and in a chapter on change and how mothers become civically engaged, we need to see poor mothers, middle-class mothers, and affluent mothers together on the same page. Carol, if she is Internet savvy, might find herself on the homepage of MOTHERS (Mothers Ought To Have Equal Rights), an organization founded by authors Ann Crittenden and Naomi Wolf, and the National Association of Mothers' Centers.[14]

The MOTHERS homepage is framed with assumptions of middle-class life. There are requests for volunteers and for new members to "Join the team of 'midwives' birthing the MOTHERS initiative for the economic well-being of caregivers"; a link for sending donations to

MOTHERS; and a link to iGive.com, the website that donates a percentage of profits to nonprofit organizations. This is a page for middle-class women—not the super-affluent, whose trust funds or inheritances or stock portfolios or partners' salaries make ordinary financial concerns like Social Security seem petty, but women of stable if modest means.

This website aims for the majority of ordinary mothers, women who are the focus of MOTHERS's political calling card: "The work of caring for children and other dependent family members is still unpaid or grossly underpaid, disrespected, and unacknowledged by all of the major institutions in our society. We believe that correcting the economic disadvantages facing caregivers is the big unfinished business of the women's movement."

Mothering may seem private, something we do at home, with our families, and in the social networks of our neighborhoods and communities; after all, we inherit a cultural legacy that insists domestic life and care are not work, are not public. MOTHERS insists on reminding us that mothering happens within public view, and that it happens within public policy, and that we probably want to open that letter that comes from the Social Security Administration once each year—the one with the chart on the second page that predicts just how much money we will draw down when we turn sixty-five—because any mother or father who leaves full-time work, either to work fully at home with the kids, or to work partially for pay and partially not, will find that decision reflected in her or his Social Security benefits. The putatively private, domestic decision of how to care for one's children, and how to do so amid a life of wage-earning work, turns out to be tracked by that most public and federal of agencies, the Social Security Administration. These are private decisions with public consequences, which renders false the claim that they ever were private in the first place. Our society, our government, does not count unpaid caregiving labor in the GDP, the gross domestic product, the accounting of all the work that is done. Neither does unpaid caregiving accrue any Social Security retirement benefits. As a result, stay-at-home caregivers—whether they're mothers or fathers—find themselves outside this fundamental safety net for old age.

MOTHERS's current political campaign highlights the issue of Social Security credits for homemakers; on Mother's Day 2004, it asked members that in addition to brunch or breakfast in bed or flowers and cards they fax lawmakers on these issues. When asked why they are so focused on the credits issue, the group had several answers. The issue hits a nerve around the country: Those zeroes are powerful—can it be that the government truly puts zero value on raising children? Other organizations have taken up issues like paid leave—but amid the ongoing discussions about privatizing Social Security and turning it into personal savings accounts, MOTHERS notes, no one else is raising critical questions about what happens to mothers. Mothers, they argue, would do even worse under the Republican-proposed system.

MOTHERS wants fathers to share. In its vision of how to offer Social Security credits, one suggestion is to have spouses share equally the credits earned during marriage. Husbands would earn fewer, home-making wives more—again, a division that wouldn't matter much if they stay together, but would provide equity for childraising labor if they don't. In this proposal, other taxpayers don't pay, but neither is the mother's labor really accounted for in terms of the whole family, which just ends up with the credits the father earned anyway. In another suggestion, the U.S. Treasury could shoulder some of the cost or its entirety. Families could pay in for their retirement; in other words, if a father is working, he could put two thousand dollars a year into a Social Security credit for the mother of his children, and the fees involved could be done on a sliding scale to make the option affordable to lower-income families. There could be a five-year cap on the home-making credit. Any of these options would provide more security for mothers in their old age.

MOTHERS doesn't want the government to pay women directly for having children, but it does want some recognition of the work that mothers do, and of the economic sacrifices that mothers make. Motherhood is the largest risk factor for sinking into poverty. Theoretically, nannies get Social Security, but mothers don't, despite doing the same work. Put this way, the issues facing middle-class home-makers are not all that different from those facing lower-income women. Women who quit their jobs for children face career loss and loss of salary, and they earn less over the course of their lives. Some of this doesn't matter as much as long as they stay with their partners, as long as money and its control is something that can be shared, no matter who earns it. But if it can't, or if the marriage falls apart and the children's other parent leaves, a mother sinks far and fast, and then security becomes a major issue.

So where's the playground revolution, the mothers and fathers who start talking out loud and acting together to make change? It might look like the women of WEEL, in Montana, who took on the huge issue of valuing mothering and succeeded in enacting very specific programs that did just that. The women of WEEL also challenge the stereotype that you have to be well educated and middle-class to be a leader and promote change. When I last checked in, it was fall 2004 and they were full steam ahead with their strategies for getting At-Home Infant Care funded once the Montana legislature returns to session in January 2005.

Or it might look like ordinary mothers and fathers resisting the Mommy Wars media out loud. Talking about it. Writing letters of complaint to newspapers and magazines and TV shows that continue to use outdated and harmful models for writing about women's lives. What might happen when we do start talking, asking questions, wondering what the policy people are up to? Or calling up the U.S. Census Bureau, as Kristin Rowe-Finkbeiner did, asking for numbers about women and motherhood and work, and moving into action when the bureau couldn't answer her questions because it wasn't really paying attention to how mothers are raising kids in and around work and home?

Rowe-Finkbeiner was a young mom. She was newly and unexpectedly at home. Her baby had been quite ill with asthma and allergies and all sorts of immune system problems. The combination of long hours and her son's health needs made it too difficult to continue work. Eight years later, he's healthy and Rowe-Finkbeiner's an at-home mom, a political consultant, and the author of *The F-Word: Feminism in Jeopardy*. *The F-Word* got started because one morning, Rowe-Finkbeiner was home with the baby and curious. "How many other stay-at-home mothers are there?" she wondered. So she picked up the telephone and she dialed the U.S. Census Bureau.

Of course, by the time she became a mother, Rowe-Finkbeiner had lots of number-crunching hours under her belt. She'd been a policy analyst and left the workforce as the political director for an environmental political action committee. She was used to calculating life in numbers, whether it was how people voted, precinct by precinct, for candidates, or how many mothers were home with their kids. The year was 2000, and after several fruitless conversations, it became clear to Rowe-Finkbeiner that the U.S. Census had missed something vital in its questions. It didn't know how to count full-time parents. "They couldn't tell me," she says. "They really couldn't tell me."[15]

How can we even know what's going on in the land of motherhood and parenting if our Census Bureau doesn't count us? Its latest study of American families at least offers some numbers and analysis of stay-at-home mothers and fathers, but there are no plans to add more detailed questions about why parents leave the workplace to parent. The Census Bureau wrangles over how to formulate and present these numbers. How can we even have policy discussions without reliable numbers? How can our society start valuing parents' unpaid labor if we don't even know what they're doing, if their work doesn't matter enough to be counted? Rowe-Finkbeiner was intrigued and continued dialing. Tracking down an economist from the Bureau of Labor Statistics, she was told that the BLS didn't "specifically track stay-at-home moms because they aren't relevant to the labor force." Further, mothers or fathers who wrote in "full-time parent" on their U.S. Census forms would have had their occupations classified automatically as category 995, "not in the labor force." Even if they tried to be counted, they wouldn't be.[16]

Even though the U.S. Census has begun to study the labor of at-home parenting, on its questionnaires it still repeats the old pattern that counts paid work and dismisses household labor and the care of children as nonexistent. So, too, did the Canadian census, and, as it turns out, nearly every census around the world. In 1985, the third UN World Conference on Women met in Nairobi. Among other action points, the delegates directed nations to recognize all the contributions, paid and unpaid, of women: to add "those contributions of women in agriculture, food production, reproduction, and household activities" to each nation's national economic statistics and to the tallying of its gross domestic product. Ten years later, the fourth World Conference on Women backed this up and again directed governments to begin efforts to measure unpaid work in their official government statistics. "Only when women's unwaged work is acknowledged and valued will women's demands and needs be valued," explained Ruth Todasco of the International Women Count Network.[17]

When Rowe-Finkbeiner went looking, she found Carol Lees, a mother of three children who lives in Saskatchewan, Canada. One day, Lees had answered a knock on her front door to find a fieldworker from Statistics Canada. After scanning the census form, Lees refused to fill it out because it would mean that she couldn't count what she did as a homemaker and mother as "work." The Canadian government took her refusal seriously. She soon received a letter from Ottawa that threatened her with full prosecution and penalties of jail time and fines. The government ordered her to fill out the form. Lees resisted and in response created the Canadian Alliance for Home Managers; she got involved with another group, too, Mothers Are Women/Mères et Femmes. The result: In 1996 the Canadian government added three questions about unpaid labor to the census.

Mothers Are Women/Mères et Femmes (MAW) is an organization for feminist mothers. Tired of receiving support for mothers' work only from right-wing organizations, and leery of those organizations' narrowness and ideology, MAW rises almost gracefully from the contradictions we all face: the assumption that women can do whatever interests us in the world of work, combined with the ways that mothers are limited by how relatively little gender roles at home have changed, so that mothers still do much of the domestic and childraising labor, through default, their own desire, or a combination of both.

As Mothers Are Women sees it, there are women for whom being with their kids is an affirmation of feminism, even though on the face it may not seem that way. MAW doesn't stop, though, at affirming the decision to be home. MAW focuses on what new social structures mothers need in order to raise their children. "We are mothers who have chosen to be the primary caregivers of our children and believe that the ability to exercise this choice without the threat of social or economic penalties is part of the struggle for equality," its website reads. "We believe that the work of caring for our children, for our families (however we define them), and for our communities must be recognized, respected, and valued. We maintain that until the unpaid work done by women in the home and community is understood and valued as work there will be no real equality for women." This is important, even if at first it seems "politically threatening to the limited gains women have made in the public sphere in the last thirty years."[18]

MAW and others know that the next social change will need to place value on the work that mothers do—that there can be no vestiges of "men's work" and "women's work" and the gap in value between them.

❧

The playground revolution might look like Kristin Beck in Seattle. Before her child was born, Kristin lived in San Francisco. Her job wasn't the most high powered, but it was stable, and something she could have been happy doing for a long while. Kristin is the author of *Facing 30*, a book for Gen-X women hitting the big three-zero, and she was, well, really happy in her professional life. Her husband, a musician, had been delivering pizza for ten years. He was mostly home with the baby, and everything was close to ideal. She worked near her home, and her husband, her mother, and her mother-in-law used to bring the baby by to nurse.

Then her husband got involved in a music website startup, and when it was acquired by Microsoft, the whole family, baby and all, moved to Seattle. Kristin figured she'd find work, but after five months of paying for the toddler's daycare, and pregnant with a second child, she gave up looking and became a stay-at-home mother. "We were going over bills and realized that if we didn't have income coming in, we couldn't justify the money. It was an uphill battle for the first few years. It all came crashing down," she says. Whenever someone else was at home, she was supportive of their new life, but when it came to her, she felt the poignancy and unhappiness of sacrificing such a large part of her own identity. To make the transition home better, and to find some relief from the constancy of caring for children, Kristin worked out a share-care with another mother. In a cruel twist of fate, on the first day the other mother told her that she'd just gotten a job. Kristin was on her own. "Now, I've come to terms with being a stay-at-home mom, with the act of rebellion that it is," she says. "My political activity ramped up. People don't think of mothering work as worthwhile, and I'm going to be political and in your face about how hard it is and the skill set you need. You need to be Superwoman. The problems you face at work are solvable. The problems you face at home are not, and there's very little guidance."

What does it mean to be political while being a mother? "Well, MoveOn.org started and the Internet became a powerful armchair political force," Kristin says. "I'd get an email about visiting the local representative and protesting, and it was something I could do and bring the kids. I realized I had to and could do something. Plus, volunteering is free, and it should be something you can do with your kids. Now, I'm actually frustrated by how little mom-organized volunteer stuff there is to do. One day I went to make phone calls for NARAL. I brought my daughter and she was bored. She took her clothes off, she needed a cookie, she had to go to the bathroom, she wanted to play." These are normal kid interruptions. Kristin couldn't help but notice that many volunteer opportunities aren't set up around kids and parents at home, despite the fact that Seattle is very kid friendly. Its stores have toys in buckets. The movie theaters have cry rooms, soundproof rooms where parents can go with their kids. It seemed all the more odd that volunteer work didn't accommodate at-home parents and young kids. Kristin saw this as a challenge, an assumption and a problem she's trying to change: "It struck me that if a group of moms organized this, they would account for childcare, too—they would trade off watching the kids and then more of us could do political volunteer work."

Small acts of change might look like Lorig Charkoudian and her fight to breastfeed in public. If Starbucks was once the literary staging ground for stories about overprivileged mothers relaxing after their morning gym routines, such tales took a markedly different turn at the Silver Spring, Maryland, Starbucks last July. Lorig was on a day off from her job as a mediator. She'd been visiting friends and running errands. At four o'clock she stopped at Starbucks to get a cold drink and a comfy, clean spot so the baby could nurse. Lorig and her child had settled into a chair in the nearly empty coffee shop when the barista stopped by their table and suggested she cover not just herself but the baby's whole head, or take a chair into the bathroom and nurse there: "He suggested I take my baby to eat in the bathroom. No one should be asked to eat in the bathroom.[19]

"I was stunned," Lorig recalls. "I'd nursed her for fourteen months. I'd brought her to work with me for the first seven months, and nursed her in offices and conference rooms and meetings throughout the state. I've nursed her at church. I've nursed her at baseball stadiums. Only once was someone uncomfortable with this, and when he said something, we had a good conversation about it. I had heard other women tell stories about being asked to leave places, but it had never happened to me."

Maryland is one of twenty or so states that legally protects women's right to breastfeed with no restrictions or limits. Even if a woman shows lots of breast in public while she nurses, it's legal and protected. "That's the thing," says Lorig. "Everyone assumes I must have been nearly naked. I wasn't. I was covered up. All you could see was the baby's head." No one in the store had even complained—it turned out that a month before, a customer had complained, and the employees were now being extra careful to ward off nursing mothers.

"We try to keep our customers happy," explained the Starbucks rep when Lorig asked to speak with the manager, and then the district representative, and eventually, the regional vice president. "But what about breastfeeding mothers?" responded Lorig, and began a long discussion with Starbucks about breastfeeding and its virtues. The discussion was followed by letters to Starbucks officials—letters that asked, first, that Starbucks comply with Maryland law and train its employees accordingly, and second, that it adopt for its nearly six thousand coffee shops a nationwide policy that protects women's right to breastfeed.

"It's amazing to me now," Lorig says. "But as committed to breastfeeding as I am, as surprisingly pleasant as breastfeeding had been, and despite how outraged I became, my first response, when they asked me to stop breastfeeding, was shame. It's that sense of shame that's the problem. When there's shame associated with breastfeeding, women are less likely to nurse their babies or to nurse them as long as they want. Or they'll feel cooped up at home while they nurse."

When letters to corporate Starbucks yielded no response, Lorig wrote up a flyer for a Sunday, August 8, nurse-in and sent it round to all the parent listservs in the D.C. area. The nurse-in flyer spread, at the speed of many forwarded emails, around the region. "It was the easiest thing I've ever done," says Lorig. She'd been involved in community projects in the past, especially on conflict resolution and mediation, but she had never organized a nurse-in. She found three other volunteers. With the help of a techie coworker they set up a website. They called print shops and asked how quickly they could print up stickers saying, "Can you drink that latte in the bathroom, I'm breastfeeding here." Using examples on the Internet, they composed and sent out press releases.

Just before the nurse-in, Lorig received a letter back from Starbucks, apologizing for her treatment and telling her that Starbucks would set about training its employees to follow local law. Nothing was said about changing corporate policy. Though thankful for Starbucks' small steps, Lorig felt that a company that claimed to be socially responsible should go further. Even Burger King has a nationwide policy, created in response to threatened protests a few years back. And, irony of ironies, the Starbucks Foundation supports and gives money to a breastfeeding advocacy group. The nurse-in became the launch of a national campaign to change Starbucks policy.

On the day of the nurse-in, the *Washington Post*, the local ABC affiliate, and the community gazette showed up to find nearly a hundred people gathered for the event. The Associated Press picked up the story from the *Post*, and Reuters reported it as well; news spread quickly throughout the country. Radio shows followed the next day, and Lorig appeared on CNN soon after. The debate raged in the *Washington Post* for a week, fueled by a particularly nasty style section piece that compared breastfeeding to picking your nose or farting in public, and follow-up letters, a political cartoon, and a supportive editorial.

It didn't stop there, either. Kathie Sever, a clothing shop owner and mother in Austin, Texas, read about the nurse-in on Mothering.com's list of action alerts. Excited, she sat down at her computer and sent a message about the nurse-in to her AustinMama listserv and included a link to www.nurseatstarbucks.org, the homepage that Lorig's techie coworker had drawn up. Within a few hours, four hundred Austin mothers read about what the Maryland mothers had done. So did Kim Lane, the editor of AustinMama.com, who suggested online that the moms exercise their right to peaceable assembly and show support for breastfeeding mothers everywhere. Within days there was a nurse-in coordinator, a location, a time, announcement postcards, and stickers and handouts for the event itself. People emailed back to say they'd be there. Sixty people showed up at a Starbucks in Austin, Texas, as did the *Austin Chronicle*. The nursing mothers breastfed their babies. Others handed out flyers and talked to passersby. The Starbucks customers were receptive, curious, and outraged. They wanted a corporation that built its reputation and sales by being socially responsible to be truly responsive to mothers, too.

"Nothing quite compares to the energy of a group with a purpose," says Lane. "Even more so when it's a group of women and mothers who often feel voiceless, underestimated, and underrepresented in this society. I noticed people making longer eye contact and easily chatting to passersby. The energy spread very easily and the spirit is moving beyond the walls of Starbucks. AustinMama now has an informal, and again, peaceful, group calling itself the Wandering Lactivistas who choose a local location for mass public nursing, announce it to our group; those who can make it meet, nurse, and chat."

Parents, and mothers in particular, are incredibly well wired, and the Internet teems with discussion boards and listservs, online mothering communities, and parenting sites. Mothers may be isolated at home, but they're connected online, and this changes everything. Michelle, a stay-at-home mother, has been on a mothers' listserv since she was pregnant with her daughter in 1997. Every day the list keeps her in touch with mothers across the United States, Canada, Australia, and the Philippines. "This has been the greatest thing for me," she says.

> Zoe was born a preemie, eleven weeks early, and that first year I was so isolated; we needed to keep her at home, keep her from getting sick. I didn't have a mothers' group or friends nearby to talk to about all the normal mom stuff. Over the years we've really helped each other. They rallied around me when I was diagnosed with cancer, and we did the same for another woman with a very serious cancer. We sent her care packages and flowers and gift certificates, and we even paid for someone to do some housekeeping for her when she was sick. I love the fact that I have the experience of forty or so moms who have the same age child. It's kind of a huge family.

And you can be sure there's no Mommy War on Michelle's listserv—just a bunch of moms doing a mix of work and parenting, supporting each other.

"The Internet has changed the face of mothering in such profound and numerous ways," says Lane. "It's like having to explain how the advent of electricity or modern plumbing might have changed one's life from day to day. The ability to communicate, extend, receive, commiserate, and learn—especially the ability to form whole, productive, thriving virtual communities without the limitations of travel, location, or scheduling conflicts—has provided all new paths to enriching a mama's life. To a demographic that is often overlooked and misinterpreted, the Internet has a clear voice, power to make changes rapidly, and the ability to be heard."

Small changes might also look like Andrea Lieber, who lives in the Pennsylvania countryside. She's a working mother of one, and a young professor at Dickinson College, and when she gave birth to her first child, her university gave her a semester off, with full pay. There's a subsidized, high-quality childcare program on campus, and Andrea and her husband, who also works on the campus, can both stop off during the day. Andrea is pregnant now with her second child, and her college has reiterated its commitment to family leave.

Each year, she needs to attend a professional conference, where she presents her research, catches up with the field, and networks with colleagues. In 2003 the conference was set for Boston in December, just before Christmas, during a week when her own childcare program was closed. She called the professional society's office, and found out that no, it had no plans to offer childcare. Some professional conferences offer childcare, but this one didn't. Before she had kids, she had never noticed; now it was a glaring affront that her profession demanded that she leave her nursing child for three days—that in its view, one cannot be a mother and a working professional too. It was all the more outrageous to her given how supportive her own college is of working parents. Their generosity made the professional society's stinginess all the more apparent.

Andrea took things into her own hands. She could have scraped up the funds to pay a student to attend the conference with her and provide childcare; she could have asked her regular babysitter to come along. But Andrea had a larger vision. Women were dropping like flies from her profession. The lack of workplace concern for their lives as mothers was the prime reason. The University of California at Berkeley had just issued a major report, sponsored by the Sloan Foundation, that studied in detail all the places in the professional pipeline where women fall out, and each one involved women becoming mothers.[20]

Rather than find a private solution, Andrea organized. "I was an activist before I became a mother," she explained. "I'm a mother now and I'm still an activist." She gathered other women and men around to help. Some were mothers and some were not, but all saw childcare as a *public* responsibility, as something shared by all. They were tired of losing female colleagues when they became mothers and had no support for continuing their work. They understood that quality daycare is a political issue, one of many confronting parents. They understood that in real life, families are not distractions but part of the work we do.

Together, and with a lot of work, these women and men made childcare happen. They culled their contacts. They found people they knew in Boston, where the conference was held. They discovered the grapevine that led them to good caregivers. They advertised for kids and they fielded complaints from older women, colleagues, who were appalled that they were raising these issues. "Childcare should not be a women's issue," Andrea was told by some members of the academic society's Women's Caucus. They were stuck in an old-fashioned feminist model, in which children cannot be mentioned in the workplace; in which we pretend we are the ideal, male workers, and never point out what we need specifically as women and mothers. There was fear, and embarrassment, at linking professional women with children so publicly. Andrea's response: "Perhaps not—maybe it's not a women's issue. But women's work lives and childcare certainly are a feminist issue." A senior colleague with several children complained that the services were too expensive (at five dollars per child per hour), and that she could bring her husband from home to watch them for free. Andrea responded by reminding her that quality childcare costs money, that subsidies were available to those who needed them, and that although she could afford her own babysitter, others could not. Andrea asked this other mother to think politically. She asked her to support the group's communal efforts even though she herself had the resources and support to go it on her own.

Andrea gathered the supplies—cots and cribs and a TV/VCR and Cheerios and goldfish crackers. She convinced the professional society to provide the room for free. She and the others sought donations to cover the fees for families who needed financial help. At a late-night party during the conference, cashmere sweaters collected from second-hand shops were auctioned, and this raised another three hundred dollars. Andrea asked people who were bringing children to bring their kids to the play center, even if they had a private babysitter (or the other parent was present). She and the other organizers felt that people should not stay alone and apart in their hotel rooms. They should show their support. The play center room should be abuzz.

The childcare efforts were a major success. The on-the-ground activism convinced the society to come through with a limited endorsement of childcare, and to provide some in-kind contributions toward it for future years. It's fair to say that the society didn't want to deal with childcare, and that the showy efforts of a few put the issue on the table and kept it there. Childcare will now be an ongoing annual feature of that conference, even though Andrea and her team still have to raise the money privately to fund it. By the second year, the society's leaders were solidly behind the childcare project.

Or small changes might look like this. At a playground in Candler Park, my old Atlanta neighborhood, the playscapes and swings were old and rickety, the sun-worn wood filled with spiders on top and pill-bugs underneath; we called them splinters waiting to happen. Most families stayed away, or just used the swings, which were old but relatively safe. The city didn't think it was bad enough to warrant improvements. When neighbors complained, the city responded by weaving orange caution tape through the worst of the danger spots. It posted signs of condemnation, and eventually sent in bulldozers to tear the offending playscapes down. That didn't mean, however, that the parks people planned to replace them.

Playgrounds are an in-between kind of space: domestic, because, after all, they are the delight of children and parents; and public, too, funded by cities and towns, by the tax dollars we all pay. Playgrounds are among the remaining few public squares. Few places encourage neighbors to hang out and talk like parks do. They offer one of the few ends to isolation; you can always pop over to the park and see who's around and what's going on, stay as long or as little as you like. No one has to prepare food or clean up afterward. Kids can run and play, and parents can talk, provided with such easy ways to start a conversation. But it's more than that. Parks also offer old-fashioned support and community for adults in a way that feels almost nostalgic. Playgrounds and parks are where we go to be with people, to see friends and neighbors without the armature of phone calls and calendars. You don't need to buy anything to be present, not even a cup of coffee or tea.

A group of neighborhood mothers took up the challenge of a new playground. They found the right city committees to work with. They engaged a landscape architect to draw up plans. They circulated the plans, and gained community support. They met with state representatives, wrote grant proposals, and sold sidewalk bricks; through bake sales and clothing sales and old-fashioned door-to-door talking with the neighbors, they raised nearly $100,000. Much of it came through small donations from local families and businesses.

When the new playground finally opened, the neighborhood gained new life. "I feel like I've up and moved to a new community," said one longtime resident as her kids played. People now came out at all hours, and from several neighborhoods around. This neighborhood had been one of the first in Atlanta to have racially integrated institutions. The city's first integrated preschool resided in the basement of a neighborhood church, and its public golf course is a nine-hole sculpted vision of what golf in a postracist society will look like.

The rest of America might have wondered at Tiger Woods and his effect on golf, but here in Candler Park black and white men and women have long been teaming up on this little course, renting hand-dragged golf carts, paying five dollars for the privilege of walking the course on a sunny Friday afternoon or weekend morning. The new playground was similar. The majority of Candler Park's residents were now white, but a block away—across DeKalb Avenue and steps away from the literal train tracks that ran parallel, over where old Atlanta had changed the street names even when the roads were the same, reflecting their move across the tracks from white to black—the neighborhoods became increasingly African American. Everybody came out to the new playground in Candler Park. It was the nicest playground for miles around, and the neighborhood still was reputed to be friendly to all.

The new playground put people at ease. They met, they talked, and their kids borrowed each other's tricycles. The playground mothers had wanted a nice place to gather where their kids could play. They could have just pooled their money for a fabulous playscape in someone's backyard. I've known other groups of friends to do that. One family buys the big playscape, another sets up a large trampoline, another installs a pool, and everyone shares. These neighbors' vision was larger than that. Instead of seeking a solution for their small group alone, they created something public, for everyone. With hard work and persever-ance and in good company they made it happen, while they raised their own children, and while some worked their own part- or full-time jobs. They improved family life for everyone—especially for all those moth-ers and children I had first been surprised to see at the 10:00 A.M. play-ground, what now seems like many years ago.

Motherhood can feel so private, so isolating. How then do we con-nect it with building new playgrounds and political activism and changing public policy? This is our challenge, the next feminist chal-lenge, the work left to do. The story told by new mother activists is that many of us reject classic feminism's rejection of home and family, much as we benefited from feminist inspiration, not to mention the expanded opportunities we received. With children of our own, though, collapsing under the weight of the double shift, rejecting the long hours we are asked to work, and garnering our generation's sense of female entitlement, we sought other lives: lives with children, lives partially split between home and part-time work, lives that refuse the classic idea that body is split from mind, that domestic life is separate from work, that the mother cannot be public. Second-wave feminism, though, was energized by housewives, by women who were able to look at domestic life and motherhood with a critical edge. Perhaps this can happen again.

Today, as commentators Amy Hudock and Judith Stadtman Tucker note, it's the mothers who feel the double shift's squeeze, who are buckling under ten-hour work days, the ones who temporarily quit the feminist dream of public paid work, the ones who make change with babies at hip and breast—all these mothers are now the startling new energy of a reviving women's movement.

EPILOGUE

As I was finishing this book, several media pieces on motherhood caught my eye. The *Dr. Phil* show aired Mom vs. Mom, episode two, and the *New York Times* op-ed page printed "Mom vs. Nanny: The Time Trials." Letters in response appeared two days later. Is our national conversation on women, parenting, and work stuck? I wondered as I watched and read. Or, as I hoped, is it moving forward with more complex and fresh ideas to be found?

On September 3, 2004, TV viewers were reintroduced to Sonja and Leah, both from the first Mom vs. Mom show, and asked to consider "Who's got it tougher: Sonja, the working mother, or Leah, the stay-at-home mom?". "These are passionate differences," Dr. Phil told us. "Should a woman stay at home or contribute financially?" Or, to recap the audience's jugular extremes, should you drop your kid in filthy daycare or get your nails done? Sonja's African American, a middle school teacher, and the mother of a school-age son. Leah's white and has several younger children, and like Sonja, she has somewhat extreme positions about what mothers should do. To Leah's "Just because you don't earn a paycheck doesn't mean you're not valuable," Sonja tosses back, "Why waste your education just to stay home with children?" When Sonja says, "I come home and drop everything to spend time with my son; just because you're working doesn't mean you're not a sensitive and nurturing parent," Leah counters with, "I grew up in daycare and I wouldn't do that to my kids. My kids are happy and well adjusted and safe."

Dr. Phil keeps the battle pitched so that viewers will stay tuned through the commercial breaks. At each point when Sonja and Leah have moved toward recognizing each other's humanity, he finds a new bone of contention. "We're going to get into the schoolyard battles when we get back," he tells us, preparing us to debate whether stay-at-home moms rule our nation's PTAs and prevent working parents from being active at their kids' schools. In contrast to the singular way that Dr. Phil moderates the show, when audience members get the microphones they speak to more complexity. Heidi Brennan (of the Family and Home Network) tells the audience that motherhood is challenging, and there's not just one description: "Our culture had created mythic Mommy Wars, when in fact, the real Mommy Wars are between motherhood itself and our culture." She wants us to think about what separation from their parents means for children. They can tolerate some separation, and she resists those who might want to put a number on that, but she wants us to consider that kids need to be near their parents to feel safe and secure.

Joan Peters, author of *When Mothers Work*, speaks with some audience members who have proposed versions of having it all. "Our society could not be what it is without working moms," one stay-at-home mom offers. "My daughter says she wants to be a dentist or a doctor and a stay-at-home mom, too." To which Peters responds that she thinks that's a wonderful goal—yet wholly unrealistic given our workplace and parenting strictures. Sadly, the woman's daughter's dream is a utopian idea. There are moments of understanding—from the same stay-at-home mom: "There are women who are better moms because they are working. There are wonderful working moms. My best friend is. It's just not me," she responds. Her voice speaks reason, but throughout the show, the issues remain within the lines of whether mothers can respect each other.

Although the show is more balanced than "Mom vs. Mom" part one, it still focuses on the Mommy Wars, if a slightly kinder version, and it offers no alternate vision; the central issue facing mothers is still that we judge each other. We know that underneath we're sorting our way through complicated issues: what we think our kids need, our commitments to them, our ability to pay our bills, our opportunities to be creative, and our know-how to navigate between all of these desires. We still need a national conversation about the real issues at stake, about workplaces that don't support mothers and fathers who want to work less than full-time and still be treated fairly and paid well.

The conversation on the *Dr. Phil* show can only be at its best when offering soothing advice. Dr. Phil's own wife is called upon to speak from the audience. After her first child was born, she worked for a year as an industrial engineer. She wanted to. But her passion was to be a mother, and she considered it a privilege to be able to stay home. "I've been uncomfortable with the judgment," she says. "I wish [the mothers in the room] could have compassion for each other as women raising a child in this world." At every turn, the explanations are interior, as if mothers live in a world apart. Great faith is expressed that we women can show more compassion, and throughout the show, mothers give and receive platitudes or semantic turns of phrase aimed at making the difference go away. "I'm a stay-at-home working mom. We all love our kids." "All moms are working moms." "I've done both and the proof is in the pudding. I'm here with my [adult] son, and he got along fine whether I was or wasn't working." "Parenting is a crapshoot. I don't think it matters whether you work or not."

These expressions of kindness lead to the show's end, in which Dr. Phil addresses the studio and home audience. He reminds us to be good stewards of our children, since both sides want the same thing: children who are healthy and happy and nurtured. "The key is not about hours. The kids need to feel special at home, so they feel special when they go out into the world. If they don't feel special they won't expect it when they go out in the world, and they won't hold people to a standard of treating them with dignity and respect."

After watching, I too found myself feeling reassured. I recommitted myself never to lose patience and raise my voice against my daughter, in order to shore up her expectations of good treatment. How can I disagree with this? Yet, Dr. Phil wrapped it up too nicely and neatly. I know—this is the MO of daytime TV. Still, this is a piece of our national conversation, and we need to be able to point out what it accomplishes and what it fails to do. When parenting is discussed on a national level, we need better terms, more imagination, more commitment to dealing with real issues.

Instead, TV that day gave us self-help solutions, and that's mostly what we get from the parenting magazines and websites. The widespread focus on self-help aims to improve our lives. But it can't. Not really. If all the mothers in America plan, grocery shop, and cook more efficiently, as the magazines exhort, that won't change the real issue, which is that in pretty much every family I know, women and not men do this labor—and not because they always want to, but because classic gender roles keep structuring our lives. Helpful household tips cannot solve this problem. The self-help model means we've bought into the American mythology of individual solutions. If only we could find the right way to organize our kitchens, the right plastic containers in which to store the children's toys or to pack their lunchboxes. If our lives continue to feel hectic and rushed, then it's our fault—for not following the right advice. If we're stuck after a five-year résumé gap and can't find decent work with part-time hours, well, it must mean we haven't hired the right life coach, the new millennium's antidote to real social and psychological reflection. Self-help is okay for a moment. Sometimes it can be very helpful. But the stresses of work and attentive parenting cannot be answered entirely by making our households run better, because the problem really isn't located at home. Women's very real frustrations are submerged beneath self-help parenting advice—decent, perhaps well-intentioned advice, but, nonetheless, advice that makes women's competing desires about work and parenting vanish.

Here's what was never said on *Dr. Phil:* There's a workplace issue
at stake. There are structural issues. All the mothers feel defensive,
which means that all the mothers feel under attack. Single mothers get
little support. Married mothers carry a huge burden of the housework.
If all the mothers in the room feel defensive, judged poorly by other
women and by society at large, whether they work or stay at home, then
we have a problem, an attack against women. Questions like "What's
this attack about? Why? What might make things better for all mothers?" and "What can we do to make it better?" can't reach the floor of
the studio set.

I do understand that daytime talk shows don't usually delve into
the technical details of social problems and how to fix them. But the
New York Times does, with regularity, and prides itself on being among
the nation's smartest and most nuanced newspapers. On the opinion
page, regular columnist Paul Krugman leads us through the complex
logic of political economy. Senators, former vice presidents, international prime ministers, and Ivy League professors present thoughtful
accounts of current problems, and their articles rarely try to dumb
down ideas. A strong argument, solid evidence, and something interesting to say about current events is considered good enough. On
September 9, 2004, when "Mom vs. Nanny" ran in the lower left hand
corner, the lead editorial featured Richard Pipes of Harvard University
("Give the Chechens a Land of Their Own"). To sort through the
article, readers had to consider that Chechen rebels and al Qaeda were
not the same, and reflect on the nuances in different types of terror-
ism. We were reminded of aspects of Soviet history going back to
Stalin and the closing days of World War II; Russian leadership
throughout the '60s; and how Chechnya was never a nominally independent republic and that's why it couldn't secede from the Russian
Federation when the Soviet Union collapsed. We read analogies to
French colonial strategy in Algeria (which ended in Algeria's independence in 1962), because Pipes believes that Charles de Gaulle was

courageous in letting go of Algeria, and that Russia should do the same and grant Chechnya independence. I consider myself well educated, and I follow international news, and I had to read this article slowly to keep the pieces in place.

In other words, the *New York Times* assumes we are not idiots, that we come to the page with some level of historical and political sophistication and knowledge, and that we prefer these types of renditions of current events to the more superficial accounts available elsewhere.

Not so with opinion pieces about motherhood, it turns out. It seems like there's a different standard for these. They're allowed to sidestep the issues of economy, society, and politics that are the mainstay of the op-ed page and instead present us with relative fluff that, policy-wise, is years behind the times. "Mom vs. Nanny: The Time Trials" is written in the form of a running interior commentary from a working mother as she compares the hours and minutes she spends with her two young daughters against the nanny's daily ten hours with them. The tally is her "Official Scorecard of Quality Time." I have empathy for the author, who's a magazine editor. She likes her job, she needs her job, she misses her kids. Like many women and men I know, she's torn between good work, a workplace that demands long hours, a commute that eats time, and the wish to spend more time with her children. She's wracked with the same ambivalence, the same competing desires, that we all are. Her kids are ten months and two and a half years old. It's especially hard when they're preschoolers, and that little, a working parent can't even rationalize that they're in "real" school seven hours a day anyway.

Like the *Dr. Phil* show, the article feeds off many platitudes, frustrating platitudes that prevent us from getting at the real issues. Does this article reflect the limits of what can be printed in public about the politics of motherhood, parenting, work, and time? In the middle of "Mom vs. Nanny" there's a paragraph that invokes imagined other mothers and sets up the usual Mommy Wars conflict: "Stay-at-home moms will ask,

'Do you know how much you're missing?' Other more well-adjusted working moms might remind me that I have a choice in the matter and if it's so torturous: 'Why don't you find a job that's more flexible? Why don't you work part-time? Why don't you quit?' All valid questions. And all questions you're welcome to discuss with me at 3:00 AM when I'm staring at the ceiling trying to figure out the answers myself."[1]

The questions this paragraph raises are at the target's center. But the questions are in someone else's voice, and the article surfs down from these to ask instead whether the three hours that the kids nap should actually count in the nanny's column. The author can touch the smallest corner of the big questions that mothers and fathers face, questions that might lead us out of pretending that the personal approach will solve the problem. I was left wondering, "Has she asked for part-time hours? Does her workplace, *Real Simple* magazine, the product-oriented bo-bo mag marketed at upscale readers, have family-friendly policies? Do they encourage the basics, like flextime and working from home? Do they offer part-time options with prorated benefits, room for advancement, and proportional pay?" That's what I want to hear about.

Sidestepping these crucial and very political issues, the article concludes that love is the answer. Mom and nanny scorecards aside, the author's daughters receive love from their parents and from their nanny. The more love, the better. It's not about hours, it's about love. She's not wrong. Love is great; I'm all for it. I love my daughter and I love my husband. As an answer to our problems, it's beside the point. All our love for our children and partners together won't solve our problems as women and mothers. I am struck by the similarity of this article to the *Dr. Phil* show. Real frustrations about working time and family time are shifted into psychological terms and quickly, easily resolved. If a mother can convey self-esteem to her kids, then it doesn't matter how stretched-tight or vulnerable she is. If a mother can find inner peace and quiet her competition with her nanny, then family life is okay.

And where are the fathers? In the article, the kids are clearly fine; it's the mom who wants help, real help. Perhaps the father, too, wants something different for his life. We don't hear from him. Perhaps he too would like a job that didn't keep him out of the house from 8:30 AM to 6:30 PM. Perhaps he can help the mother. We desperately need to have conversations about motherhood, fatherhood, family life, and work that don't so entirely erase social and structural problems, which don't run slipshod over women's needs, and which don't ignore fathers.

Are the letters to the editor helpful? Do they push forward our national conversation? A letter in response to the article, from Elizabeth Schwartz of New York, asks similar questions to mine: "Where exactly does her husband fall into the schedule with the children, what is the hourly breakdown of his own quality time, with them and how much anguish does he feel about working? The true anguish is that women still fall into the career versus good mother trap, even when they are married." Yes, where are the fathers? And how come it's still so easy to talk about motherhood as if the father's right to work continues unabated, that in the normative way that these conversations go, it's mothers who feel like their work is expendable, who feel like it's even up for question? "Where are the dads?" is a helpful way forward.

Dean Brier also writes in, a working father who hates that he has to go to work while his three-year-old daughter's home having fun. He says he's comforted by knowing that his wife is there with her, even though she has great earning potential. Forward-thinking points? I'm heartened when he uses the phrase "working dad." For too long, it's only been mothers who become a slogan the minute they give birth. Dads too need to modify their names, as moms do. They too should take on an adjective every so often, and see how it feels. "I'm a working dad" says that you don't consider it automatic that dads are at work while moms might be anywhere. It keeps open the idea that dads too must wrestle with family and work, with choice and options. It says that one could be a father who doesn't work for pay or who works less; that to father and to work should be up for question, not simply a foregone conclusion of being a man.

So, is the media changing its position on the Mommy Wars and expanding its definitions of what makes a good mother? As I was finishing this book, *Family Circle* again held a cookie bake-off between the presidential candidates' wives. Recipes for Laura Bush's oatmeal chocolate chunk cookies and for Teresa Heinz Kerry's pumpkin spice cookies were published in the magazine, and readers were again asked to whip up the recipes at home and send in their ballots. I was surprised to find that since the original flap between Hillary Clinton and Barbara Bush, in which cookies became the metaphor distinguishing working and at-home moms, the cookie bake-off has become an institution. Candidates' wives still have to prove their domestic skill. The newest round, between Bush and Heinz Kerry, pits two mothers who stayed home with their children against each other, each battling for the crown of domesticity—and, apparently, for a prediction of whose husband will win, since the bake-off winner has apparently coincided with the victorious presidential candidate since its inception in 1992. (PS: Laura Bush's cookies won.)[2]

In the same election year that Bush and Heinz Kerry were forced to compete over cookies, Republican and Democratic strategists created and then courted "Security Moms," the updated phantasm of suburban motherhood. We were to imagine that mothers across America were trading in their minivan keys and khaki pants for handguns, Hummers, and camouflage. At least one website sells Security Mom T-shirts, busty little garments emblazoned with your choice of handgun or human target. We were first told that Security Moms were traditionally Democratic mothers who might swing Republican based on fear of terrorist attacks. It became clear that they were not a swing group, but conservative exurban married mothers, the darlings of the right wing, who never had any intention of voting Democratic anyway. In October 2004, just before the election, the national press was filled with articles denouncing the new attempts to describe women this way. Even Fox News and a prominent conservative like American Enterprise Institute resident scholar Karlyn Bowman expressed skepticism as to whether Security Moms actually exist—but the political attempt to once again manipulate images of motherhood remains intact.[3]

And what's most awful: Despite wanting to heighten our motherly fears to gain votes, neither candidate truly cared much about raising issues that would comprehensively help mothers and fathers. Neither the Democratic nor the Republican National Convention included childcare for the delegates who needed it.[4] Has the national discussion moved forward? The question, the future, remains open and ours to claim.

Mom vs. Nanny. Mom vs. Mom. Mommy Wars. Nanny Wars. War metaphors and conflict still abound. Using war images to describe our family lives is cruel and misleading. The truth is, many mothers and fathers feel under attack. What happens when we start talking out loud about the lives we really lead? Because of the pressure to uphold the cheeriness of motherhood, it can feel confusing to both criticize the institution and also say, "I love my kids." But we must, because the situation is untenable. It has quietly reached crisis proportions, and we owe it to ourselves, to our families, and to our daughters and sons to get about creating a more just world where they won't have to face the same trade-offs.

It's humbling and hard to shift from being a generation of entitled feminist daughters to being a generation of feminist mothers with rights left to secure. To be a feminist mom is not about being righteous or smug. It's about being a mother with a critique of what's wrong, and even more so, about being a mother with a vision of what can be done to make life better for all women, for all mothers, for all parents. To say one is a feminist mother is not celebratory. It's not to boast or brag that you've figured out life's answers. It certainly doesn't imply that due to your own fabulous parenting your daughter shuns Barbies or Bratz dolls, or that your son doesn't have a truck-and-swords-and-wrestling fetish like other little boys. To say you're a feminist mom, a feminist parent, is much more humbling. It's not that you've escaped gender or risen above our society's various sexisms. It's to admit that we don't have the answers, that life is not perfect. It's recognizing new terrain—or actually, old terrain—that needs to be reclaimed and reconfigured. It's a sacred task, because there's lots to fix; it's daunting to think about what it takes, in terms of power and in terms of the fearfulness of actually raising one's voice in public, risking disapproval—and, harder perhaps, in front of friends. It's hard to break out of the relative ease of being one or the other, a working mom or an at-home mom, to really question the order of things.

I've been a mother for six years, my daughter no longer fits on my hip, and she's having a blast in first grade. In those six years, I've come to grips with the current strife between active parenting and active working. I understand it in a way I didn't at the beginning. There are still times when I can't actually believe it, when I look around and my ingrained, entitled feminist-daughter self says, "No, it can't really be this bad." I can still fall prey to the judgment that says, "Look at your own privilege. You have a great life. Don't complain."

My husband, Rob, has been a dad for six years, too. In these years, we've had some whopper arguments about these issues, though many fewer as of late. We've come together on a story about our marriage that acknowledges that his work life has been central, even if, when we met, our dream was mutuality and equality. We've been able to share a similar critique of what happened when we had a baby and our lives took different paths than we could have ever imagined. I've stopped being mad at him when I should be mad at bigger, wider, but less identifiable structures, like society, the workplace, and ideal worker expectations. He has learned to stop counting his domestic chores as if they're a favor to me. When recently he invited lots of family over to celebrate his father's birthday, he did all the labor. He planned, he shopped, he left work at three-thirty that afternoon to cook, clean, and set the table. We've both become aware of who does the housework, and of how much there is, and that we don't have to pretend it's invisible. He works at a foundation, and recently he hired a woman who is also a mom and who wanted to work part-time. From watching me, from our conversations, and from seeing so many women friends locked out of decent part-time work, he did the right thing: He hired Heather for a high-quality part-time job. He allowed her flexibility, which included her working from home one day a week. He fairly prorated the salary—the full salary he would have paid to a full-time worker—and he prorated the full-time benefits to fit her part-time position. He even made sure she got the keys to her own office, standing up to others who thought that part-time work wasn't serious enough to warrant it. He's seen up close what happens to mothers and fathers who want real flexibility and real fairness. He did the right thing, and I'm proud of him. And if he can figure out how to arrange high-quality part-time work, so can managers and workplaces across our nation.

I've been hugely affected by the personal stories of the women and men I've interviewed for this book, both the ones who can just get through the day and the ones who have enough resources left over at the end of it that they can look out at the world and start fixing it. Often we're afraid to speak out, afraid of being wrong, afraid of not having all the facts right and of being tossed out at the start.

Yet change happens both incrementally, person to person, and on a broader scale. When I first started writing about motherhood, I wrote in the first person. I wrote about my experience and I tried to find a context to explain that experience. Coming up against brick walls, I had to shift: talk to others and write about all sorts of people, media, policy, and grassroots change. And as this book came into being, people would ask about it, and then tell me their stories. Then they wanted stories in return. What do other moms and dads do? How do they make ends meet?

Are we talking more now? I hope so, but then again, I'm always on the lookout for stories. Like one mother I met who spends long hours at her job in the insurance industry, and who, along with her best girlfriend, feels squeezed by the hours she works. Her daughter's dad picks her up at school and helps her with homework. But she doesn't get home many nights till eight or eight-thirty, and she feels out of the loop. She's not quitting, though she's looking around for a job with less commute. She and her friend want to be able to talk about the whole issue, the gains and the losses, together. As does the at-home mother of three who tells me plaintively, "I wish I was in one of those jobs where there's part-time work," or the single dad I meet who runs a small restaurant, but was for fourteen years an at-home dad, and asks me, "Aren't there lots more dads like me?"

We must keep talking, for starters, because it ends the usual isolation of family life, motherhood, and parenting; and because there's something magical that happens when large groups of people make their voices heard. The advocacy group WEEL began as three Montana women talking at a backyard barbeque. *Brain, Child,* the magazine that's added so much to the lives of mothers who want more, began when two writer friends compared notes about how hard it was to get their articles on motherhood published. Real conversation happens because of organizations that support mothers, like Mothers & More, MOTHERS, and Mothers Movement Online. Magazines like *Hip Mama* and *Brain, Child* and *Mothering* have brought together communities of women, and websites like

TheNewHomemaker.com and AustinMama.com are important new links bridging the isolation that used to mark mothers' lives. Stay-at-home dads talk and meet through sites like rebeldad.com and Slowlane.com and DadsAtHome.com, and the burgeoning blogging community is yet another venue for mothers and fathers talking, with love and with critique, about the way things are and the way things might be. In the past, mothers and fathers could never be organized; we could never easily be pulled together as a political and social force because we were locked away in our own homes with our own ways of getting through the days. How much difference it makes to look at another parent's experience and know, "I am not the only one. I am not failing. Something bigger than me is making it harder to do what I have to do." And how much difference it makes to look at another parent and feel not judgment, but empathy.

Is there a social movement happening? Judith Stadtman Tucker of Mothers Movement Online thinks we are at the beginning of one, that we can see the rumblings and the groundwork of a movement that hasn't happened yet. "On Mothers Movement Online, we document this work," she says. "Whatever happens in history, people will know we were formulating what this can mean. There's a mothers' movement, yes, in an embryonic stage."[5]

What will it take to gather all the people affected by motherhood, mad at the restrictions, wanting real choices and more support, to come together? The women who once worked on Wall Street or for top law firms, the Hip Mamas and the AustinMamas, the poor rural mothers from Montana and the poor urban mothers from North Philadelphia, the middle-class mamas, the suburban moms, the mothers all over the country, in every city and every small town, who love their kids and are tired of workplaces based on someone else's ideal life, on promises of success and stability that don't incorporate having and caring for kids? When I listen to Tucker, I can't help but feel her excitement that we're on the national cusp of something new.

Throughout these six years, I've been convinced that the new trend of women quitting their jobs for motherhood is not just retrograde. It's a more complexly mingled brew of desire and discontent. It may look like a return to an imagined housewife tradition, but actually, it's a quiet expression of something new, something quite radical. I know this analysis doesn't seem to fit with common sense. Everyone loves the new stay-at-home dads and applauds them. Gay dads who stay home with their kids make the front-page news.[6] Like many women, they too are shifting gears away from the workplace, at least temporarily. The new stay-at-home moms and all the moms wanting part-time instead of full-time work have been treated more harshly. If stay-at-home dads are the vanguard, the new stay-at-home moms are supposed to form the rear-looking edge of gender culture. I don't buy the conventional wisdom. Instead, I am convinced that in their refusal to do the second shift, in their refusal to work all day for pay and to work all evening at home, in their refusal to bear the exhaustion of our mothers, these mothers are teaching us something new: to value all kinds of women's work, paid and unpaid. In boycotting, if you will, a labor market that does not value our labor, these mothers are, with their bodies and their actions, saying something new that needs a voice.

It may look like a retreat home, and the media may spin it that way. And today's mothers and fathers are bearing sacrifices that quite possibly won't be made right. But it's not a politically retrograde choice to leave a workplace that squeezes you too tight, that can't organize its expectations around your family responsibilities. That's called resistance, but it needs a voice, and it needs a path. It's not resistance when we slink away. We need to be vocal about what we're doing. We have to explain, even, especially when it's uncomfortable and no one seems to understand.

It's funny, but it took me years. And it took hearing so many stories to make it real. The story that affected me the most was that of

Andrea, the thirty-four-year-old professor who organized childcare at her professional conference because she just couldn't believe that her profession made it so hard for female parents to be professionals. I had met up with Andrea and some mutual friends in New Hampshire, and heard her story of how hard, still, it had been to get through graduate school, where there were no models of female professors who had active family lives. Still, as she described her life and how much support her college workplace gave her—when she explained the on-site, subsidized childcare and the no-questions-asked extended paid family leave—for the first time, I found myself really angry. As Mariella, artist-curator-teacher-mom, once said to me, these issues of motherhood and work are not linear. They don't go away, but circle back around, coming at you from different directions when you least expect it. Of course she's right; how can they get resolved until so many structures and workplaces and legal foundations change? In the talk with Andrea, it all came back round to me, yet again.

In these six years, and as I've started talking, people have often asked me if I regret quitting my job. It's the elephant-in-the-closet question, second only to "Do you work?" as the question most hard to ask a mother. Given the way things have worked out in my life, and knowing the big picture that I know now, do I regret it?

My answer is still no. I don't regret my decision. I don't think I'd be happier had I stayed at my old job. Had my family moved to northern Florida—and as a newly tenured professor—quite honestly, I could have scaled down on hours and spent a lot of time with my baby. After all, I had the ultimate job protection. I could have slacked off, done little else besides teach my two classes each semester, and you know what, they couldn't have fired me. Even had I not quit, I could have cut back or downshifted. But I don't like doing things second-rate. Certainly I couldn't have worked in the way my profession truly demands, not without my husband quitting his job or working part-time. I took a risk on another path.

I don't regret the years I spent as a stay-at-home mother, despite some mind-numbing boredom, tedious afternoons, wistfulness about my friends whose careers continued, and the sadness I felt one October when it seemed like everyone in my life was being interviewed on CNN. Rob appeared in *Education Week*. My best friend, Laura, was profiled as one of "Forty Under Forty to Watch Out For" in a local magazine. My friend Barry was doing press conferences in Costa Rica with the Powerpuff Girls. A mom at the park returned to work as the press secretary to a U.S. senator. Even my neighbors Bobby and Joe were interviewed for an Election 2000 article on undecided voters. True, most months aren't like that. Still, everyone was contributing to society in explicit and recognizable ways, and there I was, hanging out at the playground with my daughter and chatting away the afternoons. Public life continued on without me, and I often felt envious. I wasn't ready to give that up. Six years later, I realize that in the long span of my life, there's room for me to get back in. I'm writing, I'm teaching part-time. And I got to experience something incredible: day-to-day life with a child, something I never knew I would like ahead of time, and an experience that has unutterably changed the way I see the world. I would not give this up for anything.

There is *one* thing I regret: that I didn't make a bigger fuss. I didn't complain publicly about my job's lack of real maternity leave or on-site childcare. I just took a patched-together sick leave plan and stayed quiet. I didn't raise it as an issue with my department. I didn't go to the faculty union; I just assumed they wouldn't care, and besides, they didn't seem very effective advocates anyway. I didn't know then the nuances of raising a general problem—parents deserve paid family leave and real leave time and considerable support for childraising—given that I myself was protected by a husband whose salary could cover us. Still, I regret that I didn't even try. I regret that I didn't pen an editorial to the school newspaper, with its fifty-thousand-plus circulation, and explain what was wrong. Perhaps I didn't have all the facts, and as I was a newly pregnant woman who didn't even feel comfortable enough in my male-dominated workplace to be openly pregnant (and thank goodness the semester ended before I really started to show . . .), it's understandable that I didn't raise my voice, that I just got the hell out and started a new life with a baby at my hip. It takes a lot to raise a fuss. It can feel ridiculous—but as my friend Elizabeth always says, "Better to feel slightly ridiculous than totally passive."

Six years later, I've had lots of experience with a certain young lady who's quite excellent at a couple of things: having a fabulous time in life and raising a fuss when she doesn't get her way. Perhaps that, the experience so familiar to parents, is what I wish I had done, and what we all need to do. Take a lesson from infants, toddlers, and young children everywhere, who expect life to be great, and know what to do when it isn't. We must expect our lives as parents to be filled with joy, and when we don't get our way, when our society shows how little it values our work—whether as mothers or as fathers, and as workers of all kinds—we must, indeed, raise a fuss.

Notes

Introduction

[1] These statistics come from Vicky Lovell, *40-hour Work Proposal Significantly Raises Mothers' Employment*, Institute for Women's Policy Research Publication #D460, June 2003. That 63 percent of mothers aged twenty-five to forty-four with kids under eighteen at home work less than full-time is confirmed by Joan Williams, author of *Unbending Gender* and professor of law at American University, based on the Current Population Survey, March 2004.

[2] Bureau of Labor Statistics, *American Time Use Survey*, September 2004.

Chapter 1: Do Real Women Have Mommy Wars?

[1] Eric Boehlert, "Going Negative," *Salon*, March 15, 2004, http://archive.salon.com/news/feature/2004/03/15/castellanos/.

[2] Thomas B. Edsall, "US Electorate 'Moving Steadily to the Left': As Nation Changes, Parties Are Warned They Need New Tactics to Woo Voters," *Washington Post*, July 8, 2001.

[3] Quoted in Jacob Weisberg, "Soccer Mom Nonsense," *Slate*, October 12, 1996.

[4] Ceci Connolly, "Columbine Alters the Landscape of Debate on Guns," *Washington Post*, www.polkonline.com/stories/050699/nat_columbine.shtml.

[5] Laurel Parker West, "Soccer Moms, Welfare Queens, Waitress Moms, and Super Moms: Myths of Motherhood in State Media Coverage of Child Care" (working paper, MARIAL Center, Emory University, 2002).

[6] Barbara J. Berg, "Mothers Against Mothers," *Washington Post*, January 3, 1986.

[7] Stephen J. Rose and Heidi I. Hartman, *Still a Man's Labor Market: The Long Term Wage Gap*, Institute for Women's Policy Research, www.iwpr.org/pulbications/pdf.htm#recent, May 2004.

[8] Susan Douglas and Meredith Michaels, *The Mommy Myth: The Idealization of Motherhood and How It Has Undermined Women* (New York: Free Press, 2004).

[9] Ralph Gardner Jr., "Mom Vs. Mom," *New York*, October 21, 2002.

[10] Mothers & More can be found at www.mothersandmore.org.

11 Greg Bonnell, "Metrosexual Man!: The Evolution of Man, or a Marketing Flash in the Pan?" www.canoe.ca/lifewiseStyle0311/1114_metrosexual-cp.html November 2003. See also Mark Simpson, "Metrodaddy Speaks," *Salon*, January 5, 2004.

12 Euro RSCG Worldwide, "The New Moms: As America Celebrates Mother's Day, Euro RSCG Releases Findings on Five New Categories of Modern-Day Moms," press release, May 4, 2004. See also the company's website, www.eurorscg.com.

13 "Staying Home with the Kids," *CBS News*, May 9, 2004, available at www.cbsnews.com/stories/2004/05/07/sunday/main616291.shtml.

14 Reach Advisors, www.reachadvisors.com/background.html

15 Myra Stark, "The Mommy Wars: Phase 2," *2004: Ideas from Trends*, available at www.saatchikevin.com/workingit/myra_stark_report2004ideastrends.html.

16 Faulkner Fox, *Dispatches from a Not-So-Perfect Life: Or How I Learned to Love the House, the Man, the Child* (New York: Harmony Books, 2004).

Chapter 2: The Parent Problem

1 Jane Waldfogel, quoted in New America Foundation, Work and Family Program, *The Way Women Work*, March 2004.

2 U.S. Census Bureau, *Fertility of American Women*, Washington, D.C., June 2002, issued October 2003.

3 National Center for Health Statistics, "Estimated Pregnancy Rates for the United States, 1990–2000: An Update," *National Vital Statistics Reports* 52, no. 23 (June 15, 2004).

4 Phyllis Moen, ed., *It's About Time: Couples and Careers* (Ithaca: Cornell University Press, 2003).

5 Percentages have been rounded to the nearest whole number and therefore add up to 102 percent.

6 Interview with Joan Williams by author, August 2004.

7 The CPS, or Current Population Survey, is the Bureau of Labor Statistics' basic research tool; it tallies 60,000 different households each month.

8 Lovell, *40-hour Work Proposal*. Percentages have been rounded to the nearest whole number and therefore add up to 101 percent.

Chapter 3: Are Mothers Really Opting Out?

1 Maureen Dowd, "Hot Zombie Love," *New York Times*, June 15, 2003.

2 "Trading Briefcases for Strollers," letters to the editor, *New York Times*, June 17, 2003.

3 Judith Warner, "Guess Who's Left Holding the Briefcase? (It's Not Mom.)," *New York Times*, June 20, 2004.

4 Lisa Belkin, "Opt-Out Revolution," *New York Times Magazine*, October 26, 2003, 42.

5 A *Time* magazine cover story five months later used the same language in "The Case for Staying Home: Why More Young Moms Are Opting Out of the Rat Race," March 22, 2004.

6 Shoshana Zuboff, "Career Taxidermy," *Fast Company*, June 2004.

7 Summer Wood, "Freedom of Choice," *Bitch: Feminist Response to Pop Culture* 24 (Spring 2004).

Chapter 4: Mothers in the Middle

1 Lucia Herndon, "Concerning Young Women's Choices: Readers React to the Work-or-Stay-Home Debate. But What Do Young Men Think?," *Philadelphia Inquirer*, January 15, 2003.

2 See also www.wcl.american.edu/gender/worklifelaw/index.cfm.

3 Martin H. Malin, Maureen K. Milligan, Mary C. Still, and Joan C. Williams, *Work/Family Conflict, Union Style: Labor Arbitrations Involving Family Care*, Program on WorkLife Law, American University, June 14, 2004.

4 Dan Black, "Working Mom Case Sets Legal Precedent," *Rivertowns Enterprise*, August 6, 2004.

5 Joan Williams and Nancy Segal, "Beyond the Maternal Wall: Relief for Family Caregivers Who Are Discriminated Against on the Job," *Harvard Women's Law Journal* 26 (Spring 2003).

Chapter 5: We Need Some Relief

1 Theresa Funiciello, *The Tyranny of Kindness: Dismantling the Welfare System to End Poverty in America* (New York: Atlantic Monthly Press, 1993).

2 www.mochamoms.com

3 Cecelie S. Berry, ed., *Rise Up Singing: Black Women Writers on Motherhood* (New York: Doubleday, 2003), 10.

4 New America Foundation, *The Way Women Work*.

5 Betty Friedan, *The Feminine Mystique* (New York: Norton, 1963). See also Daniel Horowitz, *Betty Friedan and the Making of the Feminine Mystique: The American Left, The Cold War, and Modern Feminism* (Amherst: University of Massachusetts Press, 1998).

6 Friedan, *The Feminine Mystique*, 348.

Chapter 6: What Do You Do with Your Time?

1 Edward A. Shaw, "From the Home Front and Back: Day 6,635 of My Being an At-home Dad," www.slowlane.com/articles/from_the_home_front.html (February 2000).

2   This number is highly contested. In the study of the 2003 numbers, one million fathers with children under eighteen were out of the labor force citing illness or disability; 180,000 of these fathers cited caring for home and family as their primary reason for being out of the labor force. See Jason Fields, *America's Living Arrangements: 2003*, Current Population Reports, U.S. Census Bureau, Washington, D.C., 20–553.

3   CareerBuilder.com, "Men and Women at Work," *2004*, survey.

4   Julia Lawlor, "When Stay-at-Home Fathers Return to Work (Elsewhere)," *New York Times*, August 1, 2004.

5   Anne Marie Chaker and Hilary Stout, "After Years Off, Women Struggle to Revive Careers: Resume Gaps, New Technology Make Transition Difficult," *Wall Street Journal*, May 6, 2004.

Chapter 7: Playground Revolution

1   Karen Kornbluh, "The Parent Gap: What Arnold Schwarzenegger Can Teach Politicians About Winning Swing Voters," *Washington Monthly*, October 2002. Kornbluh is quoting Anna Greenberg, vice president of Greenberg Quinlan Rosner Research, Inc.

2   See www.familyfriendlyjuryduty.org/SiteMap/sitemap.html.

3   Katha Pollitt, "There They Go Again," *Nation*, November 17, 2003.

4   Information on WEEL and AHIC is based on telephone interviews with Mary Caferro, July 2004. See also material on At-Home Infant Care available from the National Partnership for Women & Families (www.nationalpartnership.org) and WEEL's website (www.weelempowers.org).

5   "At a Glance: At-Home Infant Care (AHIC)," www.nationalpartnership.org.

6   Julie Press, interview by the author, July 2004. "Child Care Problems and Employment Outcomes for Low-Income Mothers: Results from Wave I of the Philadelphia Survey of Child Care and Work," final report to the Ford Foundation, November 2003, unix.temple.edu/~jpress/project.htm.

7   *At-Home Infant Care Act of 2004*, HR 3595, a bill to amend the Child Care and Development Block Grant Act of 1990 to authorize financial assistance to permit infants to be cared for at home by parents, was introduced to the 108th Congress and sponsored by Rosa DeLauro and eight cosponsors. It was referred to the House Committee on Education and the Workforce and the Subcommittee on 21st Century Competitiveness.

8   Donna Lenhoff, "New Solutions for Balancing Work and Family," www.nationalpartnership.org.

9   Jody Heymann, Alison Earle, Stephanie Simmons, Stephanie M. Breslow, and April Kuehnhoff, *The Work, Family, and Equity Index: Where Does the United*

States Stand Globally? (Boston: The Project on Global Working Families, Harvard School of Public Health, June 2004).

[10] National Partnership for Women & Families, *National Survey Reveals Americans Support the FMLA and Its Expansion by Wide Margins*, May 14, 1998. See www.paidleave.org.

[11] For info on California's paid family leave program, see the state website at www.edd.ca.gov/direp/pflind.asp. For a comparison to other state programs, see National Partnership for Women & Families, *State Round-Up: State Paid Leave Initiatives in 2002–2003 State Legislatures: Making Family Leave More Affordable*, and later updates at www.nationalpartnership.org.

[12] Information on the Balancing Act is based on conversations with the congresswoman's D.C. staff, and on her website, www.woolsey.house.gov, which includes the text of the bill.

[13] Letters to the editor, *Philadelphia Inquirer*, March 6, 2004.

[14] See www.mothersoughttohaveequalrights.org.

[15] Kristin Rowe-Finkbeiner, email and telephone communication with the author, July 2004; Rowe-Finkbeiner, "Count Us In! Motherhood, Feminism and the U.S. Census," *Mothering*, March/April 2002.

[16] In November 2004, the U.S. Census Bureau published its first study ever of stay-at-home mothers and fathers, an important first step. However, there are no plans to add more detailed questions to the census forms as to why parents are out of the labor force.

[17] Rowe-Finkbeiner, "Count Us In!"

[18] See www.mothersarewomen.com.

[19] See also Lorig Charkoudian's website, www.nurseatstarbucks.org.

[20] Mary Ann Mason and Marc Goulden, *Do Babies Matter? The Effect of Family Formation on the Lifelong Careers of Academic Men and Women*, www.aaup.org/publications/Academe/2002/02nd/02ndmas.htm and www.grad.berkeley.edu/deans/mason/index.shtml.

Epilogue

[1] Jenny Rosenstrach, "Mom vs. Nanny: The Time Trials," *New York Times*, September 9, 2004.

[2] Gruner + Jahr USA, "Laura Bush vs. Teresa Heinz Kerry in *Family Circle* National Cookie Cook-Off: National Survey Finds Americans Changing Views on Traditional Roles of a First Lady," press release, June 15, 2004. For those who need them, the recipes are available at www.gjusa.com/news/pressReleaseDetails.jsp?id=4140.

[3] Kelley Beaucar Vlahos, "'Security Moms' an Elusive Voting Bloc," Fox News, October 15, 2004, www.foxnews.com/story/0,2933,135508,00.html.

[4] Kimberly Blanton, "For Some, Child Care will be a Major Issue: Convention Organizers Offer Little Help to Parents Who Plan on Attending," *Boston Globe*, July 20, 2004.

[5] See www.mothersmovement.org.

[6] Ginia Bellafante, "Two Fathers, With One Happy to Stay at Home," *New York Times*, January 12, 2004.

ACKNOWLEDGMENTS

We moms and dads chat all the time, but we don't always really talk. By happenstance I fell under the extraordinary tutelage of my agent, Sam Stoloff, and my editor, Leslie Miller. Both made sure I really talked, and pressed me further than I thought possible. This book could not have been written without them.

Gratitude goes to Rob, my partner in love and everyday life, and the delightful Miss Samira, who keeps me on my toes and reminds me what life's for; Laura Levitt, who's been my best friend for so long she's family now too; cousins everywhere; Dee, Don, Molly, Lou, and all the Bairds; my grandma Roz; and my parents, Danny and Myra Peskowitz, for modeling generosity, an open home, immensity of spirit, parental patience, and for providing childcare when I camped out at their house for a long summer month to write.

A thousand cheers for all friends, neighbors, informants, interlocutors, and those who just like to hang out and shoot the breeze: Susan Anderson, Cynthia Armstrong, Brooks Avenue, Jonathan Baird, Kristin Beck, Amy Benson Brown, Damien Bryan, Andi Buchanan, Mary Caferro, Cecelia Cancellaro, Lorig Charkoudian, Susan Clark, Amy Cohen, Marisa LaDuca Crandall, the DeDeuses, Anita Downing, Sheila Emerson, the First Wednesday of the Month Playgroup (here're your names in print: Paige, Jenny, Carolina, Liz, Jacquie, Dee, Kelly, Jennifer, Elizabeth, and the amazing Scottie Belfi), Eileen Flanagan, Jason

Francisco, Michelle Friedman, Faulkner Fox, Lonnie Golden, Monica Graves, Mary and John Halfpenny, Rachel Havrelock and Yuri Lane, Tamar Kamionkowski, Barry Koch, Phyllis Koch, Felicia Kornbluh, the Lake Claire Park Moms, Carpenter Lane, Kim Lane, Denise Larrabee and Kevin O'Donovan, Mark Ledden, Lori Lefkovitz, Eve Levy, Andrea Lieber, Peter Lighte and Julian Grant, Deborah Lipstadt, Jay Massey, Molly McCoy, Deborah Meyer, Nancy Aber Murillo, James Meyer and Patrick Garlinger, my N.Y. girls (Elizabeth Castelli and Janet Jakobsen and Barbara Kirshenblatt-Gimblett and Ann Pellegrini and Angela Zito), Jean O'Barr, Penny's Path-ers, Angie Petersen, playground moms and dads everywhere, Julie Press, Sarah Raban and John Lobron, Bill Rodenbaugh, Kristin Rowe-Finkbeiner, Sheila Ruen, Danya Ruttenberg, Laura Schwingel, Hadass Sheffer, Lynn Siprelle, Andrew Solomon, Kathy Torbit, Lisa Tosi, Michelle Trachtenberg, Judith Stadtman Tucker, Deb Valentine, Tom Weeks, Roseanne Welch, Susan Wiedman-Schneider, Joan Williams, and the invincible WriterMamas.

A thank you to all those who shared with me the intimacies of their lives as parents—those who ended up in the book, and those who didn't. And major appreciation goes to the organizations devoted to gathering data, analyzing our lives as women and mothers, and advocating for us—among them, 9to5, National Association of Working Women; the Institute for Women's Policy Research; the National Partnership for Women & Families; the Program on WorkLife Law at American University; the Work & Family Program of the New America Foundation; and many others. Their contact information is available on my website, www.miriampeskowitz.com.

About the Author

SUSAN BEARD

Miriam Peskowitz is the author of two books and many articles on an array of issues, including women, family life, and work. A tenured professor who left full-time academe when her daughter was born, she has appeared on the BBC, Discovery, A&E, and Lifetime channels. She blogs at www.playgroundrevolution.com and lives in Philadelphia with her husband and six-year old daughter.

Motherhood resources, reading group guides, and much more are available at www.miriampeskowitz.com.

For more than 25 years, Seal Press has published groundbreaking books. By women. For women. Visit our website at www.sealpress.com.

I Wanna Be Sedated edited by Faith Conlon and Gail Hudson. $15.95, 1-58005-127-8. With hilarious and heartfelt essays from writers such as Dave Barry and Barbara Kingsolver, this anthology will reassure any parent of a teenager that they are not alone.

Autobiography of a Blue-Eyed Devil by Inga Muscio. $14.95, 1-58005-119-7. The newest manifesta from the bestselling author of *Cunt* this time tackles race in America.

The F-Word: Feminism in Jeopardy by Kristin Rowe-Finkbeiner. $14.95, 1-58005-114-6. An astonishing look at the tenuous state of women's rights and issues in America, this pivotal book also incites women with voting power to change their situations.

Secrets and Confidences: The Complicated Truth about Women's Friendships edited by Karen Eng. $14.95, 1-58005-112-X. This frank, funny, and poignant collection acknowledges the complex relationships between girlfriends.

Under Her Skin: How Girls Experience Race in America edited by Pooja Makhijani. $15.95, 1-58005-117-0. This diverse collection of personal narratives explores how race shapes, and sometimes shatters, lives—as seen through the fragile lens of childhood.

Without a Net: The Female Experience of Growing Up Working Class edited by Michelle Tea. $14.95, 1-58005-103-0. The first anthology in which women with working-class backgrounds explore how growing up poor impacts identity.